Religion and Higher Educ:
Europe and North Ameri(

Religion and Higher Education in Europe and North America illuminates experiences of staff and students in higher education as they negotiate the university environment. Religious extremism has been rising across Europe, whilst recent attacks have thrown public debate around the place of religion on campus, the role of universities in recognising and managing religious fundamentalism and freedom of speech on campus into sharper focus.

Despite these debates, research exploring religion on campus has been largely absent from discourse on higher education outside of America, with policy and practices designed to deal with religion on campus largely founded on supposition rather than evidence. This book speaks into that void, including results from recent studies in the field which form an empirically grounded base from a broad variety of perspectives on religion at universities. As an attempt to offer a deeper perspective, more dialogue, and engagement on the experiences of students, *Religion and Higher Education in Europe and North America* presents us not only with an opportunity to counter growing trends of intolerance, but for people to connect with the humanity of others.

Focusing on what research can portray about staff and students' experiences, it incorporates research from different academic disciplines, including sociology, education, social policy, theology and religious studies, and across different faith and belief groups. This thought-provoking and challenging volume features chapters written by researchers involved in informing policy and practice relating to religion and belief in higher education in the UK, US, Canada, France and the Netherlands. Spanning the academic–practitioner divide, students and academics interested in the sociology of religion and of higher education, as well as those responsible for the practical management of campus life, will find this text of particular importance.

Kristin Aune is a Senior Research Fellow at the Centre for Trust, Peace and Social Relations, Coventry University.

Jacqueline Stevenson is Professor of Education Research and Head of Research in the Sheffield Institute of Education, Sheffield Hallam University.

The Society for Research into Higher Education (SRHE) is an independent and financially self-supporting international learned Society. It is concerned to advance understanding of higher education, especially through the insights, perspectives and knowledge offered by systematic research and scholarship.

The Society's primary role is to improve the quality of higher education through facilitating knowledge exchange, discourse and publication of research. SRHE members are worldwide and the Society is an NGO in operational relations with UNESCO.

The Society has a wide set of aims and objectives. Amongst its many activities the Society:

• is a specialist publisher of higher education research, journals and books, amongst them Studies in Higher Education, Higher Education Quarterly, Research into Higher Education Abstracts and a long running monograph book series.

The Society also publishes a number of in-house guides and produces a specialist series "Issues in Postgraduate Education".

• funds and supports a large number of special interest networks for researchers and practitioners working in higher education from every discipline. These networks are open to all and offer a range of topical seminars, workshops and other events throughout the year ensuring the Society is in touch with all current research knowledge.

• runs the largest annual UK-based higher education research conference and parallel conference for postgraduate and newer researchers. This is attended by researchers from over 35 countries and showcases current research across every aspect of higher education.

SRHE *Society for Research into Higher Education*
Advancing knowledge Informing policy Enhancing practice

73 Collier Street   T +44 (0)20 7427 2350   Director: Helen Perkins
London N1 9BE   F +44 (0)20 7278 1135   Registered Charity No. 313850
United Kingdom   E srheoffice@srhe.ac.uk   Company No. 00868820
                                                    Limited by Guarantee
                     www.srhe.ac.uk   Registered office as above

Society for Research into Higher Education (SRHE) series

Series Editors: Jennifer M. Case, University of Cape Town
Jeroen Huisman, University of Ghent

A full list of titles in this series is available at:
www.routledge.com/series/SRHE

Recently published titles:

Religion and Higher Education in Europe and North America

Edited by Kristin Aune and Jacqueline Stevenson

Routledge
Taylor & Francis Group

LONDON AND NEW YORK

First published 2017
by Routledge
2 Park Square, Milton Park, Abingdon, Oxon OX14 4RN

Together with the Society for Research into Higher Education
73 Collier Street
London N1 9BE
UK

and by Routledge
711 Third Avenue, New York, NY 10017

Routledge is an imprint of the Taylor & Francis Group, an informa business

British Library Cataloguing in Publication Data
A catalogue record for this book is available from the British
Library

Library of Congress Cataloguing in Publication Data
Names: Aune, Kristin, editor. | Stevenson, Jacqueline, editor.
Title: Religion and higher education in Europe and North America /
    edited by Kristin Aune & Jacqueline Stevenson.
Description: New York, NY : Routledge, 2017.
Identifiers: LCCN 2016028495 | ISBN 9781138652941 (hbk :
    alk. paper) | ISBN 9781138652958 (pbk : alk. paper) |
    ISBN 9781315623894 (ebk)
Subjects: LCSH: Church and college—Europe. | Church and
    college—North America.
Classification: LCC LC383 .R369 2017 | DDC 378/.07—dc23
LC record available at https://lccn.loc.gov/2016028495

ISBN: 978-1-138-65294-1 (hbk)
ISBN: 978-1-138-65295-8 (pbk)
ISBN: 978-1-315-62389-4 (ebk)

Typeset in Galliard
by Apex CoVantage, LLC

Printed and bound in Great Britian by Ashford Colour Press, Gosport.

Contents

Religion and higher education in Europe and North America

Historical and contemporary contexts

Jacqueline Stevenson and Kristin Aune

Introduction

This book explores how students and staff negotiate, express and wrestle with religion in higher education in Europe and North America. It illuminates the experiences of religious students and staff in the United Kingdom, France, the Netherlands, Canada and the United States, as well as of non-religious students studying on a religiously oriented campus. Drawing on new research from Europe and North America, we offer insights into the tensions and challenges faced by religious and non-religious staff and students as they navigate their different university environments. In doing so, we evidence how religion is recognised, or fails to be recognised, in universities' agendas for equality and diversity, as well as how specific institutional contexts interact with religious expressions and activities and the effect and implications this has for organisational policy and practice. Throughout the book, we seek to show how the tensions between religion and secularity, and between different religions, play out on campus and how these largely unresolved tensions can have profound implications for the day-to-day experiences of staff and students, for their identities, and for how they think about belonging and fitting in on campus.

This introductory chapter highlights the three key misconceptions or concerns which are returned to throughout the subsequent chapters. First, and a common misconception, is that universities are sites of secularisation. The reality is more complex; however, the persistence of the 'secular' misconception has significant implications for staff and students. Second, and a concern, is that when and where religion *is* recognised on campus, it is because it is perceived as a threat (for example, through student fundamentalism), or because there have been instances of religious intolerance. This too has profound implications as religion becomes perceived, therefore, as requiring surveillance and control. Instead, universities should seek to understand – and work with, not against – the diversity of student and staff religious expressions. Third, and arising from the two preceding areas, we are concerned that institutional policy in relation to religion on campus is, therefore, being crafted without an adequate or accurate understanding of staff or students' actual on-campus experiences.

Our aim therefore, is to illuminate the religion-related experiences of staff and, in particular, students, not only to make visible their experiences but also to open up an intellectual space for reflection and discussion on what has often been an under-researched and under-theorised area of academic, policy and practice interest. We begin with a brief commentary on the historical shift from religious university to secular UK campus and how this is differently experienced across Europe and North America. We then discuss the changing nature of higher education before outlining some of the contemporary discourses around religion on campus. We end the chapter by offering an overview of the scope and structure of the book.

Religious foundations and the growth of secularity

A mass global higher education system – open to those from diverse ethnic, religious, social and economic backgrounds, as well as women – is a relatively new phenomenon. For almost six hundred years, European higher education was dominated by a small number of universities, founded between the eleventh and the thirteenth centuries and educating only men from elite Christian backgrounds (Bebbington 2011). Although forms of higher education had been delivered in monasteries (and to a lesser extent nunneries) prior to the eleventh century, the earliest European universities were established in Bologna in 1088, Paris in the early twelfth century and Oxford in 1166. Other universities followed in relatively quick succession across Europe, for example the universities of Cambridge in the early thirteenth century, Toulouse in 1229 and Montpellier in (about) 1289. Operating as integral parts of the church, with academics and teachers being religious figures and lectures delivered rather like sermons (Clark 2006), these mediaeval universities educated the male, Christian elite of Europe. Within the Christian mediaeval university, inner discipline, carried by the revealed Word (from God), was the condition for understanding and constructing the external, material World (Muller 2008). Thus, the Trivium, comprising grammar, logic and rhetoric, had academic priority and precedence over the Quadrivium, namely music, arithmetic, geometry and astronomy, since understanding the Word was a prerequisite to making sense of the World. Together, the Trivium and the Quadrivium comprised the seven liberal arts taught in the mediaeval and renaissance universities.

There were differences, however, in which disciplines dominated, with the northern European universities focusing on the arts and theology whilst the southern universities focused more on law and medicine (Bebbington 2011). This meant that the scholars and students of the mediaeval period were highly mobile, moving across Europe depending on their disciplinary interests (Knight and de Wit 1995). With southern Spain still under Muslim rule in the early part of this age, European scholars also accessed the Islamic colleges of southern Spain, such as those established in Granada and Cordoba, with Islamic seats of learning contributing to the development of the Christian universities. Indeed, some academics have argued that Islamic universities actually preceded the Christian ones – although this is disputed (Makdisi 1981, 1989).

Just as the mediaeval scholars moved across Europe, Christian scholars and clergy were also amongst the earliest colonists of North America. A notable early aspect of colonisation, therefore, was the building of colleges of higher education, modelled on a highly northern European, Protestant model of the University. The first university in what would become the United States was Harvard University, founded in 1636 (although 'first university' status is claimed by more than one other institution, notably the University of Pennsylvania and The College of William and Mary). These early institutions were highly Christian in nature since their founders were tasked not only with educating the Christian sons of the colonists, but also with bringing Christian beliefs to the indigenous populations. The College of William and Mary, for example, was established by royal charter as 'a perpetual College of Divinity, Philosophy, Languages, and the good arts and sciences', whilst Harvard's 'Rules and Precepts' adopted in 1646 stated:

> Let every Student be plainly instructed, and earnestly pressed to consider well, the maine end of his life and studies is, to know God and Jesus Christ which is eternal life (John 17:3) and therefore to lay Christ in the bottome, as the only foundation of all sound knowledge and Learning. And seeing the Lord only giveth wisedome, Let everyone seriously set himself by prayer in secret to seeke it of him (Prov. 2:3).
>
> (original spelling left intact)

The beginning of the rise of science over the humanities from the seventeenth century onwards (Muller 2008), however, foretold the inevitable rise in secularity over religion on campus, beginning in Europe and spreading west. The dawning of the European Age of Enlightenment offered a secular challenge to academe, with scholars increasingly exalting the power of reason over belief and becoming increasingly sceptical towards the doctrines of the church (Bebbington 2011). Whilst the Enlightenment's 'scientific revolution' from the seventeenth century is commonly seen as sounding the death knell for Christianity, as Brooke (2012) points out, for many leading scientists, including Newton and Darwin, religion and Christianity still remained necessarily intertwined, notwithstanding a progressively sceptical attitude towards traditional religious assumptions. The commencement of the English Civic University movement, however, sharpened the decline in the religiosity of higher education across the United Kingdom. The new universities were not only non-collegiate, but their focus on the teaching of science to help enhance the economic growth of colonial Britain (Jones 1988) further enhanced the primacy of the Quadrivium over the Trivium. The building of these new 'red-brick' universities to meet the demand of the increasing middle classes (Jones 1988) thus further led to the secularisation of UK higher education. However, whilst University College London was the first university in

England to admit students regardless of their religious beliefs and (later) to admit women on equal terms with men, it was not until the passing of the University Tests Act in 1871 that religious discrimination in UK higher education was ended for non-theological courses (Gillard 2011).

Whilst both the Civic and the subsequent 'new' universities of the twentieth century – notably the 1960s or 'Plate Glass' group initiated by the 1963 Robbins Report – were founded as secular organisations, UK higher education today is not, in fact, wholly secular (Gilliat-Ray 2000). Across many universities, Theology and Divinity courses continue to recruit and thrive, whilst Islamic Studies is now offered across a range of universities. In addition, some universities such as Oxford and Cambridge remain overtly Anglican in nature, with the chaplains and the chapels regarded as essential and the language of the academies infused with religious terminology: the names of the terms at Oxford University (Michaelmas, Hilary and Trinity) and Cambridge University (Michaelmas, Lent and Easter), for example, all have religious origins. More overtly, a group of sixteen UK universities that began in the nineteenth century as Anglican, Methodist or Catholic teacher training colleges have come together to form the Cathedrals Group, stating that their mission is 'a commitment to serving the public good that springs from our faith-based values'; and even within overwhelmingly secular universities, there are also disciplinary differences, with both the sciences and the social sciences predominantly secular whilst the arts and humanities are more mixed (Gelot 2009). In addition, the whole sector revolves around a Christian calendar with teaching on Fridays and term times broken up by Christmas and Easter holidays.

Although higher education in the United States remains, arguably, more religious than secular, there too the historically Christian universities such as Harvard underwent a secular revolution from the mid-nineteenth century. Although by the outbreak of the American Civil War there were 246 college and universities in America, with the overwhelming majority founded on Christian principles, arguably the late nineteenth century saw an 'academic revolution' (Jenks and Riesman 1968), with American academics gradually seeing their role less as one of preparing good citizens through the teaching of education, religion and moral philosophy, and more as one of seeking truth via scientific methods, challenging religion in the process. The decline in the religiosity of the North American campus was hastened in the 1960s, when those who were raised in the countercultural social movements swelled the ranks of staff and students. Indeed, Marsden (1994), in his book *The Soul of the University*, describes this as a move 'from Protestant establishment to established non-belief'. The prevailing notion that US higher education has become increasingly secular, however, is one that has been challenged. Mayrl and Oeur's (2009: 272) analysis of a large number of published studies indicated that college students on US campuses 'have extensive religious and spiritual commitments, though for many students they may not be a priority during college. Religious practice declines during the college years, yet religious beliefs appear to be maintained'. Other work by Cherry, DeBerg, and

Porterfield (2001) and by Astin, Astin, and Lindholm (2010) found that religion is thriving on US campuses, whilst Smith and Snell (2009) also found that religion endured throughout students' studies. Taking a slightly different view, however, Clydesdale (2007) has argued that most students actually 'stow away' their religious (and other) identities in an 'identity lockbox' when they start college, probably because they see them as irrelevant to their university experience. Moreover, research by Mayrl and Uecker (2011) evidences that students who are religious are no more likely to liberalise their views than students outside higher education. The US university campus is not, therefore, either a secular space or a place of secularisation.

Whilst higher education across the United States and the United Kingdom is complexly both religious and secular, France is often cited as the preeminent secular nation that fully, and legislatively, separates Church and State. Religion in France is relegated to the private sphere whilst the Constitution requires the state to put in place 'state-provided, free, secular, education at all levels' (Republic of France 1946). However, as Fernando (2014) has argued, even in France, education is not wholly secular: the academic calendar is organised around Catholic holy days and the state subsidises private, mainly Catholic, religious schools across the country. Moreover, in the region of Alsace-Moselle, reintegrated after the 1905 law which separated Church and State, religious education in Catholicism, Calvinism, Lutheranism or Judaism is obligatory for public school students. However, Fernando and others also argue that the ongoing recognition of Christian, and to a lesser extent Jewish, religion does not extend equally to Islam. Indeed, the contested place of Muslim students on the French campus is indicative of broader and more global concerns around how religion is or is not recognised or valorised as a legitimate form of difference on campus. This connects to the second concern we outlined earlier: that whilst the higher education *system* might be largely or partially secular, it is comprised of a religiously diverse staff and student body that deserves respect and recognition. Unlike other aspects of diversity, religion – a fundamental aspect of the cultural identity, values and practices of many staff and students – is rarely recognised or valorised on the UK or French campus, just as religions other than Christianity do not receive adequate understanding on the North American one. This raises significant questions about how diversity is perceived and valued.

Higher education in the twenty-first century: a place of diversity?

Higher education has grown in importance as the 'knowledge economy' has become increasingly central to national and global economies. Based on the data from the UNESCO Institute for Statistics, the total global tertiary enrolments were approximately 170 million in 2009, and it is predicted that the number of students enrolled in higher education will reach 262 million by 2025 (Goddard 2012). These student populations are highly mobile. Nearly 4.3 million students were enrolled in university-level education outside their home countries in 2013 (OECD 2013), studying, in descending order, in Australia, the United Kingdom, Switzerland, New Zealand and Austria. Asian students make up 53 percent of foreign students enrolled worldwide.

As the student population has grown larger and more mobile, its constituencies have also diversified, moving from being dominated by economically and racially privileged males to a more diverse constituency in relation to ethnicity, gender, sexuality, class, religion, health and other factors. However, whilst much has been written about how these features of diversity shape the university experience, and how being at university shapes the life chances of its more diverse members, very little has been written about religion; and yet, by any measure, the majority of the world's population identify as religious, as do the majority of students. The Pew Research Center's study of over 2,500 population surveys, censuses and population registers reports that, as of 2010, 84 percent of the world's population identify as religious: 32 percent are Christian, 23 percent Muslim, 15 percent Hindu, 7 percent Buddhist, 5 percent folk religionists, 0.2 percent Jewish, 0.8 percent belong to other religions and 16 percent have no religious affiliation (Pew Research Center 2012a). Religious patterns vary widely globally, of course, with the vast majority of Hindus, Buddhists, adherents of traditional or folk religions, members of other world religions and those of no religion located in the Asia-Pacific region. Indeed, more Muslims live in the Asia-Pacific region than anywhere else, although significant numbers of Muslims also live in Africa. Christians are more evenly distributed in Europe, Latin America and the Caribbean, sub-Saharan Africa and North America, whilst most Jews live in either North America or the Middle East and North Africa (almost all of them in Israel). Of these populations, nearly three-quarters of religious people live in places where they are the religious majority; the rest live as religious minorities, with some religions – Jews, Buddhists, folk religionists and those of other religions in particular – especially likely to live as religious minorities.

These figures do not just matter in the abstract, however. They also point to the problem with a major assumption about religion in universities: that it is a concern for only a minority of people. The opposite is in fact true: religion is, to different degrees, part of the lives and identities of the majority of people in the world. In addition, as indicated above, religious students, both home and international, are present on campuses throughout the world and yet their presence is often unrecorded. This may arise in part from the fact that religion is often regarded not as a relational system, but as an affiliation category that can be easily divested or strategically shaped by actors according to context, rather than a status category (such as race/ethnicity, gender and class). In consequence, and as Barber (2010: 2) argues:

> the saliency of race, class, and gender. . . . has relegated religion to the realm of the "etc.". The common disappearing of religion into the "etc." can give the impression that religion is somehow less deserving of the analysis given to race, class, and gender, or that it is somehow different.

The assumption that religion is (or should be) a minority concern within universities, coupled with the notion that higher education has become a secularised space, further renders religious staff and students largely invisible. And yet the invisibility of religion on campus operates parallel to the sudden foregrounding of certain religious students (for instance, when religious students become linked with global political crises) when they are deemed to pose a threat to safety and security, or when there are instances of religious intolerance.

Tensions on campus

Across the globe, according to the Pew Research Center (2012b), the number of countries with high or very high levels of social hostilities involving religion reached a six-year peak in 2012, with a third of 198 countries experiencing a surge in the high level of religious hostilities, from 20 percent in 2007 to 29 percent in 2011. Of particular note is the increase in abuse of religious minorities, violence, harassment of women over religious dress, religiously motivated mob violence, religion-related terrorist violence and sectarian violence. The higher education campus is a microcosm of the global situation: in the United Kingdom, for example, the Chief Rabbi Ephraim Mirvis recently suggested that religious intolerance towards Jewish students is at such a level that Jewish students are being routinely 'vilified' on campus, with vice chancellors failing to address 'Jew hatred' (Sherwood 2016). A survey of 925 UK-based Jewish students by the Institute for Jewish Policy Research found that one-fifth said they had been subjected to anti-Semitism that academic year, and a further third had witnessed an anti-Semitic incident on campus (Graham and Boyd 2011: 49–52). Jewish students are, however, not alone in being the victims of religious prejudiced incidents in the United Kingdom. Christian, Sikh and Pagan students have reported, variously, criticism and censure in attempting to undertake legitimate religious activities, threats of violence and anti-religious sentiment (ECU 2011; NUS 2011). In addition, Islamophobic attacks have risen sharply both on and off campus: figures from London's Metropolitan police (2016) show an increase of over 50 percent in Islamophobic crimes in the twelve months prior to April 2016, with incidences in some areas of London up by over 150 percent following a spate of 'Islamic' fundamentalist terrorist atrocities in France, Belgium and elsewhere. Indeed, much of the contemporary discourse around religion on the UK campus draws on a post-9/11 'moral panic' relating to the growth of fundamentalism and global terrorism. Ever-increasing guidance is being provided to universities on how to tackle violent extremism on campus, particularly through compulsory engagement with the government's anti-radicalisation strategy, *Preventing Violent Extremism*, part of the UK Counter-Terrorism and Security Act of 2015. Guidance from the Home Office (2015) sets out specific responsibilities on higher education institutions (amongst other public sector organisations) designed to prevent people being drawn into terrorism and includes the surveillance and monitoring of staff and students.

It is notable, however, that religious hostilities have increased in every major region of the world *except* the Americas (Pew Research Centre 2012b). In her 2012 book *The New Religious Intolerance: Overcoming the Politics of Fear in an Anxious Age*, Martha Nussbaum ascribes lower rates of religious intolerance across the United States to three practices (though also noting that these are variably adhered to): (i) protecting the greatest possible freedom of conscience compatible with public order and safety; (ii) where possible, guaranteeing religious freedom of speech as well as the right to freely exercise religion; and (iii) the maintenance and adherence to an impartial and consistent civic culture and a long-standing respect for religious differences, dating back to the seventeenth century when Roger Williams founded Rhode Island, which afforded religious liberty for all. This is not to say, however, that religious hatred on the US campus does not exist: the 2014 National Demographic Survey of American Jewish College Students, for example, found that 54 percent had experienced or witnessed an anti-Semitic incident on their campus that academic year (Kosmin and Keysar 2015). Moreover, Nussbaum (2012) also draws attention to a range of religiously motivated incidences in the United States, but suggests that the fear of Muslims, post-9/11, is the main trigger in both the United States and across Europe. Indeed, concern around Islam is particularly keenly evident in France, where much of the debate around religion on campus has centred on the wearing of Islamic clothing. French Prime Minister Manuel Valls recently argued for Muslim headscarves to be banned on campus, commenting that the majority of French people do not believe the values of the French Republic are compatible with Islam (Liberation 2016). These controversies have sharpened intensely following the 2015 and 2016 terrorist atrocities in France and Belgium.

Religious students are perceived, therefore, variously as either the *victims* of racially motivated incidences or positioned as contributing to the *causes* of it. We argue that this binary is unhelpful, as the reality for most students is significantly more complex and nuanced; to challenge it, however, means illuminating the daily, micro-level experiences of religious students. To date, however, there has been little research which has done exactly that. This is an omission that we aim to correct through this book.

Researching religion and higher education

In the United States, research on the higher education campus is a more established part of mainstream theological, social scientific and educational research. This is in large part due to the higher profile of religion in the United States compared with Europe. Until recently, this body of research was almost exclusively Christian-related, theological and concerned with Christian-based universities (e.g., Anderson 2004; Astley, Francis, and Walker 2004; Henry and Beaty 2006; Higton 2012). However, the beginning of the twenty-first century has seen an upsurge of social scientific research on the variety of religion on US campuses. Mayrl (2007) attributes this to: a wider 'resurgence of public

religion' (Mayrl 2007: 1) from religious people no longer content with con-
fining their faith to the private sphere, as well as debates about religion and
freedom of speech increasing on campus; the growth of religious diversity due
to immigration; academic disenchantment with the secularisation thesis (which
had held that modern societies were becoming less religious and saw the university as an example of this); a new concern with 'spiritual development' amongst
those working in student affairs; and a renewed interest in the experiences of
religious students on campus from the scholarly community, some of whom
had begun studying adolescent religion (supported by generous funding from
the 1990s by major philanthropic foundations) and asking what happened to
those students when they entered college. The first national longitudinal study
of students' spiritual growth, for example, was funded by the prestigious John
Templeton Foundation for seven years from 2002 (Astin, Astin, and Lindholm
2010). In addition, an online bibliography of literature on student religion
in American universities has been run by the Social Science Research Council
since 2007,[1] its series of essays by key scholars in the field a useful resource
for scholars and practitioners.[2] Questions posed by the American literature on
religion and higher education have included: how can universities committed
to liberal, critical education engage with religion; how can religions' challenge
to the modernist 'scientific' knowledge upon which universities are based be
integrated into student learning; and can college engage with religion in a way
that promotes responsible citizenship?

In contrast, in Europe, the place of religion and belief on the university campus is rarely discussed, with research into the experiences of religious students or
staff notably absent from prevailing discourses relating to higher education policy
and practice. In the United Kingdom, although there has been some research
with funding from government research councils, the Higher Education Funding
Council for England and the Equality Challenge Unit (the government higher
education equality body), there remains a relative absence of studies exploring
staff and student experiences on campus, particularly compared to those exploring race, gender, age or disability. Research exploring religion on campus in other
parts of Europe has similarly been largely absent from discourses about higher
education. This means that, outside the United States, academics and policymakers know little about whether, in an apparent age of 'secularity', religion
and higher education are at odds with each other or how this plays out within
the lives of religious students or staff in 'secular' institutions; how the university
experience affects religious, or other, beliefs or practices; how religious students
and staff are accepted, or not, by their non-religious peers or by those from religions different from their own; or how students and staff are able to undertake
religious activities within specific institutional contexts, as well as the effect this
may have in terms of organisational policy and practice. And yet policymakers
continue to develop policy and practice centred on religious students and staff
despite this dearth of information. No other institutional policy making has been,
or continues to be, based on such a limited evidence base. The final aim of this

book, therefore, is to help provide well-researched and well-theorised evidence to help better inform both policy and practice. The book therefore features research which is applied, providing an evidence base for academics and policymakers working within this and related fields.

Scope of the book

The volume features research spanning different academic disciplines – including sociology, education, social policy, theology and religious studies – and different faith and belief groups (including atheism, humanism and non-belief). The language of 'religion', 'spirituality', 'faith' and 'belief' is contested and changing; for instance, the upsurge of language about 'spirituality' and 'spiritual development' (a more diffuse, more individualised and less tradition-specific formulation than 'religion') appears now to be receding, and youth attachment to religion is increasingly to tradition-based *religious* identities (see Bender 2007) – applied, of course, in multiple ways according to context and interpretation. 'Spirituality' language has been most prominent in the United States, where the 'spiritual but not religious' discourse has been especially popular since the 1970s, in line with the counter-cultural rejection of tradition and a trend towards neo-liberal individualism (Mercadante 2014). In opting for 'Religion in Higher Education', rather than 'religion and belief in higher education', 'faith in higher education' or 'spirituality in higher education', this book does not just solve the problem of ambiguous phrasing ('faith in higher education' implies someone putting trust *in* higher education itself), but also reflects what we observe as an empirical phenomenon: that taken as a collective category, 'religion' – in the form of the major world religions of Judaism, Sikhism, Islam, Christianity, Buddhism and Hinduism – attracts the largest number of students, notwithstanding the many students who identify with diffuse forms of spirituality; with agnostic, atheistic or atheist viewpoints; or who profess no religion (this latter group is growing). Religion, as this book illustrates, is diverse, its expressions both tradition-specific and context-specific: even when there are common themes – such as the Muslim headscarf debate in the United Kingdom and Turkey, or anti-Semitism in Canada and England – the histories, doctrines and practices of the religion and the reactions of others to that religion change as they are brought into contact with different national, socio-political and economic contexts.

Structure of the book

The book is divided into three sections:

1   Patterns and trends: insights from survey research
2   The religious student experience: learning from qualitative studies
3   The place of policies, structures and curricula

The first section presents quantitative research on university members' alignment with religion and non-religion in the United States and the United Kingdom. This survey research provides evidence that enables us to generalise across institutions and to respond to assumptions about universities being secularizing environments that were often based on little or flimsy evidence. More quantitative data is needed, as Weller and Hooley argue, 'to support evidence-based policy and practice in HE [higher education]'. If, for instance, policymakers discover that the majority of university students identify as religious, this provides evidence for them to take religion more seriously as an issue of diversity requiring, at the very least, accommodation.

Hill's chapter directly tackles the question of secularisation: does higher education in the United States secularize students? His chapter uses representative survey data to extend recent research on higher education and student religious faith. The findings he presents echo other research: although higher education institutions tend to be secular in ethos and structure, this secularity often does not extend to their students. Comparing young people attending university with those who do not, there is little difference in the university students' affiliation, practice or belief, apart from in two areas. First, higher education is associated with an increase in identifying with and participating in mainstream religious institutions. This may seem to be strong evidence that university achieves the opposite of secularisation and *sacralises* students; yet Hill argues that their increased participation in religious institutions says more about the students' class position than about their religious commitment, as religion 'is just one part of the middle class package'. The second difference from their non-student peers suggests some secularisation: university attendees show a small decline in belief in super-empirical entities and occurrences (e.g., angels or miracles). Yet Hill points out that most students are not very religious to start with, and even the few most devoted do not demonstrate evidence of weakened faith. That said, students attending evangelical colleges are the most likely to retain higher levels of religious commitment. Hill's analysis of survey data from the 1960s and 1970s then shows something else important: the idea that college secularises students was borne out by evidence in previous decades, but it is no longer true. University had a greater secularizing influence in the past than it does for American students today.

The survey data on the United Kingdom presented by Weller and Hooley is of a different kind. Hill analyses several large data sets from surveys carried out by others. Weller and Hooley showcase data from their own snowball-sample survey of just under 4,000 students and just over 3,000 staff in over 100 universities. The survey was designed to explore how religion or belief impacts on the ways in which students and staff gain access to higher education and how their religion or belief frames their participation. Whilst a snowball survey sample is not designed to be representative of the whole university population, it generates interesting data on religious affiliation: of those who completed the survey, the majority identify with a religion. Given that Europe is often regarded as a prime site of secularisation, this degree of religious affiliation is noteworthy. Additionally, the authors find that although the majority of students and staff are content with how their institutions treat their religious students and employees, some feel their perspective is not accommodated sufficiently in the formal curriculum, social settings (for instance, the ubiquitous presence of alcohol at social events) or assessment (for instance, scheduling exams on religious holidays).

Weller and Hooley point out that recent UK religious equality law is framed in terms of 'religion and belief', and that ' "belief" denotes "non-religious" life orientations of sufficient cogency, seriousness, cohesion and importance to function in ways similar to religion'. This is not the same elsewhere, and the study of non-religion has historically been neglected in the sociological study of religion, although it has recently attracted attention, as seen by the flourishing of the Nonreligion and Secularity Research Network (NSRN), an international and interdisciplinary network of researchers.[3] Bowman's chapter makes an excellent case for why it is important to include work on 'non-religion' in this volume. The non-religious form part of the patchwork of university life; they are a discrete group with some notable commonalities and their numbers are growing in the United States (as they are in Europe). Moreover, as Bowman argues, in a US context where religious students (or certain constituencies of religious students) numerically dominate campus life, it is important not to overlook them. Some religiously unaffiliated students feel marginalised in universities governed by the Christian calendar, although Bowman importantly notes that all religion-related groups tend to see their group as being marginalised by others, and universities should 'work to promote inclusion and cooperation across diverse groups'. Whilst non-religious students are heterogeneous in their non-religion – some atheist, agnostic, secular, humanist or non-religious – as well as in factors such as ethnic background and gender (although males are more non-religious), they share some traits; for instance, they are less socially conservative and volunteer less. Overall, religiously unaffiliated students 'tend to fare equal to or worse than religiously affiliated students', with rates of well-being being low especially, yet they nonetheless do experience spiritual growth, and their academic achievement is comparable with religious students'.

As is clear from each of these chapters, although survey research has many benefits, measuring religious commitment amongst students is complex and no one measure is adequate: there are many options, such as mapping affiliation, attendance at a place of worship, assent to doctrinal statements, attitudes or private religious practices. It is possible to score high on one but not on another: a student may pray every day in their dorm room but never attend a religious service or pray with others. This is a problem for all sociologists of religion, so it is not unique to studying students. Religion is a slippery concept, and understanding religion in higher education is similarly complicated.

The second section of the book showcases qualitative research on students and religion from the United Kingdom, Canada and France. It begins with studies of single-faith groups (Christianity, Islam, Judaism and Sikhism) and broadens out to address the multi-faith context and debates amongst different religious groups, as well as some of the tensions experienced on campus. The themes in this section show that the religious student experience shows both commonalities and differences between different faith groups. Global politics, and the representation of global political events in media and public discourse, shape students' experiences, especially when they belong to a faith group that has been stigmatised or whose group is engaged in global conflicts related to religion. The Israel/Palestine conflict is a particular case and comes up in Sheldon's chapter on the United Kingdom, Schaillié's on Jewish students in Canada and Reid's on Christian, Muslim and Jewish students in the United Kingdom. The spectre of Islamic extremism casts a shadow over universities everywhere, leading to Muslim students being viewed with suspicion, as many of the authors discuss or at least allude to.

The section begins with Aune and Guest's chapter on UK-based Christian students' perceptions of how friendly to faith their universities are. Seventy-five Christian students were interviewed for the study, and the authors find that most students see their universities as relatively faith friendly. Provision of campus-based religious activities and freedom of religious expression are important to students. Those who thought their faith was viewed with hostility described the classroom and organised student social activities as areas of tension. Institutional ethos influences Christian students' perceptions: Christian students view Christian-foundation universities as the most friendly to faith, and the modern 'post-1992' universities as the least friendly. Aune and Guest consider the implications of these findings, especially the finding that some students would like faith to be more prominent in the public spaces of university rather than secluded within chaplaincies and Christian student societies. They conclude: 'This new moment, where public and political anxiety about campus religion is accompanied by new research evidence about faith on campus, gives universities a new opportunity to comprehend the religious commitments of their students and staff and decide whether this requires accommodation of privatised faith or, rather, a deeper structural transformation'.

Virkama's ethnographic essay on the daily practices of Moroccan Muslim students studying in French universities demonstrates the problems with current representations of Muslim students in public discourse. The rise of Islamic-related terrorism in Europe has led to Muslims being perceived only through the radical/secular binary – they are seen as either, we might say, 'good Muslims' who adapt to a secularised environment, or 'bad Muslims' who become extremists. In reality, Muslim students are diverse in their beliefs and practices. The chapter deconstructs certain Islamic practices such as fasting, wearing a headscarf or eating *halal* meat, and explores how these practices are negotiated in respondents' everyday life on campus. By focusing on their agency, this chapter shows how different factors intersect in the construction of Muslim identity in everyday life in Europe.

Global religion-related stereotypes and prejudice affect the Jewish-Canadian students in Schallié's chapter. The focus group research revealed that cultural, ethnic and religious prejudice and racialized language have a significant impact on Jewish students' identity formation both inside and outside the classroom. The politics of identification with Israel as a homeland and as a nation-state proved to be the most challenging for the students' sense of identity on campus: on the one hand, it created a sense of identity and solidarity in a global religious community, but on the other, identification with Israel provoked stereotyping and anti-Semitism by others, and some students feared that their revealing their identity would be negatively received.

Singh's chapter focuses on Sikhs in the United Kingdom, a small but significant religious community (0.8 percent of the population of England and Wales in 2011) that grew rapidly due to migration from the Punjab in the 1950s and 1960s and from East Africa in the 1960s and 1970s. The chapter examines the evolution, role and impact of Sikh student societies in British universities. These societies began in the 1990s, Singh explains, as students began increasingly identifying themselves with their religion rather than their South Asian ethnicity (a trend evident amongst Hindus and Muslims too). As the university sector doubled in the 1990s due to polytechnics (the higher education sector where the most Sikh students were located) becoming universities, there were suddenly many more Sikh students in British universities. Recently, as student societies have become more regulated and receive less funding, numbers have declined. The societies differ by location and religious composition (for instance, some have close ties to particular local *gurdwaras*) but remain effective vehicles for transmission of the Sikh religion and places for young Sikhs to find community.

Sheldon's essay uses a public debate about the academic boycott of Israel to illustrate the way secular norms of free speech as propositional, polarised and impersonal are created and maintained by privileged older male academics, whilst marginalising religious students. In place of this unsatisfactory situation, Sheldon proposes, based on her interviews with Muslim and Jewish students, an 'ethics of speech' based upon minority religious students' perspectives that would reject the impersonal secular mode and instead foreground dialogue between those who are in relationship with each other. It would involve 'not merely a juridical space concerned with protecting the rights of autonomous agents to demonstrate their knowledge – but rather a pedagogic community in which we come to know ourselves and speak in our own voices from within the context of ethical relationships', she argues.

The final chapter of the section, by Reid, addresses the multi-faith context of today's universities. A case study of one university from the 'red-brick' university sector, founded in England's major cities at the turn of the twentieth century and contrasting from their predecessors in being more overtly secular, the chapter uses data from interviews with students involved in Jewish, Muslim and Christian student societies or chaplaincies. Whilst a few students treated the university in an instrumental way, seeing it just as a means to get a qualification to facilitate a good career, most saw the 'humanistic' qualities of higher education and welcomed the opportunity (and challenge) to wrestle with their faith during academic study. Involvement in religion-based clubs and societies has positive and negative effects, Reid finds: although some students find friendship and belonging in those groups, conflicts relating to Israel/Palestine, LGBT issues and marginalisation by some religious students of others in their group who they consider not to be sufficiently religiously committed lead to alienation and misunderstanding.

The experiences of students of faith are shaped by the policies and structures of their own universities, the university sector as a whole and, wider still, government. These are the contexts the authors of Section 3 address. The curriculum is the object of investigation in two essays. Cheruvallil-Contractor and Scott-Baumann examine developments in Islamic Studies since the 2007 Siddiqui Report's proposal for curricula that position the lived realities of Islam as an inherent part of British society. Reflecting on current provision, it considers the difficulties and possibilities of developing new approaches to the study of Islam in the face of neo-liberal pressures, exaggerated dichotomisation between the secular and sacred, securitisation agendas, persistent orientalism and the relative absence of women's voices. Islamic Studies is being shaped by agendas that are not just about the furtherance of knowledge *about* Islam but also about control, exoticisation and surveillance *of* Islam, the authors argue. To be fit-for-purpose in a globalised and interconnected world, Islamic studies must be multi-disciplinary, include currently marginalised voices and develop higher education to transform today's young adults into tomorrow's citizens.

Van Saane's essay on theology and religious studies education advocates a multi-faith approach. A secular, outsider-only perspective on religion is not desirable, van Saane argues. Theology and Religious Studies education is most effective when it balances a strict academic outside perspective and a personal committed perspective on religion. This is what happens at van Saane's university in the Netherlands, where religious practitioners teach alongside the university's academics in theology and religious studies programmes. This requires a highly professional teaching team, able to transfer knowledge as well as to function as a role model for students. A multi-faith context is a constructive way to foster inter-religious debate. These forms of education are strengthened by dialogical assignments, forcing students to reframe their meaning systems. These education practices flourish in academic environments characterized by intense forms of supervision, self-directed learning strategies and development of personal leadership. In these environments, learning is not simply the learning of ideas, but it is 'a process of transformation, of change'. Moreover, it equips students not just with a degree, but with 'personal leadership' skills they can use to participate in inter-religious dialogue in wider society.

Sabri's essay also explores the role of religion in learning and teaching in higher education, using a broad approach not focused specifically on religious studies courses. Religion, she proposes, should be seen as one aspect of educational development facilitated by higher education; it should not be ignored. Religion has been overlooked within research on educational development, national policy and institutional-level policy and practice, except in general terms: religious diversity is seen as requiring some accommodation, such as prayer facilities. But this approach is limited. It paints religious identities as fixed and unchallengeable, Sabri argues, limiting the opportunities the classroom should provide for intellectual development in religion-related thinking. Religion is 'a social practice which may grow, recede or fluctuate over time', she explains, and this process should be facilitated at university. In the last decade, the UK government has turned its attention to religion in only one way: now, (Muslim) students are considered to be vulnerable to ideological radicalisation towards extremism. This exaggerated attention to Muslim students is not helpful either. Instead, she advocates, 'by bringing our intellectual curiosity to this issue, the place of religious belief in the learning process can begin to be seen less as an implacable problem and more as an opportunity for new forms of collaborative intellectual inquiry which remind us of the very purpose of higher education'.

Dinham comes to a similar conclusion. His chapter also expresses frustration with some university stances towards religion, and he was behind the 2009 establishment of the Religious Literacy Leadership Programme, funded by the government's Higher Education Funding Council for England, to equip universities to better understand and work with religion on campus. Dinham identifies the problem of religious illiteracy in universities: they tend to be secular organisations that do not know how to talk about religion, despite the fact that many of their constituents (indeed, a majority, if the UK Census figures are to be believed) are religious. Secularity is often cast as neutrality, but it tends to involve neglect of religion or suspicion of certain forms of it – namely, concern about religious extremism. 'I have observed', he writes, 'a lamentable quality of conversation about religion: at the same time, a pressing need for a better quality of conversation in order to avoid knee-jerk reactions which focus only on "bad" religion'. In talking to staff across the university sector, Dinham identified four university stances towards religion: the first two were secular, 'soft neutral' and 'hard neutral'. A third stance, named 'Repositories and Resources', was evident amongst universities who saw themselves as friendly to religious diversity. A fourth, 'Formative-Collegial', often present in those few institutions with religious foundations, held that providing for students' religious and spiritual development was part of their educational role. Religious literacy is needed, Dinham shows, perhaps for some universities more than others. How can it be developed, and how can university staff become religiously literature? Dinham, who himself runs religious literacy training workshops, proposes four things. First, religion should be understood and interrogated as a category (what is religion? what does it include? where does spirituality fit in?). Second, we should ask: what are the dispositions, emotions and assumptions that university members bring when thinking about religion? Third, what do we need to know about religion (for example, course directors of degree programmes in medicine and social work will want to know different things to help them engage with religion on their courses)? And finally, how can we improve our skills at practically relating to, or engaging with, religion (for example, how we speak to students and staff who we know to hold religious beliefs)?

Towards a religiously inclusive university: recommendations

It would be tempting to conclude that policy change is the answer to improving the experiences of religious students in higher education, but it is just one answer. Policy changes such as religious equality legislation have aided students and staff seeking facilities for prayer or religious diets. Conversely, policies held by some universities that require visiting speakers to be 'vetted' for signs of extremism are quite possibly increasing religion-related animosity, so relaxation of these policies would quite possibly ease religion-related tensions. Policy implementation is also important, as policies can be interpreted and implemented in very different ways in and by different institutions.

The findings from these chapters suggest a range of 'answers' to the problem of universities' lack of engagement with religion:

1 Statistical recording of data on student and staff religious affiliation to inform policy
2 Government and university policies on religion to be shaped by research evidence
3 Institutional religious diversity policies
4 Religious literacy training for university staff
5 Religious diversity committees and working groups (parallel to those that exist for gender, 'race', sexual orientation and disability)
6 Involvement of religious practitioners in teaching religious studies
7 Inclusion of religious perspectives in class discussions
8 Philosophies of learning that prioritise whole-person and spiritual development
9 A dialogue-based approach to learning and communication based on relationship rather than on debating ideas
10 Understandings of religion as something that is lived and practiced and not just an idea to be studied
11 Greater engagement by university staff and managers with the perspectives of students themselves, and
12 Advocacy by students of diverse religious and non-religious positions, via student unions and societies, for religious perspectives to be taken seriously.

A final note

In this chapter, we have argued that religion is present and active in universities throughout the world and that religion deserves new attention in universities (as it does everywhere), not because it is problematic, but because it is a feature of human diversity that deserves recognition. At the least, we are arguing for greater inclusion of and respect for religious perspectives in universities. At most, we are arguing for those perspectives to be allowed to transform the structures and practices of higher education, such that religion is no longer marginalised and privatised, made to hide in prayer rooms and religious societies, but has a respected place at the table of every university committee and every classroom discussion. However, this call for a greater place for religious perspectives in higher education is not to deny that religion gives rise to conflicts, even violence. It can and it does. Many wars, conflicts and acts of violence are perpetrated in the name of religion, and this occurs at universities as it does elsewhere – we might think of the militant group Al-Shabaab's 2015 killing of 148 Christian students at Garissa University College, Kenya. Religious students, as in this example, find themselves on the receiving end of violence or prejudice by others. However, there is also an argument that religion gives rise to social progress and progressive social change (Davie 2016; Silvestri and Mayall 2015); moreover, it is a significant aspect of the identity of millions of university students, and for many is more important to how they think about themselves as students than their age, gender, race, ethnicity or social class. Recognising, debating and researching religion and higher education can, and does, polarise opinion. However, religion is incontestably present on campus and, therefore, whatever their personal beliefs and opinions, scholars and universities need to engage with it.

Notes

1 'Religious engagement among American undergraduates', see http://religion. ssrc.org/reguide/
2 http://religion.ssrc.org/reforum/
3 https://nsrn.net/

References

Anderson, C. (2004) *Teaching as Believing: Faith in the University*. Waco, TX: Baylor University Press.
Astin, Alexander W., Astin, Helen, and Lindholm, Jennifer A. (2010) *Cultivating the Spirit: How College Can Enhance Students' Inner Lives*. San Francisco: Jossey-Bass.
Astley, J., Francis, L., and Walker. A. (eds) (2004) *The Idea of a Christian University: Essays on Theology and Higher Education*. Carlisle: Paternoster.
Barber, K. (2010) Intersectional analyses of religion. Paper presented at the *American Sociological Association Annual Meeting*. Hilton Atlanta and Atlanta Marriott Marquis, Atlanta, GA, 14 August 2010.
Bebbington, D. W. (2011) Christian Higher Education in Europe: A Historical Overview. *Christian Higher Education* 10 (1), 10–24.
Bender, C. (2007) Religion and Spirituality: History, Discourse, Measurement, *Essay Forum on the Religious Engagements of American Undergraduates, Social Science*

Research Council, 4th January. Available online at: http://religion.ssrc.org/reforum/Bender.pdf. Accessed 14 April 2016.

Brooke, J. H. (2012) Science and the Christian Tradition: A Brief Overview. In *Science and Religion: Christian and Muslim Perspectives*, ed. by Marshall, David. Washington, DC: Georgetown University Press, pp. 7–21.

Cherry, C., DeBerg, B. A., and Porterfield, A. (2001) *Religion on Campus*. Chapel Hill, NC: University of North Carolina, 316 pages.

Clark, W. (2006) *Academic Charisma and the Origins of the Research University*. Chicago: University of Chicago Press.

Clydesdale, T. (2007) Abandoned, Pursued, or Safely Stowed? *Essay Forum on the Religious Engagements of American Undergraduates, Social Science Research Council*, 6th February. Available online at: http://religion.ssrc.org/reforum/Bender.pdf. Accessed 14 April 2016.

Davie, G. (2016) Global Challenges: The Contributions of Social Science. Lecture Delivered as Part of *The Cadbury Lectures 2016: Religion in Public Life: Leveling the Ground*, University of Birmingham, 10th March. Available online at: https://www.youtube.com/watch?v=jPguEvOHaSU. Accessed 29 May 2016.

Equality Challenge Unit (ECU) (2011) *Religion and Belief in Higher Education: The Experiences of Staff And Students*. London: ECU.

Fernando, M. L. (2014) *The Republic Unsettled: Muslim French and the Contradictions of Secularism*. Durham and London: Duke University Press.

Gelot, L. (2009) *On the Theological Origins and Character of Secular International Politics: Towards Post-Secular Dialogue*, PhD thesis. Department of International Politics, Aberystwyth University.

Gillard, D. (2011) *Education in England: A Brief History*. Available online at: www.educationengland.org.uk/history. Accessed 24 May 2016.

Gilliat-Ray, S. (2000) *Religion in Higher Education: The Politics of the Multi-Faith Campus*. Aldershot: Ashgate.

Goddard, B. (2012) Future Perspectives: Horizon 2025. In *Making a Difference: Australian International Education*, ed. by David, D., and Mackintosh, B. Sydney, AUS: UNSW Press, pp. 398–414.

Graham, D., and Boyd, J. (2011) *Home and Away: Jewish Journeys towards Independence: Key Findings from the 2011 National Jewish Student Survey*. London: Institute for Jewish Policy Research.

Henry, D. V., and Beaty, M. D. (eds.) (2006) *Christianity and the Soul of the University: Faith as a Foundation for Intellectual Community*. Grand Rapids: Baker Books.

Higton, M. (2012) *A Theology of Higher Education*. Oxford: Oxford University Press.

Home Office (2015) *Prevent Duty Guidance: For Higher Education Institutions in England and Wales*. London: Home Office. Available online at: https://www.gov.uk/government/uploads/system/uploads/attachment_data/file/445916/Prevent_Duty_Guidance_For_Higher_Education__England__Wales_.pdf. Accessed 25 May 2016.

Jenks, C., and Riesman, D. (1968) *The Academic Revolution*. Garden City: Doubleday.

Jones, D. R. (1988) *The Origins of Civic Universities: Manchester, Leeds and Liverpool*. London: Routledge.

Knight, J., and de Wit, H. (1995) Strategies for Internationalisation of Higher Education: Historical and Conceptual Perspectives. In *Strategies for Internationalisation of Higher Education*, ed. by de Wit, H. Amsterdam: European Associate for International Education Publications, pp. 5–32.

Kosmin, B. A., and Keysar, A. (2015) *National Demographic Survey of American Jewish College Students 2014: Anti-Semitism Report*. Washington, DC: The Louis D. Brandeis Center for Human Rights Under Law and Hartford; Connecticut: Trinity College. Available online at: https://www.jewishvirtuallibrary.org/jsource/antisemitism/trinityantisemreport.pdf. Accessed 25 May 2016.

Liberation (2016) Manuel Valls: Depuis plus de trente ans, on me demande si je suis de gauche, *Liberation*, 12th April 2016. Available online at: http://www.liberation.fr/france/2016/04/12/manuel-valls-depuis-plus-de-trente-ans-on-me-demande-si-je-suis-de-gauche_1445774. Accessed 25 May 2016.

Discourses of inclusion and exclusion: religious students in Makdisi, G. (1981) *The Rise of Colleges: Institutions of Learning in Islam and the West*. Edinburgh: Edinburgh University Press.

Makdisi, G. (1989) Scholasticism and Humanism in Classical Islam and the Christian West. *Journal of the American Oriental Society* 109 (2), 175–182.

Marsden, G. (1994) *The Soul of the University: From Protestant Establishment to Established Non-Belief*. New York: Oxford University Press.

Mayrl, D. (2007) Introduction. *Essay Forum on the Religious Engagements of American Undergraduates, Social Science Research Council*, 20th April. Available online at: http://religion.ssrc.org/reforum/Mayrl.pdf. Accessed 14 April 2016.

Mayrl, D., and Oeur, F. (2009) Religion and Higher Education: Current Knowledge and Directions for Future Research, *Journal for the Scientific Study of Religion*, 48 (2), pp. 260–275.

Mayrl, D., and Uecker, J. E. (2011) Higher Education and Religious Liberalization Among Young Adults. *Social Forces* 90 (1), 181–208.

Mercadante, L. A. (2014) *Belief Without Borders: Inside the Minds of the Spiritual But Not Religious*. Oxford: Oxford University Press

Metropolitan Police (2016) *Crime Figures. Latest Crime Figures for London*. Available online at: http://www.met.police.uk/crimefigures/#. Accessed 29 May 2016.

Muller, J. (2008) Forms of Knowledge and Curriculum Coherence. Paper presented to the *ESRC Seminar Series, Seminar 2: Epistemology and the Curriculum*, University of Bath, 26–27 June 2008.

National Union of Students (2011) *Hate Crime Interim Report: Exploring Students' Understanding, Awareness and Experiences of Hate Incidents*. Available online at: http://www.nus.org.uk/Global/NUS_HateCrimeReport_web.pdf. Accessed 25 May 2016.

Nussbaum, M. C. (2012) *The New Religious Intolerance: Overcoming the Politics of Fear in an Anxious Age*. Cambridge, MA: Harvard University Press.

OECD (2013) How Many Students Study Abroad and Where Do They Go? *Education at a Glance 2013: Highlights*. OECD Publishing. Available online at: http://dx.doi.org/10.1787/eag_highlights-2013–12-en. Accessed 20 May 2016.

Pew Research Center (2012a) *The Global Religious Landscape*. Available online at: http://www.pewforum.org/2012/12/18/global-religious-landscape-exec/. Accessed 23 May 2016.

Pew Research Center (2012b) *Religious Hostilities Reach 6 Year High*. Available online at: http://www.pewforum.org/2014/01/14/religious-hostilities-reach-six-year-high/. Accessed 24 May 2016.

Republic of France (1946) *Preamble to the Constitution of 27 October 1946*. Available online at: http://www.conseil-constitutionnel.fr/conseil-constitutionnel/root/bank_mm/anglais/cst3.pdf. Accessed 18 August 2016.

Sherwood, H. (2016) Chief Rabbi: 'Zionist-Bashing on Campus Has Gone Unchallenged. *The Guardian*, 8th May 2016. Available online at: http://www.theguardian.com/world/2016/may/08/chief-rabbi-ephraim-mirvis-zionist-bashing-university-jewish-students

Silvestri, S., and Mayall, J. (2015) *The Role of Religion in Conflict and Peace-Building*. London: British Academy.

Smith, C., and Snell, P. (2009) *Souls in Transition: The Religious and Spiritual Lives of Emerging Adults*. Oxford: Oxford University Press.

Section I

Patterns and trends

Insights from survey research

Chapter 1

Religion and higher education in the United States

Extending the research

Jonathan P. Hill

> To say that college does something to the average student's religion is to state a truth which will be conceded by anyone who has given the matter a moment's thought. Nine young men and women out of ten who will receive their degrees this June would probably admit, if they were called to testify, that education has acted as a poison to their faith. In many instances the virus generated by the reasoning processes induces only mild distemper of skepticism, but in others it works like an acid, eating its way into the bump of credulity until in the end this estimable organ is completely corroded.
>
> Philip E. Wenthworth, *The Atlantic* 1932

> All thinking men and women in America today are alarmed at the appalling prevalence of drunkenness, debauchery, lawlessness, and licentiousness among students of our higher institutions of learning. They are doubly disturbed by the fact that even where gross immorality itself is not apparent, there is present, only too often, a dangerous form of unmorality: an indifference to moral values, an ordering of youthful lives without reference to Christian ideals.
>
> Dan Gilbert, *Crucifying Christ in Our Colleges* 1933

Few would disagree that the institutional history of higher education in the United States is characterised by secularisation (Burtchaell 1998; Smith 2003). From the founding of Harvard in 1636 to the period before the American Civil War, higher education in the United States was largely Christian in form and purpose (Marsden 1996). Harvard College's seventeenth-century 'Rules and Precepts' instructed that every student should 'be plainly instructed, and earnestly pressed to consider well, that the main end of his life and studies is, to know God and Jesus Christ which is eternal life (John 17:3)' (Morison 1935: 333). With the turn toward the German research university model in the late nineteenth century, and the professionalisation and balkanisation of various academic disciplines, institutions began to divorce themselves from both their sponsoring religious denominations and the religious ends of university education (Reuben 1996). This institutional exile of religion is often assumed to have been accompanied by an emptying of religious faith and piety from the student population. The opening quotations of this chapter illustrate the common belief that higher education corrodes religious faith. Whether it is the critical reasoning Philip Wentworth points to in his 1932 essay in *The Atlantic,* or the immorality of student life emphasized by Dan Gilbert in his diatribe against secular education, it was assumed that a secular institution will beget a secular individual. The purpose of this chapter is to critically interrogate this assumption. Does higher education in the United States secularise students?

There are good reasons not to make this leap from the institution to the individual. Secularisation theorists, in recent years, have cautioned against collapsing the various levels of secularisation together into one master narrative. While few will argue with the decline of religious authority at the institutional level (Chaves 1994), the privatisation of faith and the changing nature of individual religious identity, practice, and belief occur in complex ways within these institutional contexts (Casanova 1994; Dobbelaere 2002).

But perhaps the best reason to not leap to the conclusion that higher education secularises students is the simple fact that this is an empirical question. We can, and should, rely on data to make our assessments about the impact of college on student faith identity, practice, and belief. Social scientists who have been doing just this in recent years have found some counterintuitive results. In sum, despite the secular nature of most higher education in the United States, there is little evidence of widespread disaffection from religious faith among students (for a review of this literature see Mayrl and Oeur 2009).

This chapter sets out to further this investigation by taking up some key questions left in the wake of these findings. By using several nationally representative studies, I extend these established findings in three directions. First, given the fairly narrow range of religious factors accounted for in the existing literature, I expand the range of religious and spiritual measures beyond the small handful typically relied upon. Second, I pay careful attention to the differential effects of college by institutional type and student characteristics. While college may not have a unilateral secularising effect in aggregate, some types of institutions (especially explicitly religious ones), and some types of students (especially highly religious ones) may experience the intersection of college life and faith differently. Last, I use available data to examine the recent past and assess whether higher education impacted student faith differently for previous generations. Perhaps higher education has little impact on faith today, but has this always been the case?

Previous research

Some of the earliest social scientific studies of college and faith compared first-year college students with graduating seniors. The general finding was that seniors were less orthodox on measures of Christian belief, and practiced their faith (both publicly and privately) less frequently than first-year students (see Feldman and Newcomb 1969: 23–28). One reasonable conclusion would be that college is exerting a secularising effect on students. The longer they attend, the more their faith is chiselled away. But this is hard to square with another reasonable way of assessing the data. More recent studies have used national surveys of the entire adult population to examine the correlation between religious faith and educational attainment. These do not show a clear-cut pattern of secularism associated with attending and graduating from college. College graduates are actually more likely to practice their faith and say it is important in their daily life. They are no more likely to disaffiliate from a religious faith (although they do appear more likely to shy away from exclusivist claims about the Bible and more likely to switch to a mainline Protestant denomination) (Schwadel 2011). Why the different results? There are several factors at work here. The first method – comparing freshman to seniors – makes the assumption that the college experience accounts for the change. But this cannot be entirely true. Similar changes are evident in religious practice and belief during this same age range (roughly age 18 to 22) among young people not in college (Smith and Snell 2009). Methodologically, there is no way to separate out the college influence from changes rooted in other cultural and developmental changes. These studies need to compare college students to those who are not in college to assess the relative differences in change. It might seem counterintuitive, but college could theoretically have a positive impact on faith even when there is an apparent decline on most religious measures between freshman and senior year.

The second method – using general population surveys – ignores the fact that those who end up attending and graduating from college may be different from the rest of the population for reasons that have little to do with college itself. Most importantly, some of these religious differences may be the result of upbringing. This is commonly referred to as selection bias. Those who end up attending and graduating college could have different religious identities and practices to begin with. While there are some ways to mitigate the influence of selection bias (e.g., statistically controlling for parents' educational attainment or using retrospective reports of faith identity and practice prior to college), there is no fool-proof way of ruling this out in general population surveys.

The third factor to consider is the sheer complexity of this relationship. Higher education has gone through substantial historical shifts that may mean the religious impact from a generation ago no longer holds today. On top of this, the various types of institutions and educational models are unlikely to be uniform in their influence on faith. Add this to the diversity of backgrounds in the student body, and the result is a complex mix of factors that undermine any single story about higher education and religious faith. This is not to say that no general patterns exist. It is simply a recognition that any account of college and faith needs to specify the conditions under which the relationship holds.

Is there an overall secularising effect from higher education in the United States?

To confidently isolate the impact of college, nationally representative panel data is needed. Panel surveys, unlike standard cross-sectional surveys, follow the same group of people over time. If we begin following a national sample of adolescents, we can measure their faith at multiple points in time. Some of these young people will go off to college. Others will enter the workforce. Some may do neither. This type of data is precisely what has been analysed in recent years. The results are somewhat surprising. For the most part, going to college does not substantially alter the religious trajectories of young people (Hill 2009, 2011; Mayrl and Uecker 2011; Uecker, Regnerus, and Vaaler 2007). If we use the best survey for measuring this, the National Study of Youth and Religion (NSYR), there are no substantial differences between college students and other young people across more than a dozen measures of religious identity, practice, and beliefs (once their faith as teenagers is taken into account). Out of twenty-three measures I examined, fifteen show no statistical significant differences. This includes belief in God, closeness to God, belief in an afterlife, belief in a future judgment day, importance of faith in daily life, frequency of prayer and Bible reading, identifying as 'spiritual but not religious', and several measures of religious exclusivism (e.g., can someone practice more than one faith? Is there only one true religion?). College does not seem to alter the religious trajectory of these measures. And, among the few differences that we can find, the results do not support a clear secularising narrative.

Before discussing the few differences that are found, it is worth considering the 'non-findings' in more detail. What can account for the general lack of influence from college for recent graduates? Should not the worldview pluralism on many campuses, the secular commitments of many university faculty (Ecklund 2010; Gross and Simmons 2007), the hermeneutic of suspicion that animates much of science and philosophy, and the student party culture (to name just a few potential secularising sources) undermine a commitment to religious faith? I am not trying to claim that these are never stumbling blocks for the religiously committed on campus; I am quite certain that they are for some. But we need to recognise that most students do not come to campus with strong religious commitments in the first place. The sociologist Tim Clydesdale (2007) has studied students the first year out of high school and finds that most new college students tend to take their religious identity and place it in a metaphorical 'lockbox'. Young people mostly follow a script that tells them religion has very little to do with this phase of their life and can be safely set aside for a few years. Donna Freitas (2008), in her study of sexual activity and religion on college campuses, finds that most students (with the exception of students attending evangelical colleges) see no real connection between their sex life and their faith. If religious identity is fragmented and private for most 18- to 23-year-olds, then why should we expect college to have any influence?

With the 'no effect' story as the default backdrop, let us look at a few exceptions. The exceptions can be classified into two groups. On the one hand, college appears to have a positive influence on institutional belonging. The most notable example of this is church attendance. Figure 1.1 below compares those who have never gone to college (both high school graduates and high school dropouts, but not anyone currently enrolled in high school who would not have had the chance to go to college), current college students attending non-religious institutions, and college graduates. Some emerging adults do not fit in these categories, but comparing these particular groups, let us see if education leaves a mark on religious belief, identity, and practice. The top bar for each group shows the 'raw' percentage – the percentage within each group who attend church weekly when measured at age 18 to 23. The bottom bar ('adjusted percent') controls for the frequency of church attendance when they were age 13 to 17, as well other religious and demographic factors. In this case, these additional control factors make little difference to the general findings. Put simply, the graph tells us that the further one has gone educationally by age 18 to 23, the more likely she or he is to be attending a place of worship regularly.

Similar trends can be found if we examine those who do not identify with any faith (most likely among those who have not attended or graduated from college) and those who believe a religious congregation is necessary to be truly religious (most likely among those who have attended or graduated from college). These all suggest that attending and graduating from college results in young people identifying more with the institutional side of religious life.

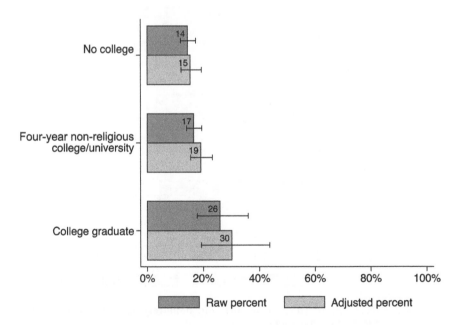

Figure 1.1 Percentage of 18–23-year-olds attending worship services weekly by educational attainment.

Source: National Study of Youth and Religion 2002–3, 2007–8.

Again, it is worth pausing to consider why this might be. Given the lack of increase (or decrease) in most other measures of religious belief and practice, it seems unlikely that the increased institutional commitment is due to an increase in personal faith. The more likely explanation, I would contend, is the class-based distinctions in trust and participation in mainstream social institutions. Those with a college education are more likely to participate in all sorts of social institutions and aspects of public life – religious and non-religious. The disenchantment (and often distrust) of mainstream social institutions has grown disproportionately among the working classes and those without a college education (Wilcox, Cherlin, Uecker, and Messel 2012). Whether marriage and family life, political participation and volunteering, or religious participation, all of this is relatively stable for college graduates but declining among those without college degrees (Murray 2012). College, increasingly, is the link to middle-class life in the United States. Religious involvement is just one part of the middle-class package.

The other notable exception is the slight decline in some measures of super-empirical beliefs associated with attending and graduating from college. In the NSYR data, the decline is associated with measures of miracles, angels, and demons (but not belief in a personal God, a future judgment day, or an afterlife). Figure 1.2 shows the percentage who 'definitely' believe in miracles by

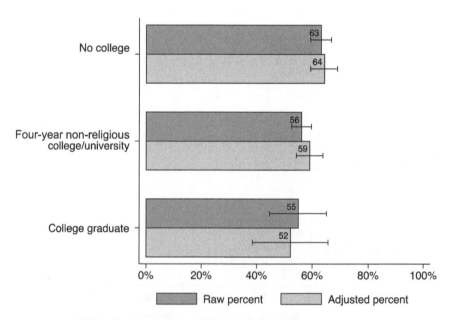

Figure 1.2 Percentage of 18–23-year-olds who definitely believe in miracles by educational attainment.

Source: National Study of Youth and Religion 2002–3, 2007–8.

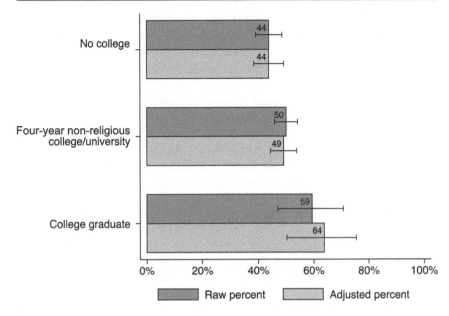

Figure 1.3 Percentage of 18–23-year-olds who have had at least a few doubts about their faith by educational attainment (only includes those who identify with a faith tradition).

Source: National Study of Youth and Religion 2002–3, 2007–8.

college status. Even when controlling for what the respondent believed at age 13 to 17 (this is what the 'adjusted percent' accounts for), the gap between never going to college and graduating from college is about 12 percentage points (64 percent versus 52 percent). Likewise, if we ask those who identify as religious if they have had any doubts about their religion, those who attend and graduate from college report at least having a few doubts at a higher rate (Figure 1.3).

So what can we conclude? College in the United States is most certainly not a catalyst for total disaffiliation or atheism. By most accounts, it actually strengthens affiliation and identification with the institutional side of religious life. Still, there are some types of beliefs, particularly the belief that supernatural forces and entities are active in the world, that appear to decline among those in college. Nevertheless, by any stretch of the imagination, college is not a unilateral secularising force.

Individual and institutional variation

Still, this does not settle the matter entirely. Perhaps college is not a poison to faith for most young people, but might that be because most do not enter it with anything like a robust, vibrant faith life? What about the highly religious? According to Christian Smith and Melissa Denton (2005), only about eight percent of adolescents could be considered 'devoted' in their faith (by this they mean that there are consistent high levels of identification, practice, and belief across a number of measures). To investigate, I have restricted the sample to only those who could be classified as devoted at age 13 to 17 (for an explanation on the measurement of religious 'ideal types', see Smith and Denton 2005: 219ff). Although it is difficult, because of the reduced sample size, to be certain whether there are any differences between the religiously devoted who go to college and those who do not, there is virtually no indication that college has a greater negative influence on this group than the general population of young people. In fact, most results point in the opposite direction, indicating that the highly religious actually fare better going to college than not going. Still, none of these reach statistical significance.

Why does college not have a negative effect for these students? While it is impossible to know solely from the survey data, these findings are less surprising than they may appear at first. We can reasonably suppose that religious students coming to a secular campus will be very aware of their minority status. For those that are determined to hold on to their faith, they will likely find like-minded others (perhaps through parachurch organisations such as Campus Crusade for Christ or Intervarsity) and develop a general posture of guardedness, a readiness for conflict (for an overview of campus parachurch organisations, see Schmalzbauer 2007). Christian Smith (1998) has made this argument about evangelicals in American culture more generally. From a social psychological perspective, embracing a minority identity allows for a clear 'us' and a clear 'them'. Intergroup conflict only serves to strengthen intragroup solidarity. The diversity of the student population on most secular campuses, then, allows students of all types to find their place and reinforce their identity.

In all of this, I have purposefully avoided analysing religiously affiliated colleges and universities. This is because most concerns about the influence of higher education are not targeted at these institutions. After all, many religiously affiliated institutions have religious and spiritual formation as an explicit goal. But do they succeed on this front? I think the answer is likely 'yes', but we need better research to confirm this. In the NSYR data, those who attend religious colleges and universities do show considerable positive effects for religious practice (church attendance, Bible reading, frequency of prayer), and the negative effects on super-empirical beliefs are not evident at these institutions. Unfortunately, there is not an adequate way to separate out the type of religious institution (e.g., Catholic, mainline Protestant, evangelical, Mormon, Jewish, etc.) without reducing the sample size to an unacceptably low level. This is one of the difficulties of relying on a national sample. Small subpopulations that are of interest to the researchers are sometimes out of reach.

One alternative is to use data that oversamples on religiously affiliated colleges. The Spirituality in Higher Education survey data, collected by the Higher

Education Research Institute at UCLA, rely upon a college-based sample. Although these data run into some of the difficulties mentioned at the outset of this chapter (namely there is no non-college sample to compare to), they do have adequate numbers of students attending Catholic, evangelical Protestant, and non-evangelical Protestant colleges to compare them to students attending other institutions. Students were measured as incoming freshman and again during the second semester of their junior year. On every measure of religious practice and identity, students attending evangelical Protestant colleges decline considerably less than their counterparts at other schools. For example, only two percent of students at evangelical colleges who enter with a religious affiliation report having no affiliation by the end of their junior year (compared to eight percent at public institutions). Eighty percent of students at evangelical colleges who were attending religious services 'frequently' as incoming students are still attending frequently by the end of their junior year. Only 47 percent of students at public institutions are doing the same. Seventy-three percent of students at evangelical colleges who prayed daily continued to do so, while 56 percent of students at public institutions continued to do so. In all of these instances, students attending Catholic and other church-related colleges and universities are much closer to the public university students than the evangelical students.

Does this mean that the evangelical colleges are the sole cause of these higher rates of religious practice and identification? Probably not. These students could likely be different in a number of ways that the survey does not easily capture (e.g., more supportive religious households, higher religious expectations from parents and home church, youth pastors who stay in contact with them, friends from home who support them spiritually, etc.). On the other hand, it would be extremely unlikely for the curricular and co-curricular aspects of evangelical colleges to have no influence on these types of outcomes. By all accounts, it is a safe bet that evangelical colleges are relatively successful in nurturing faith among their students. The success rate at Catholic and other church-related institutions is less clear.

Historical variation in the effect of college

But what about placing this (non)finding in historical context? While college does not unilaterally undermine faith in any straightforward fashion for current students and graduates, perhaps it did in the near past. Higher education has rapidly expanded since the 1960s when some of the earliest studies of faith and college first emerged. Not only this, but incoming students have different expectations of their college experience today than several decades ago (Astin 1997). Two sociological studies from the 1980s tracked the religious beliefs and practices of students over time at specific institutions (Hoge, Hoge, and Wittenberg 1987; Moberg and Hoge 1986). Students at Marquette (a Catholic institution) and students at Dartmouth (an elite secular university with Protestant roots) both exhibited declines in the percent who believed and practiced traditional faiths from the early 1960s to the 1970s. However, both campuses also saw an increase in faith and practice by the time surveys were conducted in the 1980s. Still, these surveys tell us little about the changing impact of college on faith over time because of the narrow sample and absence of a non-college comparison group (it is quite possible that all emerging adults were becoming more religiously traditional in the 1980s and higher education had nothing to do with this).

One way we can assess this is by looking at a survey that repeats questions on religion and educational attainment over time – such as the General Social Survey (GSS, administered since 1972). I have pooled all of the years of the GSS together and separated out respondents by the decade within which they were born (ranging from before 1920 to 1980 and after). We can then measure the difference between those who have a four-year college degree and those who do not by birth cohort. If the gap is positive – if college graduates measure higher – then the bar graphs are positive. If the gap is negative – with college graduates measuring lower – then the bar graphs are negative. This allows us to see if the impact of college tends to be changing over time. As before, we cannot be sure whether the gap is due to college or due to the initial differences in the types of people who went on to receive a college education. To help mitigate the second possibility, I include adjusted differences that control for household background factors, including measure of religious tradition and religious fundamentalism at age 16 (these are retrospective questions for respondents). I also control for gender, age, race/ethnicity, and parents' educational attainment. The results tell us that college, for those born in early decades, was more of a secularising force in the past than it was today. The church attendance 'boost' from college was much smaller in the past than it is today and earlier generations were more likely to disaffiliate if they went to college, while those born in the 1970s are actually more likely to disaffiliate if they do not go to college. In earlier generations, college graduates prayed less. In recent birth cohorts, they pray more or show no difference.

These graphs illustrate the general trends (space does not permit including them all). Figure 1.4 shows the gap in evangelical Protestant identification. The negative bars indicate that those with a college degree are less likely to identify with an evangelical denomination. This gap was largest for those born in the 1930s. In recent decades, the gap is virtually non-existent once we control for the respondents' religious affiliation growing up. The next figure (Figure 1.5) shows the changing belief in an afterlife. There is a clear negative to positive trend in the data, indicating that college graduates from more recent birth cohorts are actually more likely to belief in an afterlife (there is a glaring exception for those born in the 1980s – the sample size is much smaller here so it is probably worth gathering a few more years of data before anything is concluded about a renewed secular influence from college among those born

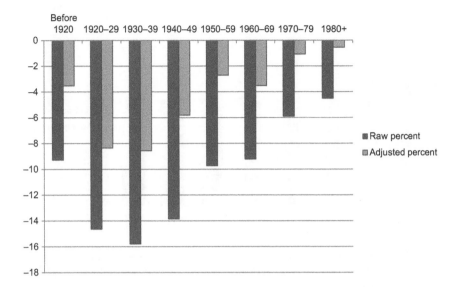

Figure 1.4 The percentage point gap in evangelical Protestant affiliation between college graduates and everyone else by birth decade, age 25+.

Source: GSS 1973–2012.

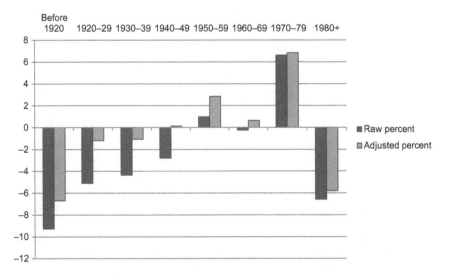

Figure 1.5 The percentage point gap in belief in an afterlife between college graduates and everyone else by birth decade, age 25+.

Source: GSS 1973–2012.

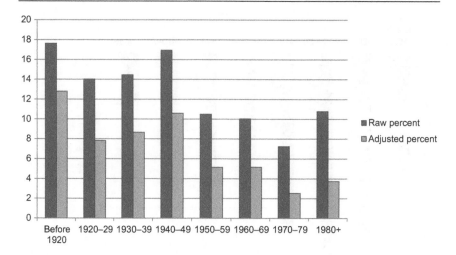

Figure 1.6 The percentage point gap in belief that the Bible is a 'book of fables' between college graduates and everyone else by birth decade, age 25+.

Source: GSS 1984–2012.

after 1980). Lastly, Figure 1.6 shows the changing gap in belief that the Bible is a book of fables. Although college graduates tend to be more likely to affirm this belief about the Bible, the adjusted gap (controlling for some religious measures growing up) is only about two to four percent in recent birth cohorts compared to about 13 percent for those born before the 1920s. In sum, most measures from the GSS seem to indicate that college had a greater secularising influence for past generations, and, consistent with the other data we have been reviewing in this chapter, recent generations show a mixed religious influence from college.

Still another way to assess this is to compare two panel data sets (data that follows people over time) from different time periods. We have already examined some of the research that has used data from those born recently. But what if we look at a similar study from an earlier generation? The Youth Parent Socialization Panel Study began with a national sample of high school seniors in 1965 and followed up with them in 1973. Does college impact their faith trajectory from the first wave to the second? The answer appears to be yes. In models that control for some confounding factors (Hill 2008), those who graduated from college in the late 1960s and early 1970s were nearly twice as likely to disaffiliate as those who did not graduate. They were also substantially more likely (about two and a half times) to believe the Bible was not divinely inspired. Interestingly enough, the typical positive influence of higher education on church attendance is absent in this data as well. College graduates were no more likely to attend church than those who never went to college.

In sum, despite concerns about the secularising influence of higher education, college tends to have a few positive (in the form of institutional belonging and practice), a few negative (in terms of certain super-empirical beliefs), but mostly no influence on religious faith. This can even be said for those who are highly religious and attend secular institutions. By most accounts, there is not any mass defection from the faith in which they were raised. Also, by most accounts, religiously affiliated colleges and universities, particularly evangelical ones, tend to be doing a better job nurturing faith than public institutions in the United States. Lastly, I examined the changing influence of college on faith over time. Although we often lack the historical data we need, it is possible to use long-standing surveys to provide reliable estimates of the changing impact of higher education. Most items point to college being a greater secularising influence in the past than it is today.

References

Astin, A. W. (1997) The Changing American College Student: Thirty-year Trends, 1966–1996. *The Review of Higher Education* 21 (2), 115–135.

Burtchaell, J. T. (1998) *The Dying of the Light: The Disengagement of Colleges and Universities from Their Christian Churches*. Grand Rapids, MI: Eerdmans.

Casanova, J. (1994) *Public Religions in the Modern World*. Chicago: University of Chicago Press.

Chaves, M. (1994) Secularisation as Declining Religious Authority. *Social Forces* 72 (3), 749–774.

Clydesdale, T. (2007) *The First Year Out: Understanding American Teens after High School*. Chicago: University of Chicago Press.

Dobbelaere, K. (2002) *Secularisation: An Analysis at Three Levels* (Vol. 1). New York: Peter Lang.

Ecklund, E. H. (2010) *Science vs. Religion: What Scientists Really Think*. New York: Oxford University Press.

Feldman, K. A., and Newcomb, T. M. (1969) *The Impact of College on Students*. Piscataway, NJ: Transaction Publishers.

Freitas, D. (2008) *Sex and the Soul: Juggling Sexuality, Spirituality, Romance, and Religion on Americas College Campuses*. New York: Oxford University Press.

Gilbert, D. (1933) *Crucifying Christ in Our Colleges*. San Francisco: Alex Dulfer Printing Company.

Gross, N., and Simmons, S. (2007) *How Religious Are America's College and University Professors?* Available online at: http://religion.ssrc.org/reforum/Gross_Simmons.pdf. Accessed 9 August 2016.

Hill, J. P. (2008) *Religious Pathways during the Transition to Adulthood: A Life Course Approach*, PhD thesis. Department of Sociology, University of Notre Dame.

Hill, J. P. (2009) Higher Education as Moral Community: Institutional Influences on Religious Participation during College. *Journal for the Scientific Study of Religion* 48 (3), 515–534.

Hill, J. P. (2011) Faith and Understanding: Specifying the Impact of Higher Education on Religious Belief, *Journal for the Scientific Study of Religion* 50 (3), 533–551.

Hoge, D. R., Hoge, J. L., and Wittenberg, J. (1987) The Return of the Fifties: Trends in College Students' Values between 1952 and 1984. *Sociological Forum* 2 (3), 500–519.

Marsden, G. M. (1996) *The Soul of the American University: From Protestant Establishment to Established Nonbelief.* New York: Oxford University Press.

Mayrl, D., and Oeur, F. (2009) Religion and Higher Education: Current Knowledge and Directions for Future Research. *Journal for the Scientific Study of Religion* 48 (2), 260–275.

Mayrl, D., and Uecker, J. E. (2011) Higher Education and Religious Liberalization Among Young Adults. *Social Forces* 90 (1), 181–208.

Moberg, D. O., and Hoge, R. (1986) Catholic College Students' Religious and Moral Attitudes, 1961 to 1982: Effects of the Sixties and the Seventies. *Review of Religious Research* 28 (2), 104–117.

Morison, S. E. (1935) *The Founding of Harvard College.* Cambridge: Harvard University Press.

Murray, C. (2012) *Coming Apart: The State of White America, 1960–2010.* New York: Three Rivers Press.

Reuben, J. A. (1996) *The Making of the Modern University: Intellectual Transformation and the Marginalization of Morality.* Chicago: University of Chicago Press.

Schmalzbauer, J. (2007) *Campus Ministry: A Statistical Portrait.* Available online at: http://religion.ssrc.org/reforum/Schmalzbauer.pdf. Accessed 9 August 2016.

Schwadel, P. (2011) The Effects of Education on Americans' Religious Practices, Beliefs, and Affiliations. *Review of Religious Research* 53 (2), 161–182.

Smith, C. (1998) *American Evangelicalism: Embattled and Thriving.* Chicago: University of Chicago Press.

Smith, C. (2003) *The Secular Revolution: Power, Interests, and Conflict in the Secularisation of American Public Life.* Berkeley: University of California Press.

Smith, C., and Denton, M. L. (2005) *Soul Searching: The Religious and Spiritual Lives of American Teenagers.* New York: Oxford University Pres.

Smith, C., and Snell, P. (2009) *Souls in Transition: The Religious and Spiritual Lives of Emerging Adults.* New York: Oxford University Press.

Stokes, C. E., and Regnerus, M. D. (2009) The CCCU and the Moral and Spiritual Development of Their Students: A Review of Research. *In International Forum on Christian Higher Education*, Atlanta, GA.

Uecker, J. E., Regnerus, M. D., and Vaaler, M. L. (2007) Losing My Religion: The Social Sources of Religious Decline in Early Adulthood. *Social Forces* 85 (4), 1667–1692.

Wentworth, P. E. (1932) What College Did to My Religion. *Atlantic Monthly* (June), 388.

Wilcox, W. B., Cherlin, A. J., Uecker, J. E., and Messel, M. (2012) No Money, No Honey, No Church: The Deinstitutionalization of Religious Life among the White Working Class. *Research in the Sociology of Work* 23, 227–250.

Chapter 2

How religion or belief frame participation and access in UK higher education

Paul Weller and Tristram Hooley

Introduction

The relation between religion or belief and higher education (HE) remains a complex and varied one. Within the HE system of the United Kingdom, there is a wide variety of different kinds of institution. These range from the ancient, collegiate universities (such as Oxford, Cambridge and Durham); through civic universities of late nineteenth and early twentieth century foundation (such as the universities of London and Manchester); universities created in the 1960s (such as Kent and Lancaster); former polytechnics that became universities in the early 1990s (such as Nottingham Trent and Sheffield Hallam); former Church of England Colleges of Higher Education, many of which are now universities (such as the Universities of Winchester, Chester and York St. John); continuing colleges that deliver HE; the private University of Buckingham; to, more recently, a new generation of corporate providers of specific fields of HE such as the University/College of Law and BPP International, which is focused on business and the professions. There is also substantial contemporary diversity in terms of what is variously identified as 'religion', 'faith', 'spirituality', 'belief', 'secularity' and 'secularism'. Each of these terminologies has specific emphases in relation to the phenomena that they seek to describe. Some also have areas of overlap with others. But all are contested. In this chapter, we use the terminology of 'religion or belief' on the basis that it is this terminology (within which 'belief' denotes 'non-religious' life orientations of sufficient cogency, seriousness, cohesion and importance to function in ways similar to religion) that shapes currently applicable human rights and equality law in the United Kingdom, as well as much social policy and practice that is framed by, and flows from, such law. Bearing in mind both the diversity of the HE context and the range of phenomena associated with religion or belief, there is, therefore, a range of ways in which the relationship between them can be explored. However, in this chapter, we focus on the practical questions, to be informed by specific project research findings and other, wider discussion, of how religion or belief impacts on the ways in which students and staff gain access to HE and how their religion or belief frames their participation.

Issues of access and participation can include seemingly straightforward matters where religion or belief directly impact on an individual's ability to access

HE. For example, there are Jewish students whose observance of the Sabbath means that they are unable to attend late lectures on Fridays during the winter. However, the intersection between religion or belief and access and participation is rarely this clear cut and can raise complex issues around the focus of curricula and the ability to express religious perspectives. For example, consider how a biology lecturer might react to a student who wished to approach a question on evolution from the perspective of intelligent design. In addition to these issues, which are concerned with the ability of students, and potentially also of staff, to access and participate in the formal aspects of HE, there are also a range of issues which relate to its informal aspects. For example, invitations to participate in post-seminar discussions in the bar may exclude those with particular religion or belief positions that preclude the drinking of alcohol and/or socialising in environments in which alcohol is present.

Issues of access and participation can be bounded on one side by issues of freedom of speech and on the other by concerns about discrimination. Many such issues might be experienced when accessing any kind of service, while others are specific, or at least reframed, by the fact that they take place in the context of HE. Further complexity is added by the fact that HE itself is a social phenomenon around which people mobilise a range of different ideologies and belief systems.

The evidential base on participation and access

Given the prominence that both HE and religion or belief have in society, the issues of access and participation have received relatively little attention. For example, the Higher Education Funding Council for England (HEFCE 2015) has published a strategy on access, participation and success for students in English HE. It highlights inequalities that exist around age, disability, ethnicity and socio-economic status, and strategises responses to each. However, religion or belief are not mentioned, despite these being among the 'protected characteristics' recognised in the Equality Act of 2010. However, this question has not been neglected altogether by policy and funding bodies: HEFCE has also funded a project on 'Religious Literacy Leadership in Higher Education', which made an intervention into the field of practice (Dinham and Jones 2010).

However, at least in the United Kingdom, issues of religion or belief – both in general, and also in relation to HE in particular – still attract relatively less attention at the level of policy and regulation than do some of the other 'protected characteristics' of equality law, and the issues have still received comparatively little attention from researchers. In what research there has been (e.g., Ahmad 2007; Guest et al. 2013; Modood 2006), participation and access have rarely been the primary areas of focus. A notable exception is Stevenson (2013) who argues that the omission of religion from discussions of participation and access is concerning and can result in some issues becoming racialised and poorly understood.

In comparison to evidence that exists on discrimination and harassment (e.g., Weller and Hooley 2016), or more recently on radicalisation and extremism (e.g., Brown and Saeed 2015), there has been less attention to the more everyday experience of how religion or belief influences the accessing of, and participation in, HE. Because of this, we have returned to a previous study we conducted which included these themes as a primary focus. This research was conducted in the United Kingdom during 2010–11 for the Equality Challenge Unit (ECU), which works to advance equality and diversity in UK universities and colleges (see http://www.ecu.ac.uk/). Although this was carried out in what is now some years ago, no similar studies have been subsequently undertaken. Nevertheless, this chapter seeks to move on the debates that were reflected in both the setting up of the original study and its results by contextualising that project's findings in a more contemporary discussion.

The ECU research explored issues around participation and disclosure in relation to religion or belief identities, the accommodation of religion and belief observance, discrimination and harassment relating to religion or belief and good relations on campus. It did so using a mixed-methods approach to gain as rounded as possible an understanding of the position of religion or belief in HE. The overall approach is discussed in Hooley and Moore (2011). Key elements of the methods used included:

- a consultation with a wide range of national stakeholders;
- a literature review (Weller, Hooley, and Marriott 2011);
- two national online surveys (of staff and students) resulting in responses from 3,077 staff from 131 HE institutions and 3,935 students from 101 institutions (see Hooley and Weller 2015) to which recruitment was secured via a variety of national networks and gatekeepers including religion or belief groups, HE institutions, trade unions, professional associations and social media.
- seven institutional case studies from across the four nations of the UK were chosen and the sample was informed by a typology of different 'types' of UK HEIs [HE institutions] (Weller, noted by Gilliat-Ray 2000: 7n).

We will use the data from this project to examine a number of themes that emerged in relation to participation and access. We will begin by looking at the issue of the collection of monitoring data on religion or belief in HE, moving on to look at how religion or belief impacts on formal and informal experiences of HE. Finally, we will explore how the institutional context frames issues of participation and access.

Understanding and monitoring access

At the point at which the ECU project research was undertaken outside of Northern Ireland, statistical data on the religion or belief identities of staff and student populations had not been routinely collected across HE institutions in the United Kingdom, although some HEIs had done this on a voluntary basis (see Weller 1991, 1992). However, if the HE sector seeks to address issues of participation and access, it is necessary first to build an understanding of its religion or belief composition since issues around participation and access relating to ethnicity, gender and class have, generally speaking, proceeded from concern about the under-representation of certain groups in either HE as a whole, and/or in certain subjects or institutions. And without monitoring data, it is impossible to identify how different religion or belief groups are represented across the sector. In tackling issues of access and participation, data therefore precedes strategy and implementation. Therefore, in the project, we sought to explore how far HEIs did or did not routinely collect data on religion or belief. We also asked if HEIs should gather more data in relation to religion or belief, whether any such data collection should be compulsory or voluntary and whether the religion or belief response categories used in the national census should also be used in collecting religion or belief data in HEIs.

At the same time, despite our advocacy of the need for better quantitative and other data on religion or belief to support evidence-based policy and practice in HE, it is important to recognise the limitations of what such – especially quantitative – data can offer (Voas and Bruce 2004; Weller 2004). Depending on how such questions are asked, they may variously provide information about identification, affiliation, beliefs, commitment or practice based on religion or belief. These questions and the quantitative data that the answers produce provide us with different information with which to inform policy and practice. To put it crudely; just because a lot of students tell you they are Christian does not mean that the university chapel will be full.

Table 2.1 shows how staff responded to the ECU survey question 'In relation to employee matters does your institution ever monitor religion or belief?'

Table 2.1 Institutions' approaches to monitoring staff religion or belief

	Number of occasions when this response was chosen	Percentage of the total responses
On an equal opportunities form when you applied for your job	1146	33.4%
On HR forms related to your actual employment	408	11.9%
On your employer's pension scheme forms	34	1.0%
At your institution's health centre	38	1.1%
None of the these	598	17.4%
Don't know	1209	35.2%
Total	3433	100.0%

Table 2.2 Institutions' responses to monitoring student religion or belief identities

	Number of occasions that this response was chosen	Percentage of the total responses
On forms when you applied to the university/college	1204	25.61%
As information you are asked for when you access services at university/college	243	5.17%
On university/college surveys	630	13.40%
On enrolment at the university/college	777	16.53%
None of these	1847	39.29%
Total	4701	100.00%

Table 2.2 shows how students responded to a similar question about the monitoring of student religion or belief.

Responses suggested that the monitoring of religion or belief identities was not widespread across the sector. However, where such questions are asked, for students this was most likely to be during application processes, while for staff it was in connection with job applications.

Against this background, the project also sought to establish the extent to which students and staff might be prepared to disclose their religion or belief. In total, 3,911 students and 3,056 staff responded to this question, with the results indicating that an overwhelming majority of respondents would be prepared to do so – including 80.3 percent of staff and 84.3 percent of students (Weller, Hooley, and Moore 2011: 30). Of course, it is possible that these results might only reflect those who, in the first instance, have in any way been willing to engage with a survey that is concerned with matters of religion or belief in HE. But the results are not incompatible with pilot research conducted by the Office for National Statistics prior to the introduction of a religion question in the 2001 decennial census question for England and Wales. While over a decade had passed since that time, during which such questions have been included in a wide range of contexts concerned with institutional policy and practice, there remained some respondents who did not feel comfortable about giving such information, as set out in Tables 2.3 and 2.4.

The fact that relatively high proportions of Buddhist student respondents (32 percent) and Pagan staff respondents (34 percent) were uncomfortable with providing answers to such questions is consistent with some prior research. In a study conducted prior to the introduction of the religion questions in the census, Buddhists were less comfortable with such questions than many other religious

Table 2.3 Numbers of students who do not feel comfortable with disclosing their religion or belief identity to their university by religion or belief group (*n* = 3911)

	Number of responses indicating that students do not feel comfortable disclosing their religion or belief	Students as a percentage of total respondents to the survey (by religion or belief group)
Buddhist	25	32.0%
Spiritual	56	30.0%
Uncodable	1	25.0%
Pagan	17	21.5%
No religion	254	20.3%
Jewish	15	20.0%
Muslim	64	18.0%
Other	12	17.1%
Hindu	13	16.9%
Sikh	5	13.9%
Christian	153	8.9%
Total	615	

Table 2.4 Numbers of staff who do not feel comfortable disclosing their religion or belief identity to their university (*n* = 3911)

	Number of responses indicating that staff do not feel comfortable disclosing their religion or belief	Staff as a percentage of total respondents to the survey (by religion or belief group)
Uncodable	8	61.5%
Pagan	15	34.0%
Spiritual	45	32.6%
Other	18	28.1%
No religion	311	27.7%
Hindu	11	20.8%
Jewish	7	17.9%
Buddhist	7	17.0%
Christian	169	11.7%
Muslim	10	11.1%
Sikh	1	3.4%
Total	602	

groups (Weller and Andrews 1998), while other research has shown that Pagans sometimes have concerns about their religious identity becoming known in employment contexts because of fears about misunderstandings, prejudice and discrimination (Weller, Feldman, and Purdam 2001: 42). Even so, there is more recent evidence (Weller, Ghanea, Purdam, and Cheruvallil-Contractor 2013: 208) that with the impact of equality and human rights legislation relating to religion or belief, Pagans are now more confident to 'come out'.

More generally, there is evidence (Weller et al. 2013: 166, 169–170) to suggest that some religious minorities have worries about surveillance by the state and its institutions. Some of these concerns have been debated subsequently in the light of the UK government's Prevent (counter-terrorism) agenda. Such debate has been particularly focused around Muslims, although Muslim respondents were not among the groups expressing most concern in 2010/2011. The debate around this has not just raised issues for those who are being monitored, but also from university staff who are charged with identifying potential violent extremism and who question the appropriateness of their becoming part of the security apparatus via their participation in surveillance conducted on behalf of the state (e.g., Hall 2015). However, we would argue that there are a range of ways in which quantitative data collection for the purpose of informing access and participation can be organised to minimise the possibility of individual surveillance taking place. Among those who described themselves as having 'no religion', another possible reason for reluctance to engage in quantitative data collection on religion or belief identities may be related to the idea that HE should have a 'secular' basis. In such a position, the 'secular' or 'secularism' (see Weller 2006) is articulated as the idea that HE institutions should be 'religion-or-belief-blind' and that therefore they should not concern themselves with what staff or students believe in these terms. The collection of religion or belief data therefore can be viewed as an abandonment of such a secular approach.

Despite the reluctance found among some groups, the majority of both staff and students who participated in the ECU project were content to disclose information on their religion or belief identity. This led to the project recommending to the ECU that there would be no widespread fundamental opposition to developing the routine collection of this data, although institutions would need to be sensitive to the concerns of some groups and individuals. Indeed, one of the policy impacts of this project was that, in 2012–13, the Higher Education Statistical Agency (HESA) adopted the ECU's recommendation, made on the basis of this research, for religion and belief data voluntarily to be collected in HEIs (see, respectively, for staff and students, Higher Educational Statistics Agency 2015a, 2015b). Of perhaps particular interest in the implementation of this is that, in their recommended forms of questions and optional answers, HESA included the response option of 'spiritual' used in this project's survey and selected by 4.5 percent of staff and 4.8 percent of student respondents to our survey despite this response category not having been offered in the UK decennial censuses (see Cheruvallil-Contractor et al. 2013). HEFCE (2016) has recently noted, however, that the return rate on religion or belief data is lower than for some of the more well-established 'protected characteristics', with religion or belief data being returned in 2014–15 on only 40 percent of staff and 44 percent of students (although this is already an increase from 31 percent and 34 percent, respectively, in 2013–14). It is not clear how far this is evidence of a limited commitment from HEIs to collect such information and how far it represents an unwillingness by staff and students to disclose. This is an area that would be worthy for further investigation.

Accessing and participating in the formal aspects of higher education

Higher education institutions perform a range of functions. These are sometimes simplified into a tripartite model of teaching, research and 'third stream' activities (outreach and entrepreneurship). It is possible to imagine ways in which religion or belief might intersect with each of these. In relation to the United Kingdom, only teaching has received any substantial attention within the literature, although it should be noted that the Cambridge Inter-Faith Programme at the University of Cambridge conducted a project on 'Religion and the Idea of a Research University' (see http://www.ideaofauniversity.com/about/) during 2011–13, which was associated with the work of Professor David Ford. Similarly, in the United States, Eckland's (2010) study of academic scientists and religion is of note. In this chapter, we will largely confine our discussion to the issue of teaching and learning within HE. This is a critical area of focus as it constitutes the main business of HEIs in terms of the interaction between staff and students. The curriculum provides a site within which ideas are transmitted and debated. Many within HE would see the active contestation of received truths, freedom of expression and the pursuit of rationality as being core values. However, the curriculum is arguably not an idealised space for critical debate, but rather a space within which hierarchies of power can be exercised and some truth claims can come to be privileged over others. Thus, even where freedom of expression is strongly supported, students may feel that articulating certain ideas associated with their religion or belief might result in a poor grade. Similarly, staff may seek to create conceptual walls between the ideas that they feel are part of their role and those that relate to their religion or belief. Because of this, participation in the curriculum may become a context for conflict and challenge around an individual's religion or belief.

Within the ECU project, we explored how students and staff experienced the intersection between religion or belief and the content and/or teaching of the curriculum. In relation to course content, 48.1 percent of students stated that they did not consider religion or belief relevant to course content. In contrast, 9.6 percent of respondents said that they did not feel that their course context was sensitive to their religion. Furthermore, 46.9 percent of students felt that their religion or belief was not relevant to how their course was taught, while 10.5 percent reported that the teaching on their course was not sensitive to their religion or belief. The survey also found that students were – at over 95 percent of responses – overwhelmingly satisfied with their course and with their general experience of being a student (Weller, Hooley, and Moore 2011: 35).

While there was a dissatisfied minority, most students either felt that their religion or belief was not relevant to their experience of participating in HE or that they were satisfied (or at least not dissatisfied) with the way that it was handled. Despite this positive finding, it was clear from the case studies that the intersection between religion or belief and the curriculum often required careful negotiation. An example of this was given by a Hindu life sciences student who discussed the dissection of animals and explained how the institution managed some of the tensions that can arise:

> The great thing about this University is at the end of the experiment, when you have got a dead animal in front of you, we have a ten or fifteen minute discussion at the end. We think about whether it has been useful. Was there any point in having this animal put down in order to learn? How can we change it for next year? They are constantly asking us about this so that we don't take things for granted. At the end of the term they ask the same question to the whole student group. I like the fact that it's out in the open. Sometimes I agree sometimes I don't. Often it's; [*sic*] come and have a go if you want to. I really appreciate their consideration.
>
> (quoted in Weller, Hooley, and Moore 2011: 39)

The inclusion of reflection and ethical discussion in this activity was seen by the student as a good way of handling a potential conflict situation. In another example, a medical student explained that because their course involves a lot of interaction with the public around sensitive issues such as death and dying, 'If you come from a particular faith, you will approach issues from the perspective of your faith so, for example, you may believe in the afterlife whereas your patient might not, or vice versa' (quoted in Weller, Hooley, and Moore 2011: 39). Again, the willingness of the course to address this openly was viewed as supportive of participation and respectful of particular religion or belief perspectives. Among the minority of student respondents who felt that either the course content and/or the teaching of it was not sensitive to their religion or belief, Table 2.5 shows how this concern varied across different religion or belief groups.

In connection with this, it is noteworthy that the proportion of Christian respondents is relatively higher than among Christians expressing broader concerns about their treatment in HEIs. Thus, a Christian student on a Religious Studies course referred to their experience of fellow students when personal belief systems entered into the academic discussion of religion: 'Because we are studying it academically, if someone gets out of hand people just shoot you down. They'll say; [*sic*] out of order, it's an academic class. Just chill out!' (quoted in Weller, Hooley, and Moore 2011: 38).

More generally speaking, where courses are not themselves directly concerned with matters of religion or belief, but do include discussion of issues that have a strongly ethical dimension, students can find themselves articulating

Table 2.5 Student concerns about the sensitivity of teaching and course content

Religion or belief	Percentage of students who disagreed or strongly disagreed that programme teaching is sensitive to my religion or belief	Percentage of students who disagreed or strongly disagreed that course content is sensitive to my religion or belief
Muslim	16.1%	15.0%
Buddhist	15.1%	12.8%
Christian	12.8%	12.0%
Jewish	11.6%	11.6%
Other	8.3%	11.4%
Hindu	8.2%	8.9%
Sikh	7.8%	6.7%
Spiritual	5.9%	6.5%
Pagan	3.8%	5.6%
No religion	3.7%	4.2%
Uncodable	0.0%	0.0%
Total	N = 410 or 10.42% of all respondents	N = 378 or 9.61% of all respondents

*Percentages may not total 100% due to rounding (Source: Weller, Hooley, and Moore 2011: 36–37)

positions that are informed by the values related to their religion or belief. As one student explained, sometimes during discussion they find themselves defending a position that aligns with their own religious standpoint, and experience criticism for the fact alone of introducing religion into the argument. Within some subjects in particular, there can be heightened sensitivity among academics to views expressed from a religion or belief perspective. As one law academic explained:

> I am conscious of the way I interact with students who may or may not be religious. I teach modules which include discussion about ethical issues. I teach a class on canon law. I am more aware of the need to keep it academic as opposed to when I am teaching criminal law.
>
> (quoted in Weller, Hooley, and Moore 2011 39)

An inclusive curriculum officer that we spoke to explained that some academics are very concerned about addressing religion or belief in the curriculum while others are uncertain about how to deal with students who use religious doctrines to illustrate academic arguments. To address this, HEIs are likely to need to find ways of bringing some of these concerns to the surface in order to try and reach some kind of working consensus among staff and students about how such issues might most fairly and equitably be addressed.

Informal participation

Participating in HE is not only about the completion of the formal curriculum. Higher education also serves a social and cultural function. It is where friendships are made, boundaries tested and ideas developed. Given this, it is important to consider how religion or belief shape access and participation of these informal aspects of university life. Some commentators have argued that the increasingly internationalised, multi-ethnic and multi-religious campus can provide a space where students learn to live in a pluralistic society (Valverde and Castenell 1998). However, for many students, the experience of being 'thrown together' is an uncomfortable one which is managed through the creation of a series of personal and group geographies through which the same spaces can be inhabited while the boundaries between different groups are maintained (Andersson, Sadgrove, and Valentine 2012).

In terms of participation and access, this may mean that different religion or belief groups are effectively accessing different non-formal experiences of HE. In the ECU research, we found that alcohol was a very important way in which these different campus geographies were maintained. As Piacentini and Banister (2006, 2009) have argued, students who do not wish to partake in this 'excessive drinking culture' are likely to experience considerable difficulty. This is particularly true for some groups of students whose attitudes towards alcohol consumption are defined by their religion or belief. In some cases, this can limit their ability to participate in a wide variety of activities and may leave them feeling isolated. Our ECU project results underlined the extent to which the wide use of alcohol is a problem for student respondents from a range of religion or belief groups, including Muslims, Hindus and some Christians.

Some student participants in the study-related stories of feeling isolated at particular times, such as during freshers' week. This was usually centred around dietary needs and the extent to which students were presented with a large number of alcohol-related activities, with only a limited range of social activities that did not involve the use of alcohol:

> It has affected my social life. In Malaysia the tradition is not to get drunk and this has been part of the foundation of my belief system. I have had to make friends with people who have a similar value set.
>
> (quoted in Weller, Hooley, and Moore 2011: 48)

In the ECU research, we identified various HEIs and Students' Unions which sought to actively address this by providing alternatives that can be supportive of an attempt to build a diverse campus where good relations are the norm. Thus, the organisers of some Students' Union Freshers' Weeks have developed a range of alcohol-free activities such as trips to local museums, shops, cultural activities and walks around the city. However, such activities only work where there are sufficient numbers of students who wish to take advantage of them. There is also a danger that such events could have the effect of ghettoizing those students who do not drink alcohol and separating them from the main student body. As one student in a collegiate university told us:

> Each college doesn't have many Muslims, and we need to meet students from different colleges. It takes you out of the college. You are chatting less with the people in your college. The whole year knows each other but they don't know you because you don't go to their entertainment events. It is difficult to socialise. Some people think Muslims are quite insular. It's not that we don't want to socialise. We would love to. I don't feel comfortable in these situations.
> (quoted in Weller, Hooley, and Moore 2011: 49)

For students with a religious affiliation, a student religious society can provide a valuable source of friends and sociability. However, this can also reinforce the separateness of religious students and lead to a stereotypical view of their unwillingness to mix. The prevalence of alcohol was also an issue for some staff. Higher education institutions offer a number of social, academic and networking events that are often associated with alcohol, such as cheese and wine evenings, Christmas celebrations and drinks receptions. This can be an issue for many who come from a religious, cultural, belief or other background in which one abstains from alcohol. Where this is the case, there is a perception that not attending such events might be potentially harmful to career progression as it removes a valuable networking opportunity. Alcohol therefore provides a particularly visible example of the way in which the experience of non-formal participation in HE can often become differentiated by religion or belief. From the point of view of those concerned about access and participation, this is clearly an issue which merits further consideration.

Accommodation and/or institutionalisation of religion or belief

The majority of HEIs organise their academic year with reference to the Western Christian calendar, and this can bring challenges for those of other than Western Christian religious traditions. The ECU project highlighted that some degree of accommodation was affected by implementing a variety of special arrangements, particularly in relation to examination. At the same time, there was often a lack consistency in the way that institutions deal with such matters. As explained by a Students' Union equality and diversity practitioner:

> When it comes to students, the academic timetable does not account for your religion at all. If you get the right programme leader you might be ok. It's down to their understanding and cultural awareness. There is no consistency within the institution; it actually comes down to the programme leader themselves.
> (quoted in Weller, Hooley, and Moore 2011: 39)

In some HEIs, the institutionalised presence of specific forms of religious presence and expectation can cause difficulties for people of no religion and/or other religions. For example, a number of HEIs often use religious (mainly Christian) buildings to accommodate examinations or degree ceremonies and others incorporate prayer (and sometimes hymns or acts of worship) into the fabric of institutional activities. As a Chaplain describing the graduation ceremony at the local cathedral explained:

> The reality is that it should be a ceremony but . . . [member of the senior management team] insisted that we have a hymn. I have complained that this is inappropriate. This is a ceremony and not a service. If it was a service it should be described as such.
> (quoted in Weller, Hooley, and Moore 2011: 39)

Or, as an atheist lecturer explained, 'As an atheist I am told to go to religious ceremonies and I feel compromised by the compulsion' (Weller, Hooley, and Moore 2011: 57). However, this is not necessarily a matter of a tension between the religious and the non-religious, but rather can be part of a wider tension between institutional norms, expectations or cultures and the consciences and practices of individuals. Thus, just as an expected alignment between an institution and a particular religion can potentially create concerns for the non-religious, it can also do so for those with a different religion than the one which shapes the ethos of the institution, and even for those whose religion it is that shapes the institution, but who feel uncomfortable with their own religion being so institutionalised.

In other HEIs, there can be at least a tension, and sometimes a conflict, for people of religion or belief between their value systems and perspectives and those which perceived to be the dominantly 'secular' or even 'secularist' ones of the majority of HEIs. While following up research conducted in 1999–2001 in a British Government Home Office commissioned project on religious discrimination (Weller, Feldman, and Purdam 2001), research in 2010–13 on religion and belief, discrimination and equality indicated an improvement in attitudes over the decade (Weller, Purdam, Ghanea, and Cheruvallil-Contractor 2013). But it also found that continuing 'unfair treatment or comments' appeared to 'stem from a dichotomy between religious and non-religious perspectives' and that HE institutions were generally seen as 'providing a space for the pursuit of "rational" knowledge and, for some, religion was perceived as "illogical" and "irrational"' (Weller, Purdam, Ghanea, and Cheruvallil-Contractor 2013: 97).

At the same time, institutions have to find ways to balance their institutional ethos with a multi-religious and pluralistic student (and staff) body. Dinham and Jones's research (2010) for HEFCE highlights how HEIs have variously sought to find such ways. In doing so, it highlighted a range of 'indicative' modes of response to religion, which they describe in terms of 'soft neutrality' or 'hard neutrality', while others saw religion in terms of 'repositories and resources', and still others in terms of it having a 'formative-collegial' role. While there are a number of institutions that have religious foundations or a strong association with a secular perspective, there is at present not very much evidence about the extent to which prospective students have much awareness of these institutionalised positions and/or use them to make choices about HE.

Conclusion

In this chapter, we have argued that religion or belief should be understood as one of the factors which shape individuals' access to, and participation in, HE. Our historic research with the ECU highlighted a range of ways in which this operates, but there remains much in this area that is not known or which has, so far, been only superficially explored. We believe that there would be value in a much stronger focus on these everyday questions about participation and access.

The issues that we have raised in this chapter have implications for policy and practice as well as research. In the ECU research, we set out a number of reflective questions that were designed to help HEIs, and the sector as a whole, to address the issues identified by the research. Those relating particularly to participation and accessibility asked institutions to consider whether they should gather more data about religion or belief and whether this should be compulsory or voluntary; how they should address the issues that emerged around the curriculum and teaching and learning; and how they could best support access and participation in the informal aspects of higher education, notably those relating to food and alcohol. Serious consideration of these questions (for their original form, see Weller, Hooley, and Moore 2011: 15), as well as a robust approach to discrimination and equality issues relating to religion or belief issues, should help HEIs and the HE sector as a whole to develop itself in ways that might make it still more accessible to participation on the part of staff and students of varied religion or belief. A future opportunity to conduct the research in ways similar to the conduct of the original ECU project might help such consideration to be informed by longitudinal comparison of the results of the original project and their evaluation.

References

Ahmad, F. (2007) Muslim Women's Experiences of Higher Education in Britain. *American Journal of Islamic Social Sciences* 24 (3), 46–69.

Andersson, J., Sadgrove, J., and Valentine, G. (2012) Consuming Campus: Geographies of Encounter at a British University. *Social & Cultural Geography* 13 (5), 501–515.

Brown, K. E., and Saeed, T. (2015) Radicalization and Counter-Radicalization at British Universities: Muslim Encounters and Alternatives. *Ethnic and Racial Studies* 38 (11), 1952–1968.

Cheruvallil-Contractor, S., Hooley, T., Moore, N., and Purdam, K. (2013) Researching the 'Non-Religious': Methods and Methodological Issues, Challenges and Controversies. In *Social Identities between the Sacred and the Secular*, ed. by Day, A., Vincett, G., and Cotter, C., Ashgate, Farnham, pp. 173–189.

Dinham, A., and Jones, S. H. (2010) *Religious Literacy Leadership in Higher Education: An Analysis of Challenges of Religious Faith, and Resources for Meeting Them, for University Leaders.* York: York St John University, Religious Literacy Leadership in Higher Education Programme.

Eckland, E. (2010) *Science v. Religion: What Scientists Really Think.* Oxford: Oxford University Press.

Guest, M., Aune, K., Sharma, S., and Warner, R. (2013) *Christianity and the University Experience: Understanding Student Faith.* London: Bloomsbury.

Hall, M. (2015) Universities Must Not Become Part of the Security Apparatus. *Times Higher Education,* 8th January 2015.

Higher Education Funding Council for England (2015) *Delivering Opportunities for Students and Maximising Their Success: Evidence for Policy and Practice 2015–2020.* Bristol: HEFCE.

Higher Education Funding Council for England (2016) Don't Ask, Don't Get: Improving Diversity Data for Staff and Students. 22nd March 2016. Available online at: http://blog.hefce.ac.uk/2016/03/23/dont-ask-dont-get-improving-diversity-data-for-staff-and-students/. Accessed 24 April 2016.

Higher Education Statistics Agency (2015a) *Staff Record 2012/2013 Religion or Belief.* Available online at: http://www.hesa.ac.uk/index.php/component/option,com_studrec/task,show_file/Itemid,233/mnl,12025/href,a%5E_%5ERELBLF.html. Accessed 31 January 2015.

Higher Education Statistics Agency (2015b) *Student Record 2012/2013 Religion or Belief.* Available online at: http://www.hesa.ac.uk/component/option,com_studrec/task,show_file/Itemid,233/mnl,12051/href,a%5E_%5ERELBLF.html. Accessed 31 January 2015.

Hooley, T., and Moore, N. (2011) *Religion and Belief in Higher Education: The Experiences of Staff and Students. Appendix 1: Project Approach.* Derby: International Centre for Guidance Studies.

Hooley, T., and Weller, P. (2015) Surveying the Religious and Non-Religious Online. In *Digital Methodologies in the Sociology of Religion,* ed. by Cheruvallil-Contractor, S., and Shakkour, S. London: Bloomsbury, pp. 13–37.

Modood, T. (2006) Ethnicity, Muslims and Higher Education Entry in Britain. *Teaching in Higher Education* 11 (2), 247–250.

Piacentini, M. G., and Banister, E. N. (2006) Getting Hammered? Students Coping with Alcohol. *Journal of Consumer Behaviour* 5 (2), 145–156.

Piacentini, M. G., and Banister, E. N. (2009) Managing Anti-Consumption in an Excessive Drinking Culture. *Journal of Business Research* 62 (2), 279–288.

Stevenson, J. (2013) Discourses of Inclusion and Exclusion: Religious Students in UK Higher Education. *Widening Participation and Lifelong Learning* 14 (3), 27–43.

Valverde, L. A., and Castenell, L. A. (1998) *The Multicultural Campus: Strategies for Transforming Higher Education.* Walnut Creek, CA: Altamira Press.

Weller, P. (1991) Religion and Equal Opportunities in Higher Education. *Cutting Edge* 2, 26–36.

Weller, P. (1992) Religion and Equal Opportunities in Higher Education. *Journal of International Education* 3 (November), 53–64.

Weller, P. (2006) 'Human Rights', 'Religion' and the 'Secular': Variant Configurations of Religion(s), State(s) and Society(ies). *Religion and Human Rights: An International Journal* 1 (1), 17–39.

Weller, P., and Andrews, A. (1998) Counting Religion: Religion, Statistics and the 2001 Census. *World Faiths Encounter* 21 (November), 23–34.

Weller, P., Feldman, A., and Purdam, K. (2001) *Religious Discrimination in England and Wales* (Home Office Research Report 220). London: Research, Development and Statistics Directorate, Home Office.

Weller, P., and Hooley, T. (2016) Religion and Belief, Equality and Inequality in Higher Education. In *Religion, Equality and Inequality*, ed. by Llewellyn, D., and Sharma, S. London: Routledge, pp. 89–101.

Weller, P., Hooley, T., and Marriott, J. (2011) *Religion and Belief in Higher Education: The Experiences of Staff and Students: Appendix 3. Literature Review*. London: Equality Challenge Unit.

Weller, P., Hooley, T., and Moore, N. (2011) *Religion and Belief in Higher Education: The Experiences of Staff and Students*. London: London Equality Challenge Unit.

Weller, P., Purdam, K., Ghanea, N., and Cheruvallil-Contractor, S. (2013) *Religion and Belief, Discrimination and Equality: Britain in Global Contexts*. London: Bloomsbury.

Chapter 3

Religiously unaffiliated students in the United States

Characteristics, experiences, and outcomes

Nicholas A. Bowman

By almost any metric, the United States is one of the most religious post-industrial countries in the world. For instance, in a survey of 30 countries (Smith 2012), 3 percent of people in the US reported that they do not believe in God versus 18 percent in Great Britain, 20 percent in the Netherlands, and 23 percent in France. Only Chile, Cyprus, and the Philippines ranked lower than the US. Conversely, 61 percent of people in the US said that they know God exists and have no doubts about it; this figure contrasts sharply with those from other post-industrial nations, including Denmark (13 percent), Sweden (10 percent), and Japan (4 percent). Moreover, according to a large-scale study from the Pew Research Center (2015), a majority of adults in the US report praying daily (55 percent) and believing that religion is very important (53 percent).

In this overall context of substantial religious observance and belief, religiously unaffiliated students at US colleges and universities merit attention. These students have an interesting place within higher education, since most institutions are not religiously affiliated, but their student populations are largely religiously identified. This chapter offers an overview of these students. First, it explores characteristics of unaffiliated students and how these attributes have changed over time. Second, it describes the experiences of these students, along with subsets of students (e.g., atheists), on university campuses. Third, it compares the outcomes of unaffiliated students with students who do identify with an organized religion or faith.

The findings from US colleges and universities can be compared with those from relatively secular countries. Recent research has explored the characteristics and experiences of atheist and non-religious university students in Scotland and Canada (Cotter 2015; Tomlins 2015) and of atheist adults in the United Kingdom and elsewhere (Bullivant and Lee 2012; Catto and Eccles 2013). Other studies have examined Christian students within the relatively secular environments of English universities (e.g., Guest et al. 2013). Despite the divergent religious contexts, some interesting similarities across the United States and other Western countries are evident, including the heterogeneity in unaffiliated students' identifications and beliefs as well as perceptions from both religiously unaffiliated and Christian students that their worldviews are marginalized.

Who are religiously unaffiliated students in the United States?

By definition, religiously unaffiliated students are those who respond 'none' when asked to choose their religion or worldview from a larger list; as a result, this group is sometimes referred to as the 'religious nones' (e.g., Putnam and Campbell 2010). As the largest and oldest study of postsecondary students in the United States, the Freshman Survey from the Cooperative Institutional Research Program (CIRP) has asked about students' religious/worldview identification for decades, and it weights its results to be nationally representative of all incoming students at baccalaureate-granting institutions. Students can choose from nineteen different response options, including 'other Christian' and 'other religion'. Therefore, all students who identify with a religion – regardless of its representation in the United States or their level of engagement in that religion – should select an option other than 'none'. In 2014, 27.5 percent of students selected 'none' (Eagan et al. 2014), which is notably greater than 17.4 percent in 2005 and 7.6 percent in 1982 (Pryor et al. 2007). More students selected 'none' in 2014 than any other response option, including Roman Catholicism; however, Protestant Christianity is divided into numerous categories (e.g., Baptist, Lutheran, Presbyterian), and this would be the largest identification if all Protestant denominations were combined into one group. This percentage of students who responded 'none' is quite similar to a figure from a national postsecondary student survey that asked a different question: 'In general, would you describe yourself more as a religious, spiritual, or secular person?' (Kosmin and Keysar 2013). Overall, 28.2 percent of students identified as 'secular', and fairly similar proportions responded 'religious' (31.8 percent) and spiritual (32.4 percent), along with 7.7 percent who reported 'don't know'.

However, religiously unaffiliated students are a more heterogeneous group than one might expect. In 2015, the CIRP Freshman Survey added two new response options to their identification question: agnostic and atheist. Overall, 29.5 percent of students identified as either atheist (5.9 percent), agnostic (8.3 percent), or 'none' (15.4 percent) (Eagan et al. 2015). These patterns differed notably by racial/ethnic group: Asian students were the most likely to be unaffiliated (39.5 percent) and to select 'none' (23.6 percent), White students were the most likely to be atheist (6.8 percent), and students from two or more racial/ethnic groups were most likely to be agnostic (10.0 percent). Black students were the least likely to identify with any of the three unaffiliated groups of 'none' (9.9 percent), agnostic (3.0 percent), and atheist (1.3 percent). Moreover, over the past few decades, male students are consistently more likely than female students to be religiously unaffiliated (Eagan et al. 2014).

Research on general adult samples provides further insight into the potential beliefs of unaffiliated students. Among religiously unaffiliated adults, 61 percent believe in God and 20 percent pray daily (Pew Research Center 2015), which illustrates that a lack of formal religious identification does not imply a lack of religiosity. About half of young adults who are religiously unaffiliated also report believing in God, whereas only one-sixth identify as atheist (Smith and Snell 2009), so these trends are not limited to older adults. Among religiously unaffiliated groups, atheists engage least in religious practice and hold the least conservative attitudes, followed by agnostics, and then other unaffiliated adults (Baker and Smith 2009). Moreover, as one might expect, religious observance is far more frequent for adults who identify with a particular religion than for the unaffiliated. Among all US adults, 50 percent report attending services at least monthly versus 9 percent of religious 'nones' (Pew Research Center 2015).

In a large-scale national study, the Higher Education Research Institute (2005) examined various religious, spiritual, and other attributes of entering postsecondary students across twenty categories of religious/worldview identification. When examined as a single group, religiously unaffiliated students were lowest on religious commitment, religious engagement, and spirituality, whereas they were the highest on religious skepticism. They also had among the lowest scores on religious/social conservatism. Perhaps reflecting the long-standing argument for the role of religion in bolstering community engagement, religiously unaffiliated students were lower than any other group in charitable involvement (mostly defined through volunteer work) and compassionate self-concept (viewing oneself as a kind and generous person).

Importantly, a lack of religious affiliation is not necessarily a stable personal attribute. In a longitudinal survey of US adults, Lim, MacGregor, and Putnam (2010) found that 30 percent of people who reported having no religious affiliation actually reported having an affiliation just one year later. The overall proportion for a lack of religious affiliation did not change over time, because approximately the same number of respondents moved in the opposite direction during that year (by subsequently reporting no affiliation when they had one a year earlier). Interestingly, people who changed in their reporting generally showed no significant changes in religious belief or practice. Nonetheless, the United States has become somewhat more secular over time, which appears to be largely driven by substantial generational differences in religiosity (Pew Research Center 2012; Voas and Chaves 2016).

Experiences of religiously unaffiliated students in postsecondary education

Almost one-quarter (22 percent) of all degree-granting colleges and universities in the United States are religiously affiliated, and almost one-tenth (9.3 percent) of postsecondary students attend one of these institutions (Council for Christian Colleges and Universities 2015). Although this means that the vast majority of students attend an institution that has no religious affiliation (including all public and most private schools), religion may still play an important role on these nonsectarian campuses (Clark et al. 2002; Seifert 2007). As several examples, 'winter break' (formerly 'Christmas break') is consistently scheduled during Christmas, a chapel or other Christian building is present on many campuses, Christian-informed prayer or reflection is common during some campus events and ceremonies (e.g., convocation, athletic team meetings), and institutions frequently accommodate Christian students' needs (e.g., serving fish in dining halls during Lent) whereas non-Christian students need to justify or advocate for their own needs (e.g., attending a week-long ceremony for a deceased relative).

Qualitative research illustrates some of the difficulties that religiously unaffiliated students – particularly those who identify as atheist – may encounter on university campuses. Regardless of their own religious/worldview identity (atheist, Christian, Jewish, or Muslim), students widely agreed that a three-tier hierarchy exists at many colleges and universities, with Christians as the socially dominant group on top, students from non-Christian religions in the middle, and atheists at the bottom (Small 2011). Campus interfaith dialogues, which often constitute an attempt to break down barriers of worldview and power, are likely to exclude students who do not identify with any formal religion (Nash 2011). The same is true in religious studies courses, in which the perspectives of non-religious students are often marginalized within the courses and/or excluded from the course content (Goodman and Mueller 2009; Nash 2011). Overall, college students' attitudes toward atheists and atheism vary dramatically, with students from religiously conservative groups holding negative attitudes overall (Bowman et al. in press).

Mueller (2012) conducted an in-depth study of sixteen students who identified as atheists. Although the single-institution sample was a limitation, these students had a substantial level of agreement with one another. They all had experiences encountering negative stereotypes about atheists: 'that they are (at best) hedonistic, unhappy, antagonistic, without belief in anything, and (at worst) amoral, dangerous, devil-worshippers' (p. 259). Many had experiences with students trying to proselytize to them. As a result, students generally did not share their atheist beliefs and tried to avoid conversations about religion altogether. They even described concerns about 'coming out' as well as being 'closeted' about their views, using language similar to students who identify as lesbian, gay, bisexual, and transgender. They found that they generally did not feel a need to discuss their worldviews, because their campus – like many others – was increasingly secular in a variety of ways.

These experiences should be contextualized by considering the experiences of students who do identify with a particular religion or faith. Muslim students report facing a hostile climate on university campuses (Cole and Ahmadi 2003; Mir 2014; Seggie and Sanford 2010; Speck 1997), as do Jewish students (Kosmin and Keysar 2015; Weinberg 2011) and non-Christian students more generally (Singer 2008; Small 2011). These negative experiences range from misunderstandings of one's religious practices to blatant discrimination and hate speech. Perhaps more surprisingly, evangelical Christian students consistently report encountering a campus climate that is antagonistic toward their views specifically and a religious perspective more generally (Brow et al. 2014; Bryant 2005; Hulett 2004; Magolda and Gross 2009; Moran, Lang, and Oliver 2007).

In short, virtually all religious or worldview groups perceive that they encounter difficulties on campus. It is important to note that students are much more likely to recognise an adverse climate for their group than for other groups (see Felix and Bowman 2015). When asked specifically about campus attitudes for acceptance of non-religious viewpoints, atheist students reported that their campus was less accepting than did religious majority (i.e., Protestant and Catholic) students; agnostic students' perceptions did not differ significantly from those of religious majority students (Rockenbach, Mayhew, and Bowman 2015). However, other research has asked about the campus religious climate in general (Mayhew, Bowman, and Bryant Rockenbach 2014; also see Bryant Rockenbach and Mayhew 2014). Using a broader indicator of climate, religious majority students perceived the worst climate, while religiously unaffiliated students perceived the best climate. Religious majority students who were strongly committed to their worldview perceived the most hostile climate of any group, differing by close to a standard deviation from religiously unaffiliated students who were strongly committed to their worldview.

Some limited research has also explored general forms of engagement on campus, and it often shows no differences between groups. Multiple studies found that religious/worldview identification was often unrelated to participation in various academic and non-academic experiences (Bowman, Rockenbach, and Mayhew 2015; Bryant 2011). Moreover, religiously unaffiliated students and religious majority students did not differ in the frequency of cross-racial interaction, whereas students from several religious minority groups (Buddhists, Hindus, Jews, and Muslims) each have greater cross-racial interaction than religious majority students (Park and Bowman 2015); these patterns occurred even when accounting for students' demographics (including race/ethnicity), pre-university attitudes, and other university experiences.

In most cases, religiously unaffiliated students differ from other groups in the availability of or interest in campus organizations specific to their worldview. Unaffiliated students who do not value their own spiritual or religious beliefs may not seek out such involvement, which could explain findings for cross-racial interaction (i.e., the greater cross-racial interaction among religious minorities may stem from their engaging in more racially diverse religious groups). In contrast, students who strongly identify with atheism may be more able and willing to connect with others who have similar views. As perhaps the best-known example, the Student Secular Alliance is an independent organisation with 270 college and university affiliate groups (Secular Student Alliance 2015). Some names of these affiliates directly counter negative stereotypes (e.g., 'Alliance of Happy Atheists!' at California Polytechnic State University) or showcase their belief in science ('Occam's Razors' at the University of Arkansas, which also alludes to their Razorback university mascot). Nonetheless, such opportunities for group membership and cohesiveness are more the exception than the rule.

Postsecondary outcomes for religiously unaffiliated students

Some research has examined the link between religious/worldview identification and a range of outcomes, including religion, spirituality, well-being, university satisfaction, grades, and retention. In general, religiously unaffiliated students tend to fare equal to or worse than religiously affiliated students. Relative to other students, unaffiliated students tended to exhibit greater decreases in religious commitment and perceived religious growth, along with greater increases in religious skepticism, during the first three years of postsecondary education (Bryant and Astin 2008; Small and Bowman 2011). These patterns persist when controlling for various pre-university attributes and university experiences, including students' actual religious engagement, which differs massively as a function of religious (un)affiliation (Brandenberger and Bowman 2013). Therefore, these findings are not simply explained by differences in religious practice between affiliated and unaffiliated students. Other dynamics seem to be at least partially responsible for explaining this gap; for instance, students may view their self-identification with a religious organisation as evidence for their religiosity above and beyond their actual participation in religious behaviors.

Most research on spirituality also suggests that religiously unaffiliated students experience less growth than do affiliated students, but this difference is largely (and sometimes entirely) explained by disparities in religious engagement and other university experiences (Bowman and Small 2010, 2013; Bryant 2007; Bryant and Astin 2008; Bryant, Choi, and Yasuno 2003). Despite these patterns for religious and spiritual changes, engaging in a spiritual quest or journey does not differ between religious unaffiliated and mainline Protestant students (Bowman and Small 2010, 2013), and students from various religious and non-religious backgrounds ask numerous spiritual questions (Brown 2012; Cherry, DeBerg, and Porterfield 2001). Such findings broach the complicated issue of the practical distinction between religion and spirituality. Some researchers argue that these two constructs are strongly related, citing high correlations between relevant indicators (e.g., Astin, Astin, and Lindholm 2011). Others argue that students distinguish readily between religion and spirituality, as they frequently categorise themselves into 'spiritual not religious' and other such distinctive groups (e.g., Kosmin and Keysar 2013; Zabriskie 2005) and have definitions of spirituality that may be largely independent from religion (Rockenbach et al. 2015). From the available research evidence, it appears that religiously affiliated and unaffiliated students often differ in terms of their religious and spiritual outcomes, but the occurrence of spiritual exploration and inquiry may be more universal.

In a potentially related domain, religious and spiritual struggle has also been explored as a function of religious/worldview identification. These studies have yielded mixed evidence; when comparing religious majority and unaffiliated students, the results indicate that religiously unaffiliated students are lower on struggle (Small and Bowman 2011), higher on struggle (Bryant 2011), or not significantly different (Bryant and Astin 2008). This variation may be explained by the different methodologies of these studies: Small and Bowman examined changes in spiritual struggle over time, Bryant examined only indirect effects on postsecondary religious struggle using a structural equation model, and Bryant and Astin predicted postsecondary spiritual struggle but did not have a true pre-test. The potential mechanisms underlying these relationships are unclear, but it is possible that the importance of worldview and the act of searching may play a role. For instance, engaging in a spiritual quest, discussing religion/spirituality with friends, and attending a religiously affiliated institution are all positively and uniquely associated with spiritual struggle (Bryant and Astin 2008). Therefore, any relationship between religious (un)affiliation and struggle is likely explained by the salience of spirituality and religion in students' lives.

Other outcomes related to religion and spirituality include ecumenical world-view (one's interest in and openness to diverse religious traditions), pluralism orientation (seeing the similarity among and desire to interact across different faith traditions), worldview commitment (how strongly one believes and cares about one's religious/worldview identification), and self-authored worldview commitment (the extent to which one arrives at a thoroughly considered commitment as opposed to relying on external sources). These constructs have recently been examined in multiple large-scale data sets. Overall, ecumenical worldview is greater among religious minority students than religious majority and religiously unaffiliated students (Bryant Rockenbach and Mayhew 2013; Mayhew 2012). For pluralism orientation, religious minority students also exhibit the highest outcomes; in addition, agnostics are higher than the average student, whereas atheist and 'non-religious' students are lower than average (Rockenbach et al. 2015; Rockenbach et al. in press). One possible explanation is that religious minority groups may particularly benefit from interfaith appreciation and cooperation, so they are therefore the most likely to hold ecumenical worldviews and pluralism orientations.

Furthermore, although religiously unaffiliated students as a whole have the weakest overall commitment to their worldview (Mayhew and Bryant Rockenbach 2013), agnostic and atheist students are higher than average in terms of self-authorship of their worldview commitment, whereas other 'non-religious' students were somewhat lower than average (Mayhew, Rockenbach, and Bowman in press; Rockenbach et al. in press). Having a self-authored lack of religious affiliation is consistent with qualitative findings that showed atheist students were often raised in religious households (Mueller 2012), so they likely arrived at their current worldview through their own consideration of religious and spiritual issues. Moreover, the disparities among atheist, agnostic, and other non-religious students may reflect the extent to which identifying as atheist is a more definitive statement of one's beliefs, whereas identifying as 'non-religious' – but not atheist or agnostic – may reflect a lower level of introspection on average.

Across various studies, religiously unaffiliated students tend to fare more poorly on measures of well-being than other students. Specifically, relative to religious majority students, they have lower overall and social satisfaction with their college or university (Bowman, Felix, and Ortis 2014; Bowman and Toms Smedley 2013; but see Mooney 2010), higher levels of depression (Phillips and Henderson 2006), reduced subjective well-being (Bowman and Small 2012), and diminished self-rated physical health (Bryant and Astin 2008). Religiously unaffiliated young adults also have lower overall satisfaction with their lives (Smith and Snell 2009). These differences sometimes persist even when adjusting for students' religiosity and spirituality, which may explain at least some of these relationships (Bowman and Small 2012; also see Koenig, McCullough, and Larson 2001; Mayrl and Oeur 2009). Some research has found no differences between religious majority and unaffiliated students in their social adjustment to university (Bryant 2007) and their changes in emotional well-being and psychological distress (Bryant 2007; Bryant and Astin 2008); however, the university experiences used as control variables may have simply accounted for the significant relationships observed in other studies.

Finally, academic outcomes have also received some limited attention. Several studies have indicated no significant differences in postsecondary grades between religious majority and unaffiliated students (Bowman et al. 2014; Bryant 2007; Mooney 2010), as well as no difference in graduation rates (Bowman et al. 2014).

Conclusion

This chapter provides the most comprehensive overview to date of religiously unaffiliated students in the United States. In the context of high religious observance, this group merits attention from researchers and practitioners alike. The chapter provides insights into the characteristics of unaffiliated students (with some surprising information about the diversity and prevalence of this group), their experiences on university campuses (along with how these contrasts with those of religiously affiliated students), and their outcomes from attending higher education (which are often less favorable than their peers).

Religiously unaffiliated students are a heterogeneous group, since they exhibit substantial variation in their belief in God, religious and spiritual practice, self-identification (other than a common lack of association with existing religions), and the temporal nature of their self-description. This group has grown substantially over the past couple of decades; the most recent estimate is that about 30 percent of undergraduates at four-year US institutions do not identify with a religious group (Eagan et al. 2015). Religiously unaffiliated students – especially those who identify as atheist – face challenges adjusting to postsecondary institutions that reflect the Christian history and present-day predominance of Christianity in the United States. However, unaffiliated students may actually perceive a more positive climate for religion and spirituality than other groups, whereas highly committed evangelical Christians report the most hostile climate on (now largely secular) campuses.

Overall, religiously unaffiliated students fare more poorly than religious majority students in their university and life satisfaction as well as changes in well-being, religiosity, and spirituality. These students' lower religious engagement likely plays a role in explaining at least some of these disparities. Nonetheless, unaffiliated students do as well as majority students in terms of engaging in spiritual searching and questioning, holding ecumenical worldviews and pluralism orientations, participating in academic and co-curricular experiences, and attaining academic outcomes.

Implications

In the context of considerable discussion about religious freedom and orthodoxy in higher education and beyond, these findings suggest that (non)religious differences are meaningful for shaping student experiences and outcomes, but they appear to be relatively unimportant for some outcomes. The fact that all students perceive a climate that is at least somewhat hostile toward their worldview group suggests that colleges and universities must work to promote inclusion and cooperation across diverse groups. Creating a positive climate is certainly not a 'zero-sum' game; that is, improving the climate for one group does not have to result in a poorer climate for another. However, part of the challenge is that efforts to make the campus more inclusive of non-Christian and non-religious worldviews may give the impression that Christianity is devalued (see Moran et al. 2007), which appears to be a problem in the United States and beyond. This tension may be particularly strong when the needs of unaffiliated students are given full attention.

Moreover, the lower levels of well-being and satisfaction for religious unaffiliated students are concerning. How can these students find community on campus in ways that serve similar functions as religious organisations? This question does not imply that students necessarily need analogous clubs or groups (such as those through the Secular Student Alliance), but they likely need outlets for forming interpersonal connections and developing purpose. More inquiry is necessary to understand this issue. In general, research on this topic is complicated by the frequent use of a single 'none' response option to capture the diverse identities of religiously unaffiliated students. Using more nuanced categories will help researchers and practitioners to better understand the experiences and outcomes of this burgeoning group of students.

References

Astin, A. W., Astin, H. S., and Lindholm, J. A. (2011) Assessing Students' Spiritual and Religious Qualities. *Journal of College Student Development* 52, 39–61.

Baker, J. O., and Smith, B. (2009) None Too Simple: Examining Issues of Religious Nonbelief and Nonbelonging in the United States. *Journal for the Scientific Study of Religion* 48 (4), 719–733.

Bowman, N. A., Felix, V., and Ortis, L. (2014) Religious/Worldview Identification and College Student Success. *Religion and Education* 41, 117–133.

Bowman, N. A., Rockenbach, A. N., and Mayhew, M. J. (2015) Campus Religious/ Worldview Climate, Institutional Religious Affiliation, and Student Engagement. *Journal of Student Affairs Research and Practice* 52, 24–37.

Bowman, N. A., Rockenbach, A. N., Mayhew, M. J., Riggers-Piehl, T., and Hudson, T. D. (in press) 'College Students' Appreciative Attitudes toward Atheists'. *Research in Higher Education*.

Bowman, N. A., and Small, J. L. (2010) Do College Students Who Identify with a Privileged Religion Experience Greater Spiritual Development? Exploring Individual and Institutional Dynamics. *Research in Higher Education* 51, 595–614.

Bowman, N. A., and Small, J. L. (2012) Exploring a Hidden Form of Minority Status: College Students' Religious Affiliation and Well-Being. *Journal of College Student Development* 53, 491–509.

Bowman, N. A., and Small, J. L. (2013) The Experiences and Spiritual Growth of Religiously Privileged and Religiously Marginalized College Students. In *Spirituality in College Students' Lives: Translating Research Into Practice*, ed. by Bryant Rockenbach, A., and Mayhew, M. J. New York: Routledge, pp. 19–34.

Bowman, N. A., and Toms Smedley, C. (2013) The Forgotten Minority: Examining Religious Affiliation and University Satisfaction. *Higher Education* 65, 745–760.

Brandenberger, J. W., & Bowman, N. A. (2013). From Faith to Compassion? Reciprocal Influences of Spirituality, Religious Commitment, and Prosocial Development during College. In *Spirituality in College Students' Lives: Translating Research into Practice*. ed. by Bryant Rockenbach, A., and Mayhew, M. J. New York: Routledge, pp. 121–137.

Brow, M. V., Yau, J., Jiang, Y. H., and Bonner, P. (2014) Christians in Higher Education: Investigating the Perceptions of Intellectual Diversity Among Evangelical Undergraduates at Elite Public Universities in Southern California. *Journal of Research on Christian Education* 23 (2), 187–209.

Brown, M. S. (2012) *The Nature of Spiritual Questioning among Select Undergraduates at a Midwestern University: Constructions, Conditions, and Consequences.* Unpublished PhD thesis. Bowling Green, OH: Bowling Green State University.

Bryant, A. N. (2005) Evangelicals on Campus: An Exploration of Culture, Faith, and College Life. *Religion and Education* 32 (2), 1–30.

Bryant, A. N. (2007) The Effects of Involvement in Campus Religious Communities on College Student Adjustment and Development. *Journal of College and Character* 8 (3), 1–25.

Bryant, A. N. (2011) The Impact of Campus Context, College Encounters, and Religious/Spiritual Struggle on Ecumenical Worldview Development. *Research in Higher Education* 52, 441–459.

Bryant, A. N., and Astin, H. S. (2008) The Correlates of Spiritual Struggle During the College Years. *Journal of Higher Education* 79, 1–28.

Bryant, A. N., Choi, J. Y., and Yasuno, M. (2003) Understanding the Religious and Spiritual Dimensions of Students' Lives in the First Year of College. *Journal of College Student Development* 44, 723–746.

Bryant Rockenbach, A., and Mayhew, M. J. (2013) How Institutional Contexts and College Experiences Shape Ecumenical Worldview Development. In *Spirituality in*

College Students' Lives: Translating Research into Practice, ed. by Bryant Rocken-bach, A., and Mayhew, M. J. New York: Routledge, pp. 88–104.

Bryant Rockenbach, A., and Mayhew, M. J. (2014) The Campus Spiritual Climate: Predictors of Satisfaction Among Students with Diverse Worldviews. *Journal of College Student Development* 55 (1), 41–62.

Bullivant, S., and Lee, L. (2012) Introduction: Interdisciplinary Studies of Non-Religion and Secularity: The State of the Union. *Journal of Contemporary Religion* 27 (1), 19–27.

Catto, R., and Eccles, J. (2013) (Dis)Believing and Belonging: Investigating the Nar-ratives of Young British Atheists. *Tenemos* 49 (1), 37–63.

Cherry, C., DeBerg, B. A., and Porterfield, A. (2001) *Religion on Campus*. Chapel Hill, NC: University of North Carolina Press.

Clark, C., Vargas, M. B., Schlosser, L., and Alimo, C. (2002) It's Not Just 'Secret Santa' in December: Addressing Educational and Workplace Climate Issues Linked to Christian Privilege. *Multicultural Education* 10 (2), 52–57.

Cole, D., and Ahmadi, S. (2003) Perspectives and Experiences of Muslim Women Who Veil on College Campuses. *Journal of College Student Development* 44, 47–66.

Cotter, C. R. (2015) Without God Yet Not Without Nuance: A Qualitative Study of Atheism and Non-Religion Among Scottish University Students. In *Atheist Identi-ties: Spaces and Social Contexts*, ed. by Beaman, L. G., and Tomlins, S. New York: Springer, pp. 171–193.

Council for Christian Colleges and Universities (2015) *Profile of U.S. Post-Secondary Education*. Available online at: http://www.cccu.org/~/media/2015%20Post%20 Secondary%20Profile.pdf. Accessed 13 March 2016.

Eagan, K., Stolzenberg, E. B., Bates, A. K., Aragon, M. C., Suchard, M. R., and Rios-Aguilar, C. (2015) *The American Freshman: National Norms Fall 2015*. Los Angeles: Higher Education Research Institute, University of California.

Eagan, K., Stolzenberg, E. B., Ramirez, J. J., Aragon, M. C., Suchard, M. R., and Hurtado, S. (2015) *The American Freshman: National Norms Fall 2014*. Los Ange-les: Higher Education Research Institute, University of California.

Felix, V., and Bowman, N. A. (2015) A Historical and Research Overview of Reli-gious/Worldview Identification in Higher Education. In *Making Meaning: Embracing Spirituality, Faith, Religion, and Life Purpose in Student Affairs*, ed. by Small, J. L. Sterling, VA: Stylus, pp. 37–57.

Gilliat-Ray, S. (2000) *Religion in Higher Education: The Politics of the Multi-faith Campus*. Aldershot: Ashgate.

Goodman, K. M., and Mueller, J. A. (2009) Invisible, Marginalized, and Stigmatized: Understanding and Addressing the Needs of Atheist Students. In *Intersections of Religious Privilege: Difficult Dialogues and Student Affairs Practice* (New Direc-tions for Student Services, No. 125), ed. by Watt, S. K., Fairchild, E. E., and Good-man, K. M. San Francisco: Jossey-Bass, pp. 55–63.

Guest, M., Aune, K., Sharma, S., and Warner, R. (2013) *Christianity and the Univer-sity Experience: Understanding Student Faith*. London: Bloomsbury.

Higher Education Research Institute (2005) *The Spiritual Life of College Students: A National Study of College Students' Search for Meaning and Purpose*. Los Angeles: Higher Education Research Institute, University of California.

Hulett, L. S. (2004) Being Religious at Knox College: Attitudes toward Religion, Christian Expression, and Conservative Values on Campus. *Religion and Education* 31 (2), pp. 41–61

Koenig, H. G., McCullough, M., and Larson, D. B. (2001) *Handbook of Religion and Health.* Cambridge: Oxford University Press.

Kosmin, B. A., and Keysar, A. (2013) *Religious, Spiritual, and Secular: The Emergence of Three Distinct Worldviews among American College Students.* Hartford, CT: Trinity College.

Kosmin, B. A., and Keysar, A. (2015) *National Demographic Survey of American Jewish College Students 2014: Anti-Semitism Report.* Washington, DC: Louis D. Brandeis Center for Human Rights Under Law.

Lim, C., MacGregor, C. A., and Putnam, R. D. (2010) Secular and Liminal: Discovering Heterogeneity among Religious Nones. *Journal for the Scientific Study of Religion* 49, 596–618.

Magolda, P., and Gross, K. E. (2009) *It's All about Jesus! Faith as an Oppositional Subculture.* Sterling, VA: Stylus.

Mayhew, M. J. (2012) A Multi-Level Examination of College and Its Influence on Ecumenical Worldview Development. *Research in Higher Education* 53, 282–310.

Mayhew, M. J., Bowman, N. A., and Bryant Rockenbach, A. (2014) Silencing Whom? Linking Campus Climates for Religious, Spiritual, and Worldview Diversity to Student Worldviews. *Journal of Higher Education* 85, 219–245.

Mayhew, M. J., and Bryant Rockenbach, A. N. (2013) Achievement or Arrest? The Influence of Campus Religious and Spiritual Climate on Students' Worldview Commitment. *Research in Higher Education* 54, 63–84.

Mayhew, M. J., Rockenbach, A. N., and Bowman, N. A. (in press) The Connection Between Interfaith Engagement and Self-Authored Worldview Commitment. *Journal of College Student Development* 57 (4), 362–379.

Mayrl, D., and Oeur, F. (2009) Religion and Higher Education: Current Knowledge and Directions for Future Research. *Journal for the Scientific Study of Religion* 48 (2), 260–275.

Mir, S. (2014) *Muslim American Women on Campus: Undergraduate Social Life and Identity.* Chapel Hill, NC: University of North Carolina Press.

Mooney, M. (2010) Religion, College Grades, and Satisfaction Among Students at Elite Colleges and Universities. *Sociology of Religion* 71 (2), 197–215.

Moran, C. D., Lang, D. J., and Oliver, J. (2007) Cultural Incongruity and Social Status Ambiguity: The Experiences of Evangelical Christian Student Leaders at Two Midwestern Public Universities. *Journal of College Student Development* 48, 23–38.

Mueller, J. A. (2012) Understanding the Atheist College Student: A Qualitative Examination. *Journal of Student Affairs Research and Practice* 49 (3), 249–266.

Nash, R. J. (2011) Inviting Atheists to the Table. In *Sacred and Secular Tensions in Higher Education: Connecting Parallel Universities,* ed. by Waggoner, M. D. New York: Routledge, pp. 72–91.

Park, J. J., and Bowman, N. A. (2015) Religion as Bridging or Bonding Social Capital: Race, Religion, and Cross-Racial Interaction for College Students. *Sociology of Education* 88, 20–37.

Pew Research Center (2012) *'Nones' on the Rise: One-in-Five Adults Have no Religious Affiliation.* Washington, DC: Author.

Pew Research Center (2015) *U.S. Public Becoming Less Religious. Modest Drop in Overall Rates of Belief and Practice, But Religiously Affiliated Americans are as Observant as Before.* Washington, DC: Author.

Phillips, R., and Henderson, A. (2006) Religion and Depression Among U.S. College Students. *International Social Science Review* 82 (3/4), 166–172.

Pryor, J. H., Hurtado, S., Saenz, V. B., Santos, J. L., and Korn, W. S. (2007) *The American Freshman: Forty-Year Trends 1966–2006.* Los Angeles: Higher Education Research Institute, University of California.

Putnam, R. D., and Campbell, D. E. (2010) *American Grace: How Religion Divides and Unites Us.* New York: Simon and Schuster.

Rockenbach, A. N., Mayhew, M. J., and Bowman, N. A. (2015) Perception of the Campus Climate for Non-Religious Students. *Journal of College Student Development* 56, 181–186.

Rockenbach, A. N., Mayhew, M. J., Davidson, J., Ofstein, J., and Clark Bush, R. (2015) Complicating Universal Definitions: How Students of Diverse Worldviews Make Meaning of Spirituality. *Journal of Student Affairs Research and Practice* 52 (1), 1–10.

Rockenbach, A. N., Mayhew, M. J., Morin, S., Crandall, R. E., and Selznick, B. (2015) Fostering the Pluralism Orientation of College Students Through Interfaith Co-Curricular Engagement. *Review of Higher Education* 39 (1), 25–58.

Rockenbach, A. N., Riggers-Piehl, T. A., Garvey, J. C., Lo, M. A., and Mayhew, M. J. (in press) The Influence of Campus Climate and Interfaith Engagement on Self-Authored Worldview Commitment Across Sexual and Gender Identities. *Research in Higher Education* 57 (4), 497–517.

Secular Student Alliance (2015) *Affiliated Campus Group List.* Available online at: https://secularstudents.org/affiliates. Accessed 13 March 2016.

Seggie, F. N., and Sanford, G. (2010) Perceptions of Female Muslim Students Who Veil: Campus Religious Climate. *Race, Ethnicity, and Education* 13, 59–82.

Seifert, T. (2007) Understanding Christian Privilege: Managing the Tensions of Spiritual Plurality. *About Campus* 12 (2), 10–17.

Singer, M. J. (2008) A Hidden Minority Amidst White Privilege. *Multicultural Perspectives* 10 (1), 47–51.

Small, J. L. (2011) *Understanding College Students' Spiritual Identities: Different Faiths, Varied Worldviews.* Cresskill, NJ: Hampton Press.

Small, J. L., and Bowman, N. A. (2011) Religious Commitment, Skepticism, and Struggle Among College Students: The Impact of Majority/Minority Religious Affiliation and Institutional Type. *Journal for the Scientific Study of Religion* 50, 154–174.

Smith, C., and Snell, P. (2009) *Souls in Transition: The Religious and Spiritual Lives of Emerging Young Adults.* Cambridge: Oxford University Press.

Smith, T. W. (2012) *Beliefs About God Across Time and Countries.* Chicago: NORC/University of Chicago.

Speck, B. W. (1997) Respect for Religious Differences: The Case of Muslim Students. In *Building Faculty Learning Communities* (New Directions for Teaching and Learning, No. 70), ed. by Sigsbee, D. L., Speck, B. W., and Maylath, B. San Francisco: Jossey-Bass, pp. 39–46.

Tomlins, S. (2015) A Common Godlessness: A Snapshot of a Canadian University Atheist Club, Why Its Members Joined, and What That Community Means to

Them. In *Atheist Identities: Spaces and Social Contexts*, ed. by Beaman, L. G., and Tomlins, S. New York: Springer, pp. 117–136.

Voas, D., and Bruce, S. (2004) The 2001 Census and Christian Identification in Britain. *Journal of Contemporary Religion* 19 (1), 23–28.

Voas, D., and Chaves, M. (2016) Is the United States a Counterexample to the Secularization Thesis? *American Journal of Sociology* 121 (5), 1517–1556.

Weinberg, A. (2011) *Alone on the Quad: Understanding Jewish Student Isolation on Campus.* Available online at: http://www.bjpa.org/Publications/details.cfm?PublicationID=13969. Accessed 28 April 2016.

Weller, P. (2004) Identity, Politics and the Future(s) of Religion in the UK: The Case of the Religion Questions in the 2001 Decennial Census. *Journal of Contemporary Religion* 19 (1), 3–21.

Zabriskie, M. (2005) *College Student Definitions of Religiosity and Spirituality.* Unpublished PhD thesis. Ann Arbor, MI: University of Michigan.

Section II

The religious student experience

Learning from qualitative studies

Chapter 4

The contested campus

Christian students in UK universities

Kristin Aune and Mathew Guest

During the first decade of the twenty-first century, several incidents occurred on UK campuses that highlighted tensions between evangelical Christian students, Students' Unions and university authorities about publicly expressed views on gender roles and homosexuality. Controversy surrounded the evangelical Christian Union at Bristol, where an attempt was made to limit opportunities for female speakers; at Exeter and Birmingham, the issue was inclusion of LGBT students. These incidents illustrate that university campuses can be sites in which conservative, counter-cultural forms of religion emerge or even thrive, an observation that sits uncomfortably alongside the common assumption that higher education is a driver of secularisation (Berger 1999; Guest et al. 2013a).

More recent controversies have tended to focus on Islam, with government rhetoric on counter-terrorism pointing to links between student Islamic societies, radical speakers invited onto campuses, and the dangers of 'radicalisation' (Brown and Saeed 2015). The Counter-Terrorism and Security Act (2015) places a legal responsibility on universities to intervene where 'radicalisation' may be occurring, its Prevent Guidelines extending the focus of suspicion to a variety of forms of 'non-violent extremism', including far-right, far-left, animal rights and environmental movements that oppose 'fundamental British values'. The university is recast as a context of anxiety and risk, with religion marked as having a subversive potential that needs careful monitoring.

Such anxiety about public engagement with contentious topics is mirrored in the growing tendency among students refusing to share a platform with external speakers whose perspective they find offensive. This censorious approach to controversy extends beyond religious matters, with some prominent feminists prevented from speaking on UK campuses. The reasons given cite the importance of protecting vulnerable groups, although 'no platforming' is also treated as a form of protest, a refusal to grant legitimacy to an opponent's position. Government approaches to counter-terrorism reveal a tendency to exclude and delimit open debate, made plain in the language universities use to justify decisions to curtail public discussions about religion (Grove 2015). Although later changing its position, the University of Warwick's Students' Union initially refused to allow ex-Muslim human rights campaigner Maryam Namazie to speak on the grounds that she might 'incite hatred' (Adams 2015). Religion has become a sensitive issue on many campuses, its expression among students especially so.

These developments stand in tension with long-established traditions of freedom of speech. While coloured by a romanticised past, universities' commitment to freedom of expression enjoys the benefit of more structural support insofar as it is enshrined in equality law. The 2010 Equality Act requires public institutions (including universities) to ensure equality for those who possess the 'protected characteristics' of age, disability, gender reassignment, race, religion or belief, sex, sexual orientation, marriage and civil partnership, and pregnancy and maternity. It directs universities to ensure equality of opportunity, elimination of harassment and good relations between those who share the protected characteristic and those who do not. It is therefore not simply a matter of 'equal opportunities', but also of wider campus relations. As supporting students and staff who are religious is now a legal requirement, universities have worked to improve their engagement with religion, such as by providing better facilities for prayer and religious diets, especially for the growing numbers of Muslim students who require Friday prayer and *halal* food. The inclusion of religion as a 'protected characteristic' presents significant challenges for universities seeking to maintain both freedom of religious expression and opposition to discrimination and intolerance. This is a difficult balance to strike, especially when religious perspectives on gender, sexuality and inter-religious relations run counter to the equality norms embedded in British culture, as became clear during the conflicts involving Christian Unions mentioned earlier.

Against this background, the status of the university as a context for the expression of religious identities is far from straightforward, and is framed by competing urges to accommodate religious difference on the one hand, and exclude or control religious radicalism on the other. Definitions of the latter are unstable and vulnerable to popular prejudice, with some scholars arguing that the 'radicalisation' agenda has focused disproportionate attention on Muslim students (Brown and Saeed 2015). But as the examples above illustrate, a culture of suspicion extends beyond Islam and renders religion a source of contention on university campuses, a trend heightened by the emergence of a self-conscious and organised secularism among the student body, often mobilised in attempts to discredit religious truth claims or the legitimacy of religion as a constituent part of university life. One aspect of this issue that remains to be explored concerns the way in which religious students perceive their campus environment: what kind of environment is it, and how does it accommodate matters of faith? Dinham and Jones's (2012: 194) qualitative research with senior university managers and students revealed that 'A majority of the VCs and PVCs. . . were keen to promote their institutions as "faith friendly"', citing provision of faith spaces and catering for religious diets. The desire to attract international students was an impetus for religious provision, implying an economic motivation, and 'a number of the religious students commented that their university only dealt with questions of religious faith at a superficial level' (Dinham and Jones 2012: 196). They conclude that the university is a place where religion is given increasing consideration and vice chancellors 'regarded religion as a potential source of enrichment and a resource on which universities could draw', but 'It remains to be seen . . . whether in a context of financial hardship they can adapt to the challenges of a world in which both religious and secular worldviews will inevitably come into more frequent contact' (Dinham and Jones 2012: 199). The research we present in this chapter explores how Christian students perceive universities to accommodate their faith, but first we draw on existing literature to highlight our analytical perspective, including its conception of institutional ethos.

Theoretical framework

American sociology has produced an abundant body of research into religion on university campuses, in part as a means of exploring the institutional dynamics of secularisation. Universities and colleges are often assumed to be major engines of secondary socialisation into a 'modern', rather than religious, perspective (Berger 1999; Hunter 1987). This assumption has been confirmed and challenged, with some scholars pointing to examples of religious or spiritual vitality within campus contexts (Bryant, Choi, and Yasuno 2003; Cherry, DeBerg, and Porterfield 2001), and others calling for a more complex understanding of how the experience of students interacts with the complex range of encounters that make up university life (Clydesdale 2007). While traditionally focusing on the educational dimension – how what students learn shapes their orientation to religion – scholarship is now more sensitive to the broader institutional cultures that students experience, including social, political and religious aspects of campus life (Bryant 2005). As Mayrl and Oeur comment in an article surveying the field, a major problem has been decontextualisation. Previous studies presented a rather two-dimensional picture of university life, failing to investigate how 'specific intuitional contexts interact with the religious engagements of undergraduate students' (Mayrl and Oeur 2009: 271).

A sociological treatment of campus religion demands a more subtle theorisation of the university experience, capable of distinguishing between the various institutional cultures that characterise the higher education sector. This kind of approach is also capable of highlighting the distinctive characteristics of the UK context; the US literature is helpful in guiding us through important conceptual and methodological matters, but UK higher education is very different; for instance, in housing a much less religiously committed population and very few faith-based universities. The following analysis builds on research undertaken as part of the 'Christianity and the University Experience' (CUE) project, which explored the ways in which the experience of university shapes the moral and religious orientations of Christian students. The CUE project involved a survey completed by around 4,500 students, of whom approximately half identified as Christian, and 100 interviews: 75 with self-identified Christian students (15 at each of five universities) and 25 with professional and religious staff and student leaders working with Christian students – for example, chaplains and equality and diversity officers (for survey findings and student demographics, see Aune 2015; Guest 2015; Guest et al. 2013a; Guest et al. 2013b; Sharma 2012). We addressed the diversity of higher education institutions in England by dividing them into five types, each distinctive with respect to geographical location, historical background, student demographics and institutional ethos. In this chapter, we take up the concept of institutional ethos – which we take to refer to the moral and aesthetic (i.e., evaluative) aspects of a given culture (Geertz 1973: 126) – and explore how a university's ethos shapes Christian students' perceptions of how Christianity is accommodated by their university.

Traditional elite universities are characterised by a long history, stretching back at least to the early nineteenth century, a heritage that comes with status. These universities – including Oxford, Cambridge, Durham and older London colleges such as University College London – maintain this high status on the basis of acclaimed academic research, reflected in high positions in university league tables and the popular imagination. They tend to be located in large and/or historical cities and attract higher proportions of students from privately educated and/or middle-class backgrounds. Their elite status fosters an ethos characterised by traditional scholarship, a sense of being set apart from the mainstream, and of continuing a centuries-old tradition of student life. By contrast, *inner-city redbrick universities* trace their origins to the late nineteenth and early twentieth centuries, established to serve the industrial age within major urban centres such as Birmingham, Leeds, Manchester, Sheffield, Liverpool and Bristol. Occupying a tier slightly below the traditional elites with respect to popular status and recruitment of social elites, the Red Bricks nevertheless maintain levels of research excellence that are on a par with those of traditional elite institutions. Still dedicated to science and industry, in the twenty-first century they attract culturally and religiously diverse populations and benefit from the opportunities afforded by commercial vitality and nightlife. Their ethos tends to reflect this, fusing wide-ranging disciplinary engagement with vibrant student politics and a social scene energised by the urban environment.

Additionally, *1960s-campus universities* were established in the wake of the 1963 Robbins Report that recommended the post-war population boom and economic growth be met with an expanded university sector. A number of brand new universities were rapidly built, most set within purpose-built, out-of-town campuses (most of the red bricks were located on various sites within the precincts of their cities). Self-consciously progressive, ambitious and experimental, universities such as Lancaster, York, Warwick and Sussex reflected an ethos of social inclusion and a mission to make university education available to all with the necessary educational credentials, irrespective of social background. At some, this came with radical politics and/or an essentially secular ethos, with only Kent establishing a Department of Theology and Lancaster pioneering the first explicitly Religious Studies Department, open to those of any faith or none. In maintaining a diverse student constituency and inclusive campus culture, the

1960s universities share much with the *post-1992 universities*, although the latter have contrasting origins and are our most institutionally diverse category. They originated as polytechnic colleges established to complement the older, more traditional universities by offering practical and vocational forms of training, often in close connection with local industry. This pedagogical focus made the polytechnics appealing to less privileged students, a tradition continued after they were gradually accorded university status following the 1992 Further and Higher Education Act. This diverse group of institutions includes a highly diverse student body. High proportions of locally based students mean the post-1992 universities often lack the extra-curricular campus vitality found at most of those in traditional elites, red-brick and 1960s-campus categories. That said, the cultural and religious diversity of universities such as Derby and Kingston has fostered innovative expressions of student faith on campus and warn against simple generalisations. Moreover, post-1992 universities' commitment to vocational education and widening access to populations traditionally under-represented in higher education fosters a shared ethos structured around values of accessibility, equality of opportunity and innovation in teaching and learning.

The final category encompasses the Council of Church Universities and Colleges (or '*Cathedrals Group*'), sixteen universities that were originally established – most in the nineteenth century – by the Anglican, Roman Catholic or Methodist Churches as colleges for training school teachers. While many have expanded to cover a range of academic disciplines, they maintain strong links with their originating denominations, affirm an explicitly Christian ethos and express this in a commitment to vocational and public-service-oriented programmes of study. Their Christian identity is also typically reflected in the prominent role they accord to chaplains, in a greater frequency of Christianity-framed public events and, in some cases, in systems of governance. Cathedrals Group universities tend to be found in historical Cathedral towns such as Chester, Canterbury, York and Chichester, but are much smaller than typical institutions in the other four categories. In professing an ethos that is Christian and church-founded, they are unique within the United Kingdom.

The notion of institutional ethos emerges as especially important in the subsequent discussion, and can be appropriately understood as arising from and maintained by the other three factors of geography, history and student demographics. Moreover, institutional ethos is conceived here not in simple, singular terms, but as pointing to a number of contested narratives – some official and public, others more informal and implicit – together informing the institutional identity of the universities that formed the empirical basis for the research. While thirteen universities featured in the national survey undertaken for the CUE project – spanning all five types and attracting responses from 4,500 undergraduates – this essay focuses on the five case study universities – one from each type – that were explored in greater detail via semi-structured interviews with 75 students who self-identified as Christian. Each was questioned about their experience of being a Christian at university, the overall aim being to ascertain how this experience had shaped their religious and moral perspectives and attempts to live out their Christian identity within a university context.

Students were asked, 'Would you describe your University as hostile, neutral or friendly to faith, and if so, in what ways?' How questions are phrased affect responses, and our open phrasing (in contrast to 'Would you describe your University as hostile, neutral or friendly to *Christianity*?') elicited responses relating to friendliness to Christianity as well as to other faiths or religion in general. This will be discussed later in the chapter. Data were coded, using NVivo, in two ways, first in terms of relative friendliness, neutrality and hostility, then second, by theme.

First, six categories were created using a spectrum ranging from hostile to friendly, based on their assent to one or more of the terms 'hostile', 'neutral' or 'friendly': 'friendly', 'neutral to friendly', 'neutral', 'friendly to hostile', 'neutral to hostile' and 'hostile'. Where students wavered between two options or, for instance, described aspects they considered friendly and others they considered neutral, we coded this 'neutral to friendly'. 'Friendly to hostile' responses were initially coded as such rather than as 'neutral' when students did not use the term 'neutral' and indicated two contrasting aspects of their university; the six responses in this category were later recoded as 'neutral' because the 'hostile' and 'friendly' aspects balanced each other out, producing something not dissimilar to neutrality. Table 4.1 displays the results.

Overall, more students perceived a friendliness than a hostility to faith in their universities. More than six in ten thought that their universities were either friendly or neutral-to-friendly towards faith. Three in ten considered their universities neutral, or thought that they encompassed elements that were both friendly and hostile. One in ten experienced their campuses as hostile or neutral-to-hostile. This is an important finding, because it suggests that Christian students do not for the most part perceive their universities as a hostile environment for those with faith.

These findings bear similarities with Weller, Hooley, and Moore's (2011) study of 3,935 students and 3,077 staff in UK universities, commissioned by the higher education equality body the Equality Challenge Unit in response to the Equality Act's religious equality requirements for universities to ensure equality of opportunity for religious staff and students. Like ours, their study found that the majority (93.9 percent) of students did not feel discriminated against or harassed. Only 4.3 percent of Christian students felt discriminated against or harassed, a lower

Table 4.1 'Would you describe your University as hostile, neutral or friendly to faith, and if so, in what ways?'

Friendly	Neutral to friendly	Neutral (includes 6 'friendly to hostile')	Neutral to hostile	Hostile	Total
35	12	21	3	4	75

figure than all religious groups other than 'Pagan'. The greater welcome experienced by Christian students in both studies is likely to relate to the partial alignment of Christianity with the dominant ethno-cultural traditions of the United Kingdom. Students with minority status were less likely to feel they were not discriminated against, especially Muslims (17.8 percent of whom reported harassment in Weller et al.'s study), Jews (10.3 percent) and Hindus (9.4 percent) (Weller et al. 2011: 76–77).

The second stage of coding was thematic. When we asked whether they thought their university was hostile, neutral or friendly to faith, students contextualised their comments in relation to four main themes, with the first two dominating discussion: 1) Christian/religious spaces and activities, 2) religious freedom and respect for faith, 3) the classroom/curriculum and 4) organised student social activities. These themes framed Christian students' perceptions of their campus contexts, feeding into constructions of institutional ethos that illuminate how religion inhabits different kinds of university spaces.

Theme I: Christian/religious spaces and activities

Forty-six students commented on this theme, and more than half of the comments about a university's friendliness to faith related to it. Christian students highly appreciate the university's provision of Christian groups and activities. This is the most significant factor in helping them to feel their universities are friendly to faith, as these comments illustrate:

> I'd say it's friendly, predominantly because it's a Church of England institution and it seeks to encourage community as a university and I think community is something that is found deeply within religion. . . . I think with the visual presence of the chapel, the visual presence of the chaplaincy at the start of the year in Fresher's Week, with the fact that there are allocated faith spaces central to each campus for people of any religion, just to freely use.
>
> (male, Cathedrals Group)

> It's pretty friendly. They have a lot of different societies for different denominations and different religions. . . . They're certainly an accepting community. . . . It is easier for Christians because [name of university] is primarily a Christian base. The churches have been around a lot longer than mosques or synagogues or anything have.
>
> (female, traditional elite university)

> I think it's friendly . . . – there's [an] Anglican chaplaincy, Roman Catholic chaplaincies . . . and the CU [Christian Union] especially is very prominent on campus. . . . There's lots of outlets if you're a Christian and . . . lots of other faith chaplaincies as well, so I think that. . . it's very sort of open.
>
> (female, 1960s campus)

There were some institutional variations. Students in traditional elite and 1960s-campus universities mentioned the annual university-run Cathedral carol service. In several universities, the predominantly Christian nature of faith-related activities was noted, whereas in the red-brick university, located in a major multicultural city, students commented positively on the inter-faith activities, describing an innovative inter-faith comedy show that had taken place on campus.

But some students described Christian activities as a more neutral facet of university life. In a classic example of what Davie (2007) calls 'vicarious religion' (performed by a minority on behalf of a majority who passively benefit), one red-brick student commented on being glad that the chaplaincy existed even though she does not personally make use of it. She praised the provision of a Muslim prayer room alongside Christian chaplaincy, and described the student body as having a 'neutral' orientation to these facilities. However, when asked whether the chaplaincy makes a contribution to her life as a student, she replied:

> Not massively because I haven't really gone to a church or institution here . . . but I think it is nice to have it as part of the University. I think it's good to have it as part of a place where they have teaching and they also have Christian services. I think it does add to the University community.

Her more muted personal commitment to faith may explain her lack of wholesale enthusiasm for the university's Christian activities. For others who see the university as neutral or friendly-to-neutral, their strong Christian commitment is what leads them to perceive university Christian activities as not signifying sufficient friendliness to Christianity. Several at the traditional elite and Cathedrals Group universities spoke nostalgically of their university as having a historic Christian heritage which was now in the background or paid lip service to.

A male student at the 1960s campus felt that granting the Christians a chapel after years of campaigning by the chaplains was a concession rather than a real commitment to faith, and compared the university unfavourably with the local Cathedrals Group institution. Interestingly, the two campuses were contrasted with reference to spatial characteristics, the Cathedrals Group university having buildings 'named after theologians' and a 'very large chapel which can be seen from all around'. This, in addition to them having a Christian Union that is 'very big and very much busier', contributed to a perception of a diminished Christian presence in his own university, where he discerned a 'vaguely anti-Christian sentiment'.

A female student from the post-1992 university also wanted more than just a carol service, an inter-faith forum and one Christian group that she felt excluded from as a black person:

> . . . it looks friendly but when you actually experience it for yourself as someone of faith, it's not really that friendly. It's not really made me think people

are really horrible and I'd never tell a Christian not to come here or anything like that, but there's not exactly a mass welcoming feeling. I think there could be a lot more Christian activities. . . . I was the only black person in the Christian Union and so there's not a lot of things for us more Pentecostal kids.

Theme 2: religious freedom and respect for faith

The second major theme cited by students discussing their universities' orientation to faith related to religious freedom and respect for faith; 42 students commented on this. Compared with the first theme, where the majority of students who commented perceived their university as friendly because it made available Christian-related activities, students who raised the issue of religious freedom were more likely to see their university as neutral, even hostile, on this issue.

Students who praised the university as friendly to freedom of religion commented on their appreciation for their university's openness to everyone's beliefs, religious or not. Words such as 'respectful', 'tolerant', 'open' and 'non-judgemental' appeared many times.

> . . . there are a lot of different people and of different faiths who come here, and I think they're very, very open to that, and I think that's good. I think they have to be, because obviously everybody's different and there are so many different students, you have to have that kind of balance, so yeah, I think they've been quite good.
>
> (female, post-1992)

This student assumes a culture of liberal tolerance ('I think they have to be [open]') and bases this on the pluralistic context of this post-1992 university. For this traditional elite student, respectfulness is based on intelligence rather than pluralism:

> Part of the nature of it being a university is [it is] full of intelligent people who are going to take things fairly sensibly. . . . People don't tend to be fairly prejudiced about faith in my experience here. Maybe other people have had different experiences. I've found it pretty good. [Names city] seems fairly secular, but within that . . . it's basically any faith goes, that's fine.
>
> (female)

Some students spoke about the institution's ethos. Others talked more about the student or staff population. Students at the red brick praised the fact that their university had made an official commitment to protect religious people from discrimination:

> I think the Student Union we belong to is very, very supporting of people from any walk of faith or any background. Equality is very much campaigned

for and supported over here, so I'd say it's quite friendly. I think in terms of the student population, it might be a different story, but that depends on the individual.

This student, interestingly, felt that the student union was more positive towards religion than some individual students might be, highlighting the distinction between institutional orientations and those perceived at a more popular level.

A somewhat larger number of more neutral comments related to two themes: student apathy and hostility to religion, especially to Christian Unions, mostly from students but also from lecturers. In relation to apathy, while students recognised that freedom of belief should also mean freedom to not believe, they resented the indifference they sometimes encountered from their peers. Answering our question directly, one student said:

> Depending on circumstance, I'd say all three. So hostile, I received hostility from certain groups of students, because of what I believe, partly when they are drunk. So I don't know whether it's true feelings or whether 'you know what, I've had a bit to drink, I'm going to play the big man and have a stab'. But then neutral, because I think a lot of people at university are like 'you know what, I'm going to embrace whatever is going on, it's good for you but I'm right here. Yes you get on with that, but I'm happy where I am'. . . . But then I've had a lot of friendliness in that a lot of my friends genuinely want to know what on earth I'm so passionate about and like they want to know, well, is it actually for me?
>
> (female, traditional elite)

> Sometimes neutral and sometimes friendly. It does depend on who you're with. It's all split down the middle. Some people are very friendly to it and some people put neutral, they don't really want to give an opinion. But I haven't seen or been anywhere where it's hostile. I think a lot of people are accepting but sometimes they have their own beliefs and therefore they don't really want to put an opinion into it because they don't want to get into an argument. . . . I think that's one thing people worry about, getting into a religious argument against another group.
>
> (male, 1960s campus)

As this 1960s-campus student noted, students' reluctance to debate religion may be more due to fear of offending others than to apathy, echoing the tendency to treat religion as a sensitive topic associated with anxiety and risk, as mentioned earlier. This tendency recurred throughout the CUE data, as Christian students attempted to affirm values of civility and inter-religious tolerance, while retaining Christian identity markers (Guest 2015), reflecting at a practical level the challenge of balancing freedom of speech with respect for religious diversity.

This male red-brick student perceived their university as neutral because it neither advocated nor prohibited religion on campus, and commented that although the institutional stance was neutral, students could be 'anti-religion':

> In terms of this specific formal policy, I'd say they're neutral, they don't advocate for faith, they don't prohibit it, they're quite, you know, open to. . . all faiths. In terms of informal interactions with the university, I'd say that the majority of students are sort of anti-religious, but they're not like aggressive anti-religious, they just like brush it off like, you know, that's, 'I don't believe in flying spaghetti monsters' and stuff like that. They like just, you know, brush it off like child's play.

Students who were more religiously conservative and belonged to the Christian Union were more likely to pinpoint hostility to it as a sign of neutrality or hostility, as this (somewhat guarded) comment illustrates.

> I wouldn't say friendly, particularly friendly, or particularly hostile but that has been just my experience, and I think people have probably found other extremes, like both extremes within the university. I think like we're so blessed to have the freedom to meet as a Christian Union, to, like, book rooms to use to, like, use our college bars to put on events to share the gospel with our friends . . . I think, like, people are quite, fairly open to, fairly open but I know within some colleges that that's not the case and there's, like, I suppose just a bit of resentment towards, like, evangelism.
>
> (female, traditional elite)

These students were also more likely to describe encountering negativity towards faith from lecturers, as those from the post-1992 university in particular did.

Theme 3: the classroom and curriculum

A small number (eleven) of students' comments on their universities' relative friendliness said what happens in the classroom was the leading issue. Universities having theology and religious studies courses were mentioned as demonstrating a university's friendliness to faith, as were those with theology study centres or Christian or Muslim youth work courses, such as those run by the Cathedrals Group university. One female student commented, 'Having a really top Theology, Religious Studies department. . . It's becoming recognised, you know, in the country. They wouldn't have that if they weren't bothered about faith and relating faith to real life, and especially practical Theology'.

Students on non-religion-based courses were more critical, especially students at the 1960s campus and post-1992 institutions. This 1960s-campus student explained that being 'expected to do field trips on Sundays' was problematic as no allowance was made for her faith.

RESPONDENT: Even though I protested, that wasn't taken into account.
INTERVIEWER: As part of your course?
RESPONDENT: Yes, despite the fact that I made it clear I wanted to be at church on those particular days. . . It was a member of staff that helped get me into the Alpha course [an introduction to Christianity course], but other members of staff – they haven't openly mocked it, but . . . I think they think it's sort of silly and they've not said it in so many words, but you know you'll have tutorials and I did a dissertation on church architecture. So conversations came up about my faith. . . I think from an academic point of view they find it foolish.

She went on describe being allocated course readings that said that God was dead. The most explicitly hostile example was given by this female student at the post-1992 university:

RESPONDENT: In my classes, you know the tutors, a lot of them swear. A lot of them blaspheme.
INTERVIEWER: What would that be?
RESPONDENT: Just saying the word Jesus and whatever. For example like the tutor was like, 'oh I've got more followers than Jesus' or something, you know, comments like that. . . I think they say them to make the class laugh, because then they do get a reaction and the class laugh.
    . . . You do feel a bit sad sometimes because you're just hearing it constantly, you know, so much violence towards a religion that no one understands. Why do they hate Christianity and they don't know what it's about? Why does everyone say 'Jesus'? They don't say Mohammed or whatever. Why is it always Christianity that they use when they're cursing?

Theme 4: organised student social activities

For a smaller number still (nine), the issue affecting their perception of their university's view of faith was what happened in the student social sphere. Most comments related to the Students' Union, who were seen as positive if they supported Christians' involvement, but negative when they challenged the Christian Union to be pro-LGBT or inclusive of other faiths. At the red-brick institution, a female student pointed out that a candidate standing for election to the Students' Union was trying 'to make the Union more faith-friendly'. This post-1992 Christian Union student was also positive about her Students' Union:

We've got the multi faith centre so they're very friendly towards people having beliefs and all that kind of thing but I think like the rest of the world, they're very taken over by this politically correct stuff. . . When we did our Exec training for the CU with all the Execs for all the societies, they said every society has to make sure that it's approachable for all religions or something, and I was like, 'My society's a Christian Union so how does that work?' and she was like, 'Oh, I don't know really'.

I think if we started saying we all believe it's wrong to be gay, that would probably not go down too well but generally, they're really good. The Students' Union are very into societies in general so because we're a society, they like us because they want as many societies as they can get! They're generally pretty supportive and when I try and get things signed off, they're like, 'Well, you're the Christian Union so you'll be fine.'

Both students referred somewhat disparagingly to the university's culture of liberal tolerance, which the first student perceived as an unhelpful imposition for campus Christians. Student Unions were also criticised for excluding Christians through organising alcohol-fuelled events:

Every single event that goes on, I haven't been able to attend because it's been against my religion or whatever. Like I really want to go to one of the balls, but they've got like bands on that I won't listen to, and it's the wrong kind of environment for me. You look in the student magazine and you'll see people like half naked and totally drunk and wearing really outrageous fancy dress and everything, and I can't associate with that.

(female, post-1992)

The alcohol-focused nature of student life appears to be an almost peculiarly British 'problem', causing problems for some religious students who do not drink, as we have discussed elsewhere (Guest et al. 2013b: 122–127; Sharma and Guest 2013; see also Valentine et al. 2010; Weller et al. 2011: 47–52).

Institutional variations

While all universities included students with responses that varied between 'Friendly' and 'neutral', three observations stand out when their responses are categorised by university type, as in Table 4.2. First, Cathedrals Group students were the group most likely to perceive their university as friendly to faith, and none of their responses were on the negative side of the balance. Second, while the responses of students at the post-1992 institution ranged across the spectrum, they were the type most likely to perceive their university as hostile to faith (indeed, they were the only one that featured responses from students perceiving their university to be unequivocally 'hostile' to faith). Third, the remaining

Table 4.2 'Would you describe your University as hostile, neutral or friendly to faith, and if so, in what ways?' Results by university type

University	Friendly	Neutral to friendly	Neutral (includes 6 friendly to hostile)	Neutral to hostile	Hostile
Traditional elite	6	1	7	1	0
Red brick	6	4	4	1	0
1960s campus	8	1	6	0	0
Post-1992/ new	5	3	2	1	4
Cathedrals Group	10	3	2	0	0
Total	35	12	21	3	4

universities included responses that spanned the friendly to neutral categories, with very few indications of hostility to faith.

It is not surprising that Christians at a Christian-foundation university perceive their university as friendly to faith. Indeed, an important question is whether students of other faiths would agree; perhaps this is an institution that is positive to Christian faith but not to other faiths – our data cannot tell us, but Weller et al.'s (2011) findings that religious minority students experienced more hostility indicate that this is likely to be the case. It is perhaps more surprising that students at the post-1992 institution were the most negative about their university. Post-1992 universities are socio-economically and, like red bricks, ethnically diverse, located in multicultural cities, so a tolerant atmosphere, accepting of religion, might be assumed to correlate with this ethos. However, the students we interviewed were Christian, and this raises the issue that Christian students might not perceive a diverse university as sufficiently friendly to *their own* faith. It is here that institutional ethos appears especially relevant; does the successful fostering of a multi-religious ethos also heighten a sense of alienation among Christian students who might presume to hold the 'majority' faith? Cathedrals Group universities may be better than post-1992 institutions at nurturing a campus culture that is affirming of Christianity, but does this owe more to their less diverse student populations than any structural features they might have?

Examining the reasons why Cathedrals Group students felt their institutions were friendly to faith, they often listed their plentiful Christian activities: the on-site chapel, the chaplains' prominent welcome tepee at Fresher's Week, the city's Christian heritage (it has a Cathedral) and the city's many churches which welcomed students. They also praised the university's tolerance and friendliness towards other faiths – for instance, the fact that the institution ran a Muslim youth work course – but the most important aspect seemed to be the institution's Christian activities. In the post-1992 institution, which had fewer Christian activities and a multi-faith centre rather than a bespoke chapel, the Christian Union and Chaplaincy's existence were praised, but there were perceptions of a more negative climate elsewhere in the university, with a Students' Union who were not always understanding of Christian students' social or religious needs, and teaching staff who were critical of and mocking towards Christianity. There was also a perception that other faiths, especially Islam, were treated more positively.

In what way might Christian students' varying experiences of friendliness, neutrality or hostility relate to the institutional ethos that each university is attempting to foster? Large-scale research is needed to test out any typology of university stances to religion, but Dinham provides a useful starting point. Dinham (in this volume) describes four university stances towards religion: 'hard neutral' (the university asserts its need to protect itself from religion), 'soft neutral' (the university is conceived as neutral and avoids mentioning religion as far as possible), 'repositories and resources' (the university sees religion as a learning resource and supports religious diversity) and 'formative-collegial' (the university offers education 'for the whole person' and sees spiritual development as central to this, as is common in religious-foundation universities such as the Cathedrals Group). Ethos can be gauged by university mission statements and annual reports and from more informal institutional cultures (and the two may diverge), but gauging ethos from the university's multiple constituencies makes this a difficult task. Moreover, how might students' perceptions, and staff behaviour, differ from the institution's intention?

At the post-1992 university, it is unlikely that lecturer criticism of Christianity relates to formal institutional ethos, given that all universities have policies promoting respect for religion. However, it may indicate that this university had not, at the time of research, promoted religious inclusion sufficiently through staff development courses, given that the Equality Act only came into being in the year our fieldwork began.

In contrast, religious-foundation universities are arguably distinctive in focusing on provision for students' spiritual needs; as the Cathedrals Group's introductory web page says, 'there is a strong commitment to providing a high quality education for students, supporting personal and spiritual development within a challenging learning environment' (The Cathedrals Group n.d.a). The Cathedrals Group's strategic priority document describes their mission statement as:

To present a distinctively ethical perspective in the higher education landscape, that celebrates our heritage as Christian foundations, influences national and local agendas and supports our Member institutions to offer the highest quality experience for our students, staff and partner organisations.

(The Cathedrals Group 2013)

As a report on the Cathedrals Group found, for this group, the 'student experience' does not mean a consumer experience (as Sabri 2011 argues has been increasingly the case as universities have improved their facilities to compete for increasing numbers of home and international students), but means that these universities support and respect students as individual members of their community.

> A key – perhaps *the* key – distinguishing characteristic of Cathedrals Group institutions lies in the nature of the student experience. Following the major shift in emphasis to the student as customer, consumer and funder, the high value placed on the student relationship must be a critical factor in distinctiveness to which the Group should play strongly. . . Each institution supported individuals on a day to day basis and was concerned about personal values of dignity, trust and respect.
>
> (Wooldridge and Newcomb 2011: 5)

The small size (less than 10,000 students) makes it easier for these universities to create a sense of community. The group's commitment to 'building communities that embrace and value diversity' and 'social justice' (The Cathedrals Group, n.d.b) exists alongside a commitment to their Christian heritage. This tension is keenly felt, the 2011 report found, with some within the group more 'reticent' (The Cathedrals Group, n.d.b: 3) about their Christian values than others, especially in promotional material. The Christian students we spoke to value both, but emphasised their university's Christian activities more than they mentioned the ethos of diversity. The Cathedrals Group have to work to retain their distinctive ethos, and Warner (2013: 348) observes 'a secularising trajectory' among them, as they come under pressure to remove the occupational requirement that senior managers share their Christian values and chaplaincy is 'redefined as essentially pastoral counselling' (Warner 2013: 349). Nevertheless, Warner argues that the Anglican universities (a subset of the Cathedrals Group) can retain a distinctive five-point vision of inclusivity, public service, seeing education as life-enhancing, 'faith-development friendly' (356) and being 'reflexively dependent upon a Christocentric metacritique' (355).

Conclusion

Institutional ethos, we conclude, has a bearing on how friendly to religion different universities are perceived as being among students of faith. This was most clear in the differences articulated by students in Christian-foundation universities, who perceived their institutions as most friendly to faith, and students in the modern 'post-1992' universities, who believed that the ethos of diversity meant there was less respect for Christianity. Institutional ethos, however, is shaped by many factors, and although university type – in the United Kingdom, the five are traditional elite, inner-city red brick, 1960s campus, post-1992 and Cathedrals Group – is one significant factor in framing institutional ethos, it is not the only one. Moreover, differences between the Christian students' experiences at the traditional elite, red-brick and 1960s-campus university were not large enough to draw clear conclusions.

Most Christian students we interviewed tended to view their universities as friendly to faith, but at times feel their faith is marginalised and confined to a 'private' sphere of religious activities and religious spaces. The majority of students who see their universities as friendly to faith seem to accept the partial secularisation of the university and the confinement of religion to an enclave rather than being present throughout the university's structures and activities. Which students are uncomfortable with this? We argue that minority status – which arguably results from their marginalisation by the attitudes and structures of the more privileged – accounts for some of the perceptions of neutrality and hostility. Previous research suggests that ethnic minority students perceive their university experiences less positively than white students, with some seeing their religious identity as insufficiently understood by their institutions (Aida et al. 1996; NUS 2008). While the majority of Christian students in our survey (75.8 percent) were white, Christian students from ethnic minorities demonstrated higher levels of Christian commitment as measured by frequency of churchgoing, private prayer and Bible reading (Guest et al. 2013b: 172). Moreover, our interviews indicate more discontent among these students about a perceived marginalisation of Christianity at their universities. For them, achieving 'friendliness to faith' requires a more public discussion of religion that may unsettle the fabric of the institution. Yet it is not true to say that religion is absent from everything but the faith spaces of the university, as for some institutions it is there in the fabric via graduation ceremonies in the Cathedral and religious equality policy. Where it is most frowned upon is in the classroom and the leisure and social spaces of student peer interactions.

That some religious students – particularly those of minority faiths or minority backgrounds – perceive their universities in less positive terms is not a new finding, though ours is the first investigation of this in relation to Christianity. Nor is the conclusion that faith is, to at least some extent, marginalised and privatised by higher education institutions new – it reflects Dinham and Jones's (2012) and Dinham's (this volume) conclusion. Dinham argues that the fact that most people opting to attend his Religious Literacy training events were chaplaincy and equality and diversity officers reflects a 'widespread assumption amongst our sample that "religion" is something that is done in the chaplaincy primarily, with little resonance or relevance in the wider life of the institution'. He comments:

'The risk is that religion is "bracketed off". . . rather than understood as something which pervades universities, and wider societies'. Universities have become, to greater or lesser degrees, replete with secular and secularising assumptions. This new moment, when public and political anxiety about campus religion is accompanied by new research evidence about faith on campus, gives universities a new opportunity to comprehend the religious commitments of their students and staff and to decide whether this requires accommodation of privatised faith or, rather, a deeper structural transformation.

References

Adams, R. (2015) Student Union Blocks Speech by "inflammatory" Anti-Sharia Activist. *The Guardian*, 26th September. Available online at: http://www.theguardian.com/education/2015/sep/26/student-union-blocks-speech-activist-maryam-namazie-warwick

Aida, E., Roberts, D., and Allen, A. (1996) *Higher Education: The Ethnic Minority Student Experience*. Leeds: Heist.

Aune, K. (2015) Faith and the University Experience in the UK. *Occasional Papers on Faith in Higher Education*, a joint publication of Whitelands College, University of Roehampton and Colleges and Universities of the Anglican Communion, No. 1 April. Available online at: http://cuac.anglicancommunion.org/media/153639/Occ-Papers-on-Faith-in-HE-no-1.pdf

Berger, P. (1999) The Desecularisation of the World: A Global Overview. In *The Desecularisation of the World: Essays on the Resurgence of Religion in World Politics*, ed. by Berger, P. L. Washington, DC: Ethics and Public Policy Center & Grand Rapids: Eerdmans, pp. 1–18.

Brown, K. E., and Saeed, T. (2015) Radicalization and Counter-Radicalization at British Universities: Muslim Encounters and Alternatives. *Ethnic and Racial Studies* 38 (11), 1952–1968.

Bryant, A. N. (2005) Evangelicals on Campus: An Exploration of Culture, Faith, and College Life. *Religion and Education* 32 (2), 1–30.

Bryant, A. N., Choi, J. Y., and Yasuno, M. (2003) Understanding the Spiritual and Religious Dimension of Students' Lives in the First Year of College. *Journal of College Student Development* 44 (6), 723–745.

The Cathedrals Group (n.d.a) Welcome to the Cathedrals Group. Available online at: http://www.cathedralsgroup.org.uk/. Accessed 25 February 2016.

The Cathedrals Group (n.d.b) Our Values. Available online at: http://www.cathedralsgroup.org.uk/OurValues.aspx. Accessed 25 February 2016.

The Cathedrals Group (2013) *Cathedrals Group Strategic Plan 2013–2016*. Available online at: http://www.cathedralsgroup.org.uk/Docs/47.pdf. Accessed 25 February 2016.

Cherry, C., DeBerg, B. A., and Porterfield, A. (2001) *Religion on Campus: What Religion Really Means to Today's Undergraduates*. Chapel Hill, NC and London: University of North Carolina Press.

Clydesdale, Tim (2007) *The First Year Out: Understanding American Teens after High School*. Chicago: University of Chicago Press.

Davie, G. (2007) *The Sociology of Religion*. London: Sage.

Dinham, A., and Jones, S. (2012) Religion, Public Policy, and the Academy: Brokering Public Faith in a Context of Ambivalence. *Journal of Contemporary Religion* 27 (2), 185–201.

Geertz, C. (1973) *The Interpretation of Cultures*. London: Fontana Press.

Grove, J. (2015) Sir Ken Macdonald: 'obnoxious' Anti-Radicalisation Measures Attack Campus Free Speech. *Times Higher Education*, 2nd July 2015. Available online at: https://www.timeshighereducation.com/news/ken-macdonald-obnoxious anti-radicalisation-measures-attack-free-speech

Guest, M. (2015) Religion and the Cultures of Higher Education: Student Christianity in the UK. In *Issues in Religion and Education: Whose Religion?*, ed. by Beaman, L. G., and Van Arragon, L. Leiden: Brill, pp. 346–366.

Guest, M., Sharma, S., Aune, K., and Warner, R. (2013a) Challenging 'Belief' and the Evangelical Bias: Student Christianity in English Universities. *Journal of Contemporary Religion* 28 (2), 207–223.

Guest, M., Aune, K., Sharma, S., and Warner, R. (2013b) *Christianity and the University Experience*. London: Bloomsbury.

Hunter, J. D. (1987) *Evangelicalism: The Coming Generation*. Chicago: University of Chicago Press.

Mayrl, D., and Oeur, F. (2009) Religion and Higher Education: Current Knowledge and Directions for Future Research. *Journal for the Scientific Study of Religion* 48 (2), 260–275.

National Union of Students [NUS] (2008) *Student Experience Report*. London: NUS/HSBC.

Sabri, D. (2011) What's Wrong with 'the student experience'? *Discourse: Studies in the Cultural Politics of Education* 32 (5), 657–667.

Sharma, S. (2012) 'The Church is . . . My Family': Exploring the Interrelationship Between Familial and Religious Practices and Spaces. *Environment and Planning A* 44 (4), 816–831.

Sharma, S., and Guest, M. (2013) Navigating Religion between University and Home: Christian Students' Experiences in English Universities. *Social and Cultural Geography* 14 (1), 59–79.

Valentine, G., Holloway, S. L., and Jayne, M. (2010) Contemporary Cultures of Abstinence and the Night-Time Economy: Muslim Attitudes towards Alcohol and the Implications for Social Cohesion. *Environment and Planning A* 42 (1), 8–22.

Warner, R. (2013) Re-Imagining a Christian University in a Secular Age. *Journal of Beliefs & Values* 34 (3), 347–358.

Weller, P., Hooley, T., and Moore, N. (2011) *Religion and Belief in Higher Education: The Experiences of Staff and Students*. London: Equality Challenge Unit.

Wooldridge, E., and Newcomb, E. (2011) *Distinctiveness and Identity in a Challenging HE Environment: A Unique Opportunity for Cathedrals Group Institutions: Executive Summary*. Chester: The Cathedrals Group.

Chapter 5

Invisible Islam

Muslim student migrants' everyday practices in French secular universities

Anna Virkama

Introduction

After the terrorist attacks conducted by radical Islamists in France and Belgium 2015–16, there have been calls for deeper understanding of Islam in Europe. However, as the interest in Muslims rises at a time of global Islamic terrorism threat, there is a danger that Islam is analysed only through the lens of radicalisation and security threat. This approach would not only rule out many other possible perspectives and create a potentially biased vision of Muslims' everyday life practices in Europe, but would also leave unnoticed many social and cultural aspects that shape the lives of the large Muslim majority, those who are often referred to as 'moderate Muslims'.

This chapter shares some fieldwork-based observations about the everyday life activities and practices of North African student migrants in France. It draws on qualitative research on migrant transnationalism among Moroccan migrants in France, with a particular focus on highly educated migrants and university students. The data was collected as a part of a larger research project TRANS-NET, a multi-level analysis of migrant transnationalism carried out in eight countries: Estonia, Finland, France, United Kingdom, Turkey, Germany, Morocco and India. This research project was funded by the European Union's 7th Framework Programme for Research, under the Socio-Economic and Humanities theme.

In France, the research was carried out by a team of researchers and research assistants in close collaboration with the research team in Morocco, where both Moroccan returning migrants and French residents in Morocco were interviewed. The whole data set collected in two phases in both countries consisted of 161 qualitative, semi-directive interviews, along with 40 life-course interviews. I conducted the twenty life-course interviews in France, which included fifteen men and five women. Respondents were either migrants or non-migrants who were engaged in transnational activities, meaning that they maintained cross-border ties, and they were asked about the transnational aspects of their lives in four different areas: educational, socio-cultural, economic and political (Virkama et al. 2012: 63).

These interviews comprised part of the fieldwork for my doctoral research on international student mobility and transnational educational spaces, and in this chapter I take a closer look at one of the thematic areas of my study: the student migrants' everyday practices related to religious activities. As the project's main focus was not on religion, but on transnational practices, this chapter is more exploratory than explanatory. Rather than offering an all-encompassing ethnographic account of Moroccan students' religious practices, therefore, the chapter explores and discusses some religion-related practices of the studied subjects, and shares observations from the field.

The chapter will also discuss how the diverse ways in which the subjects practice Islam in everyday life does not fit the radical/moderate binary, and it, therefore, argues for a more accurate vocabulary to describe the multitude of lived realities of European Muslims, and for Muslim migrants residing in Europe for determined periods of time. Studying Islam only as texts or discourses produced by certain, perhaps marginal, groups or religious authorities does not give a realistic perception of how the large 'silent' or 'invisible' majority of Muslims practice their religion. It also does not take into account other religious or non-religious ideologies that may influence the worldviews of Muslim subjects more than their religion.

Islam as a religion is often perceived as a major structure that governs most social aspects in Muslims' lives. In this framework of thinking, Islam is understood 'as an eternal and unchanging religion' and Muslims as being 'bound by the limits and framework set in the Holy Book'. This paradigm, which can be held both by Islamists and Islamophobes, sees that the religious text has a direct bearing on the political and social attitude of Muslims (Akbrazadeh and Roose 2011: 309–310.)

Post-colonially oriented research has demonstrated, however, how many of the orientalist assumptions of 'Muslim societies' are based on generalizations, and they have argued for deconstruction of a set of ideas through which the Muslim 'other' is perceived. In the current political climate, it is more important than ever that social scientists studying Muslim populations 'flatten their view' and 'stay close to the ground', as has been suggested by one of the most significant scholars of everyday life sociology, Bruno Latour (2005). The ethnographic method, used in the data collection of this research, is particularly useful for revealing how people negotiate the cultural ideals as well as the pragmatic concerns of everyday life.

Research questions

In this chapter I am exploring how student migrants negotiate their everyday life practices in a French secular university (both on and off campus), including what meanings students give to certain practices and why they choose to practice or not practice. I am also interested in whether their way of practicing has changed during their time in France and, if so, why. In particular, I am focusing on some tangible, 'visible' aspects of Islam – dietary restrictions, vestimentary codes, and relationships between men and women – as these are the practices that in social interactions of everyday life can mark the difference between Muslims and non-Muslims.

Most of the research questions arose during the fieldwork period as a result of observations or conversations with the informants. Although I had not particularly sought out practicing Muslims as respondents (the focus being on transnationalism), I was still surprised how flexible the students were with their religious-related practices. After some time spent on campus, I felt that instead of investigating how students practice Islam on campus, it would be more interesting to focus why they do *not* follow certain Islamic practices, such as fast at the time of Ramadan or wear a veil. Finally, in the light of my findings, at the end of this chapter, I discuss the limitations of the current terminology to understand Islam from a cultural rather than religious perspective.

Data and methodology

The paper draws on observations during fieldwork periods in Paris (2008–11). Out of the twenty people I interviewed for the project, sixteen had arrived in France with a student or scientific visa. Two female respondents had arrived in France with other types of visas (one being a resident through her mother, the other one being on a tourist visa), but carried on their studies in France, and two were not students and had arrived on other types of visas. Although one respondent was born in 1953, most students were born in the 1980s. They were all Master's and PhD students studying either in universities (*université*) or other higher education establishments such as engineering schools (*grandes écoles*). All students were from urban backgrounds: the majority of them were from Casablanca (N=4), from the North of Morocco, Tétouan (N=3), and from Rabat and Marrakech (both N=2); the rest came from other larger cities (Meknes, Nador, Salé).

My own role during the fieldwork was as participant observer. As a postgraduate foreign student myself, I shared the same educational spaces and participated with other students in their daily activities in the libraries, cafés, hobby clubs and associations without being 'out of place'. Whereas the primary data consisted of in-depth, life-course interviews, I also used my field notes from the diary I kept during the fieldwork, and media texts such as newspaper articles and online sources. All the data collected during the fieldwork process is confidential, and the anonymity of the respondents is protected by using pseudonyms in the published texts and by not discussing their personal characteristics in such detail that they could be recognised.

The study has been largely influenced by my own experiences of studying in Morocco while collecting material for my Master's thesis (Virkama 2006), as well as three- to six-month-long periods when I stayed in the country between 2001–04, and several short visits between 2008–11. The networks established during my stays in Morocco were very important in the whole process of research, start-ing from recruiting the informants: I had already interviewed one of the key informants years before in Morocco, and two other respondents were found through common acquaintances in Morocco. My previous fieldwork experience in Morocco has also been meaningful for the study in that it gave me an idea of certain everyday life aspects that were, according to my observations, different in France than in Morocco. For example, I knew that, in Morocco, the campus life adjusts to the Ramadan fasting by changing the schedules so that the students can take classes after *ftour*, the fast-breaking meal in the evening, which is not the case in France. I had been a non-fasting, non-Muslim student on a campus where the majority of other students were fasting (meals were always served for non-Muslim students). I had also been invited to students' homes for Ramadan dinners where the whole extended family would get together, enjoy home-cooked meals and exchange presents – again a very different experience from pizza dinners with friends that some respondents described when asked about their celebration of Ramadan in France.

This transnational approach does not only fit well in the larger pattern of my PhD study, which focuses on educational transnational space, but also responds to the call of avoiding 'methodological nationalism' in social scientific research (Wimmer and Glick Schiller 2003) and is methodologically influenced by multi-sited ethnography (Marcus 1995). Although research on immigrants focuses on issues of identity and belonging, considerably little attention is still given to the sending country context of immigrants, and to diverse social, cultural and educa-tional backgrounds that even migrants from the same country of origin may have.

In France, this decontextualizing approach has been criticized by Algerian soci-ologist Abdelmalek Sayad, who emphasised the importance of understanding the individual's migration trajectories starting in their country of origin, as before becoming an *immigrant*, an individual is always an *emigrant*: presence in a certain context implies absence in other place (Sayad 1999). In the study of religious prac-tices, there is a great risk of biased understanding of the role of the religion and how it determines the daily life in the sending country context. This comes clear in cur-rent debates of 'radicalisation' or 'secularisation': either it is understood that Mus-lim migrants arrive in Europe as practicing Muslims, which they progressively give up as a result of the secularisation/integration process; or, alternatively, they arrive as 'moderate' Muslims, who in Europe radicalise as a result of alienation from the secular society, or because of entering in contact with other radicalised individuals.

Many studies on Muslims in Europe have focused on vulnerable or margin-alised groups: illiterate, undocumented, second generation. The position of a researcher is different when the objects of the study are highly educated migrants who often are very aware of the political and academic discourses on immigra-tion, Islam and integration. The kind of research setting in which both respond-ent and the researcher share some common characteristics (being students and foreigners in France, sharing experience of studying in Morocco, even having friends and acquaintances in common) allows interaction on a more equal basis than conventional research with immigrants, which often involves a highly educated researcher studying illiterate, low-skilled, marginalised or vulnerable minority populations. In my case, I could say that I was rather 'studying up' (Nader 1972), as despite being 'Muslim minority' and 'immigrants', the studied subjects were in a better socio-economical position than myself in some cases, as well as equipped with better language skills since they had grown up in French-speaking environments and/or even went to French schools.

France, Islam and challenging laïcité

Islam is the second largest religion in France and very well established with mosques and prayer rooms in all larger cities, several official Muslim organizations and associations. Yet the presence of Muslims in metropolitan France has never been unproblematic. In public discourses, Islam is often perceived to be at odds with the French notion of *laïcité* (secularity), especially recently with the rise of Islamic terrorism on one side, and militant secularism as a response to the visibility of Islam in public spaces on the other.

Ever since the Muslim community in France started growing with the arrival of North African labour migrants from former French colonies after the Second World War – a migration that was intended to be temporal, but turned into a permanent settlement in the 1970s and 1980s – the perceived cultural differences of Muslim immigrants have been of interest to scholars and policymakers. Whereas the early research on labour migrants did not pay much attention to the social and cultural aspects of the immigrants' lives, this aspect became important after 1973, when France officially stopped recruiting labour migrants, and those migrants who already were in France started to settle down permanently, bringing their spouses and children through family reunification programs. This meant that instead of just policing immigration flows, public policy had to face challenges such as how to integrate immigrant children into the French school system (Fetzer and Soper 2005; Tribalat 1995: 27–33).

Since the 1980s, most North African immigrants have entered France with a student visa. Yet, considering that after the 1980s, student migration became the major channel of migration of North Africans to France, surprisingly little attention has been paid to Muslim international students in France. Some academic work has focused on the intellectual diaspora and highly skilled elites in France (Borgnogno et al. 1995; Geisser 2000; Kadri 1999), but, as elsewhere in Europe, little attention is given to Islam in the university setting, although the campus is the place where both student activism and identity politics are drawn together (Brown and Saeed 2015: 1952). It is known, though, that students who arrived in France from Muslim countries in Maghreb and West Africa have been very active in religious organizations and have contributed to shaping contemporary Islam, promoting inter-faith dialogue and creating the new Muslim elite in France (Cesari 2005: 1033–1034).

Unlike in the United Kingdom and Australia, the French policy towards minorities does not celebrate multiculturalism. Symbols of religious identity such as Muslim women's headscarf are banned in the public space as religion is perceived to be a private matter. Therefore, public universities do not take into account students' religious practices by offering, for example, a place of worship or special meals such as *halal* (or *kosher*, for Jewish students).

Radical, moderate or cultural? Limitations of the current terminology for diverse Muslim identities

The everyday life practices of Muslims have received little academic attention, whereas other themes related to Islam such as securitisation, integration or Islamic law have been more studied. The everyday practices of Muslims are not only interesting as expressions of Islamic tradition or self-fulfilment, but also as symbols of belonging and expressions of social, cultural and religious meanings that create borders between groups (Toguslu and Leman 2013: 12). In order to discuss *how* practices related to Islamic culture are present in the lives of Muslim students, and to avoid unnecessary labelling, it is important to keep the definition of 'Muslimness' open, and let the respondents define themselves. At this point, the researcher has to be attentive, and not try to force his or her respondents into a Muslim identity, but to respect the anthropological principal of giving voice to the members of the community and let the subjects define themselves. The current terminology to discuss the variety of Islamic practices is very limited, especially when it comes to the vast majority of Muslims who are not fundamentalist or radicalised, but who do not form a homogenous 'moderate' group either. We may understand the terms 'radical Muslim' or 'fundamentalist Muslim' as someone who embraces salafist or wahhabist ideas. But as far as we know, this group represents a very small minority among Muslims, and it would be inaccurate to define other Muslims only as in opposition against the radicals.

The assumed conflict between Islamic identity and the Western lifestyle is not, of course, typical for France only, but reflects a general tendency in today's Europe. For example, studies in the British context have shown that Muslims who do not openly embrace a 'British lifestyle' are living under the suspicion of radicalisation (Bartlett and Miller 2012; Briggs and Birdwell 2009; DCLG 2007; Hickman et al. 2011; Kabir 2010; cf. Brown and Saeed 2015: 1953) Yet, millions of Muslims, whether immigrants or born in Europe, adjust their religious practices in a non-Muslim majority countries and find creative solutions in order to adapt while maintaining their religious identity. Akbrazadeh and Roose (2011) use the term 'cultural Muslims' – a group generally unrepresented both in public debate and in the academic literature. Yet theoretical debates about the compatibility of Islam with modern education often remain on an abstract or theoretical level. Very little evidence is brought into discussion, drawing from lived, everyday experiences of people. This chapter therefore helps to understand the 'invisible life' of so-called moderate Muslims, and helps to conceptualise the definition of a 'cultural Muslim'.

Student life, religious practice and the construction of Muslim identity

University campuses have a high potential to be arenas of symbolic and ideo-logical struggles. In Morocco, for example, there have been violent confronta-tions between leftist and Islamist students, but students can also be involved in non-violent, culturally oriented movements such as groups promoting the culture and the rights of Amazigh (Berber) people (Virkama 2015a: 145). Ever since the first generation of North African students in France, metropolitan France, and Paris in particular, has represented a space for more freedom of political expression and action, with more diversity of ideologies and political movements than in Maghreb. It was, ironically, in Paris where the international encounters of different anti-colonialist and anti-imperialist Maghrebi nation-alists took place (Sayad 1999: 147). On a Northern Parisian campus where I was observing students, pro-Palestinian demonstrations and posters on the wall were frequently seen. Apart from that, there were student and staff strikes whenever the university took decisions that were opposed by the students' and teachers' unions, but no movements that would have been directly linked to radical, political Islam.

On the university campus, Moroccan students came in touch not only with non-Muslim peers, but also with Muslim students from other Maghreb and Sub-Saharan African countries. Whenever identity issues came up in either the inter-views or in informal discussions, respondents usually described themselves on national (Moroccan/French), ethnic (Arab/Berber) or regional (North African/ Mediterranean) terms, far more often than as based on religion identification as Muslims. But when asked about their religious practices, students made a distinc-tion between being either *'croyante'* (believer) or *'pratiquant'* (practicing) – the former referring to someone who recognises Allah as the only God and considers him/herself as a Muslim, trying to follow the guidelines of Islam, but not nec-essarily by practicing daily, and the latter meaning someone who prays daily at home and in the Mosque on Fridays.

The definition of a non-practicing and practicing Muslim is problematic, as it does not take into account the enormous variety of ways that Muslims practice the religion: practice can be regular or non-regular (for example, during Ramadan only and otherwise not), and non-practicing does not mean being atheist, as faith can as well be an important part of a non-practicing Muslim's life so that it is not only someone who faithfully observes the five pillars of Islam (fast, prayer, eating *halal*, giving *zakat, Hajj* – the pilgrimage) that should be regarded as a religious Muslim. Equally, some female students felt comfortable to veil only during Rama-dan, whereas some others expressed that if you choose to wear a veil, the decision should be taken for a lifetime and not just for a short period of time.

Halal or not? Food, socialisation and symbolic boundaries

Food is an essential part of culture, and it is often the first thing we notice in a foreign country: what do other people eat? Which food items are considered unpure and to be avoided? Food can unite people of different backgrounds around the same table, but it can also create minor social conflicts. In France, the issue of Muslim's dietary restrictions has been one of the topics of debates. The rejection of certain food items such as pork and alcohol is perceived by extreme right anti-immigration forces as a rejection of 'French way of life'. At the time of my fieldwork period, a very revealing event took place in North of Paris around the neighbourhood of rue Myrha. The prayer room of the nearby Mosque was too small for the Muslims of the neighbourhood, who often occupied the nearby streets to use as a place or prayer. This provoked a counter-reaction from some non-Muslim neighbours, who started to organise 'Saucisson et Pinard' ('Sausage and booze') themed gatherings on the street nearby the Mosque, in order to fight against the perceived 'Islamisation of the neighbourhood'. The participants sought to claim back the space that they considered invaded by Muslims, by publically displaying their right to consume in public the food items that are perceived as impure by Muslims. More recently, the rejection of non-*halal* meat by Muslim refugees was perceived as snobbery by French right-wing extremists (Résistance Républicaine 2015).

On campus, mealtimes are part of everyday life and one of the moments when students can socialise with each other. Most respondents aimed to have one daily meal at the university's dining hall for several reasons: first, there were not many other catering options near the campus. Second, the meal was inexpensive and included a starter, main course, cheese, dessert and bread. Third, the students I interviewed, especially the younger ones, mostly lived in small apartments or dorm rooms and lacked either the skills or the possibility to cook their own meals. The meal option offered at the university was considered as a 'healthy and complete meal', although it was sometimes replaced by a quick sandwich.

The university did not have any special meals for Muslims, although there was usually either a vegetarian or a fish plate available. Students had to make choices based on their taste and dietary practices, but the choice was limited to what was offered on the menu of the day. I noticed that while students were stricter about not eating pork, many of them were more flexible about eating meat in general, even if it was not *halal*, and often chose the plate including meat over vegetarian or fish choice. None of the respondents had adopted a vegetarian diet as a mean of avoiding non-*halal* meat, although vegetarian options were usually available at the university canteen and vegetarianism was gaining popularity among non-Muslim students. In Morocco, pork meat is generally available in larger supermarkets or special stores, but it is usually clearly indicated (see Figure 5.1). This is not the case in France, so Muslim students were always inquiring about the ingredients in the food.

Figure 5.1 Pork meat indicated clearly in a Moroccan supermarket.
Photo: Anna Virkama.

Students' choices at the mealtime were not only based on their religion, but also on their personal preferences and limitations of their food budget. Why would students eat non-*halal* meat, but avoid pork? As I interpret it, pork has a connotation of being considered as a ritually impure animal in Islamic tradition and, therefore, most people who grew up in Muslim-dominant country would feel repulsed by it. In conversations I had in Morocco, it often came out that pork meat was believed to cause cancer or other serious illnesses, and that was one of the reasons why it was originally banned by Prophet Mohammed. Pork was also referred to as 'Christian food' by some respondents, so it seemed to be the food item that most clearly marked the boundaries between Muslims and (Christian) non-Muslims.

Whereas in Morocco pork products (when available) are clearly indicated, in France, students who wanted to avoid pork had to make certain efforts to find out what they were served. Some meals were unfamiliar to them, and there was not always enough staff in the canteen to answer inquiries. The same applied if the students got invited to a dinner or lunch: they had to ask before what they would be served. During my fieldwork time, I heard several anecdotes of non-Muslim French students playing jokes on their Muslim peers by offering them food to taste and only revealing afterwards that the meal contained pork. Needless to say, humour of that kind did not help to increase socialisation between Muslim and non-Muslim students.

Student parties and alcohol consumption

Alcohol consumption is another area that can set the Muslim students apart from non-Muslims, as much of the socialisation outside of campus and even on campus can involve drinking. Wine being an essential element in French celebrations and culinary culture, it was not uncommon that wine was served on campus on different occasions: celebration after a thesis defence, book release or a conference reception. Therefore, a strict interpretation of Islam which would not allow a believer to spend time in spaces where alcohol is consumed would greatly limit Muslim students' participation in campus life.

Although Morocco is a country that produces wine and alcohol can be purchased in certain places such as luxury hotels, international supermarket chains and specialised stores, Muslims are not allowed to consume alcohol, and they can be sanctioned for drinking in public. Socio-economic and class differences of the students' backgrounds became more evident in this area of food choice. Students whose parents had also studied in France and who belonged to higher social classes were often socialised in French-influenced circles, where wine can be a part of a festive meal. Therefore, the ways in which alcohol is consumed or not consumed is not only a religious, but also a social and cultural issue.

Different approaches students took with regard to alcohol revealed very different takes on religion and how religious principles could be interpreted in this area of life. Three cases can illustrate the diversity of approaches:

1   A 29-year-old female engineer, who self-identified as a practicing Muslim from a middle-class family background, was already working in a prestigious information technology consulting firm at the time of the interview. After-work get-togethers and occasional parties were common practice in

her company and alcohol was often involved. She never drank alcohol herself, but said she would not mind joining her colleagues for after-work drinks even if it would take place in a pub. She would just choose a non-alcoholic beverage for herself. She said that it did not bother her if her colleagues drank alcohol, and did not feel like it was in contradiction with her Muslim faith. Having worked and studied with people from different cultural backgrounds, she found that French people were less eager to get visibly drunk than, for example, her Dutch or British colleagues.

2   A 24-year-old Master's student in Accountancy considered alcohol consumption and getting drunk an important part of French culture. In France, he consumed alcohol frequently and his socialisation with non-Muslim French mostly took place in bars and clubs. He seemed genuinely surprised when I declined his invitation of having a beer as a part of the interview session. This student raised by a widowed mother in Casablanca was from the most modest background and his contacts with the French had been limited prior to his arrival in France. In France, he was staying with his older brother, and he had partly given up studies in favour of working in his brother's *halal* butcher shop.

3   A 21-year-old young man from a well-off Casablancan family who was preparing for an engineering school said that he did not drink alcohol. He did not mind going to a party where people drank, but became quickly bored if he was the only sober person. Instead of drinking parties, he preferred to socialise around a dinner, or just going dancing with friends. He went to a French school in Casablanca, and his family in Morocco included both people who consume alcohol moderately, and those who, for religious reasons, do not accept alcohol consumption at all.

Ramadan, differently: fasting and feasting in France

Islam also requires a month of fasting, usually taking place during the month of Ramadan, considered as the holy month by Muslims. In Morocco as elsewhere in the Islamic world, the whole society lives in a different rhythm during Ramadan. Having spent Ramadan month in Morocco during my stay as an exchange student in 2004, I was able to observe all the adjustments made on a Moroccan campus during that holy month: the class schedules changed, there were long weekends off so that students could stay with family, special foods were consumed after sunset time when the fast was broken, etc. Knowing this was helpful when I was asking the students about their Ramadan habits in France, as universities in France do not officially recognise or adjust to Ramadan month and the students are expected to carry on their activities as usual. When it came to Ramadan, most respondents said they observed it. One respondent said she could not for health reasons, which is acceptable from the religious perspective, and one respondent said she had decided to stop fasting.

These two were both women. One respondent said that he tried to observe it, but found it difficult:

> Maybe I am just trying to find excuses, but I am not really practicing my religion since I am in France. Ramadan here is just not the same, there is no festive feeling. We just gather together [with some other North African students] and eat a pizza or whatever. It's not the same.
>
> (Male, engineering student)

For some students, being in a foreign country and a foreign environment was a religiously acceptable reason not to fast: 'according to Islam, if you are traveling, you are in a foreign country you don't have to fast'. For others, the fasting gained a deeper religious meaning when it took place in a setting where most other people did not fast, which provided an additional challenge.

As I observed during my several stays in Morocco, the month of Ramadan is not only an expression and confirmation of Muslim faith, but a month filled with traditions: delicious special meals shared with family, visits and spending time together watching TV shows during the long hours of fast, or going to the *souq* (market) or to a mall to buy presents and festive clothes. For some families, Ramadan may have more religious significance, whereas for others it was a month dedicated to feasts. Many Moroccans were joking about how they gain weight during the fasting month, and many hotels in the North Africa and Middle East nowadays offer luxurious Ramadan packages, which involve abundant buffet tables after the Muslims are allowed to break the fast. Therefore, for many of the students I talked with, the fasting was not the hardest part of Ramadan in a non-Muslim country, but the lack of celebration and feeling of community: 'Whenever there was some Moroccan feast I was alone and I was not surrounded by friends like in Morocco' said a female student who spent her first study year in Southern France, in a small university where she did not know many other Muslim students.

Fasting during Ramadan was also something that frequently raised the curiosity of non-Muslim students, who wanted to know how the students would make it throughout the day without eating or drinking, while the non-observation of the fast would also immediately raise questions. A female Moroccan PhD student who considered herself as Muslim by faith and tradition, but also secular and socialist, said that it was hard for her French peers to understand that she could choose not to fast during Ramadan: 'was not fasting when I lived in Morocco, so why would I fast here? They don't get it."

The students' decisions on how they interpret the Islamic dietary restrictions seemed to depend on various factors, and not solely on how deeply they identified themselves as practicing Muslims. Budgetary restrictions played a role, as much as peer influence and personal preferences. Some students' choices were based on their theological interpretations of considering the stay abroad as a travel: being away on the land of Islam, where different rules applied. They considered that not fasting, or occasionally eating non-*halal* food, was acceptable if it was for a limited period of time. Even those who considered themselves as believers agreed that Allah (God) is understanding and merciful, if the believer is temporarily unable to follow certain Islamic practices. It was perceived as more important to 'get back in order' when life permits.

To veil or not to veil? Religion, fashion and pragmatism

In 2016, the French interior minister Manuel Valls brought up again the decades old debate on Muslim veiling by stating that universities should ban the veil as the public schools have done. Currently, veiling is not forbidden in universities, as the students of higher education institutions are free to receive information and express cultural, political and economic views (Le Monde 2016). In French schools, the debate on Muslim veils was brought into public debate in early 2000 in the 'Islamic Veil Affair'. In 2004, it became forbidden by law to wear visible religious symbols in school. The difference with schools is that university students are adults, and therefore considered free to make vestimentary choices. On campus where I was observing the students, there were many Muslim women who wore a veil, but it was hard to say how many of them were foreign students and how many were French-born Muslims.

Despite the Islamic call for modesty of dress for women, female beauty is very much celebrated in the traditions of Mediterranean Muslim societies. In a traditional Moroccan wedding, bride's hands and feet are decorated with *henna*, and it is a custom that the bride changes her clothes several times during the ceremony. *Caftan*, the beautiful traditional dress used for ceremonies, has also influenced many Western fashion designers, and the *caftans* of latest fashion can also be short sleeved or sleeveless. Western-style beauty contests are also held, and the European fashion has taken over in most of the larger cities. According to my observations, there is significant tolerance towards different ways of dressing, and it is not uncommon to see in the same group of family and friends women dressing very differently: some perhaps dressed in a hooded garment, *djellaba*, which is worn by both men and women.

The practice of veiling has been interpreted in various ways: a symbol of cultural and anti-colonial resistance, symbol of religious and cultural identity, or either conformism or resistance to male norms. None of the women I interviewed in France wore a veil or headscarf, although some of them considered themselves as devoted or pragmatic Muslims. Most women seemed to think that wearing a veil is not a decision one should take lightly, as it brings many consequences into one's life. The decision of wearing a veil was perceived as something one must decide once for a lifetime. As one respondent said 'once you start wearing it, it's for life'. In some cases, the adjustment may even start long before any migration. A good illustration of this is in an interview sample of the French anthropologist Constance de Gourcy, who interviewed Algerian students about their future study projects in France. The interview took place with a 21-year-old Algerian female student in Oran, Algeria:

STUDENT: Can I ask you a question: I have heard there is racism against Arabs there [in France]
RESEARCHER: Is there something you are worried about?
STUDENT: Yes, the headscarf. You can't wear a headscarf there. I don't know why.
RESEARCHER: You are not wearing a headscarf.
STUDENT: Yes, at the moment I am not wearing it. Why? Because I want to study in France. If in France it's not forbidden to wear a scarf then I can wear it. Otherwise I can't wear a headscarf and then I take it off.
RESEARCHER: So you are not wearing headscarf as you are planning to leave for France?
STUDENT: That's it.

(de Gourcy 2009: 105) [Translated from French by the author]

Question of dress also came out in one of my own interviews, with a former Moroccan female student who, after her studies in France, was looking for her first working experience (internship) in her field, in the very competitive and masculine field of information and communication technologies consulting. She emphasised the meaning and importance of choosing correctly one's outfit for a professional interview. She did not use a veil herself, and she emphasised the need for a professional yet fashionable outfit for a job interview:

Even for finding employment, being a woman is an advantage, because being physically attractive and nicely dressed is an advantage in working life, even though in IT is not so important. - -But when you go to a work interview with the manager, as a woman you can be more elegant and also more original than a man who just needs to wear a suit. It is not the most important thing but it counts.

(Female respondent, engineering student)

Although the respondent said she is deeply committed to Islamic values, she did not consider veiling necessary, as it could form an obstacle for the professional career she wanted to make for herself – the reason why she had come to France, after all. She also added that having an Arab first name could be a reason for discrimination, but that female names would not be perceived as negatively as male names: 'also, our names, Arab female names are better, whereas a man who is called Mohammed, Hassan . . . and that is very. . . hmm'. Her reasoning may sound contradictory considering that she in many cases emphasised being a practicing Muslim, but it also made sense as a counter-discrimination strategy in the political climate in which particularly Muslim men had become regarded as suspicious individuals. Ironically, the purported discrimination against men brought her an advantage as a Muslim woman when competing for the same internships and jobs with male students from her faculty: she could stand out by being positively different from other candidates.

From the perspective of cultural adjustment and adaptation, the decision of whether to wear or not to wear a veil is interesting, as it the decision may be influenced by the desire to fit in and to be accepted by the others. The decision in migratory contexts is also more individual, less influenced by parents, relatives or Muslim peers. While for Muslims born in France, the headscarf may be a symbol of cultural resistance, for those students who came from outside of Europe, it was often not the primary preoccupation, or it could be negotiated in order to access education and jobs. In various informal conversations I had with the respondents, there were arguments defending veiling and also against it. But most students seemed to think that as it was not a European custom to veil, those who want to work and live in Europe should not wear it. At the same time, the majority found the French laws banning the veil a specific attack on the Muslims community, as they felt that Jews were still allowed to openly wear *kippahs* and were not bothered about the issue of religious symbols.

Moroccan women were often perceived as 'Westernized' or 'emancipated' by their non-Muslim peers if they worked or travelled, or had moved to France independently. The problem that female student migrants faced were not the opposition coming from their own Muslim community, but the biased, stereotyped view that the non-Muslims frequently held about Muslim women. In the eyes of their non-Muslim peers, any signs of independence (professional, financial, ideological or freedom to travel) was questioned based on the idea of Islam as a misogynistic religion.

Inter-religious friendship and facing stereotypes about Islam

Although none of the respondents had experiences of direct or violent racism, some students reported that they had felt discrimination in the private housing sector, for example, or while looking for an internship. But interestingly, they interpreted this to be related more to the fact that they were foreigners, Arabs/North Africans, not for being Muslims. Experiences of being excluded because of Islamophobic prejudice as expressed by verbal or physical abuse, such as that reported by Brown (2009) in the United Kingdom, were absent from the Moroccan students' narratives.

As I noticed, the students also used different skills they had in order to make friends and gain favours from the host nationals. The skills could have been technical, such as computer skills learnt through formal education, or soft, cultural skills such as dancing or cooking. Students were able to gain popularity among their peers by, for example, cooking traditional meals or teaching folkloric dances to their peers. Participation in clubs and associations (none of them religious or ideological) was also a way of making friends across the ethnic or religious boundaries. Cole and Ahmadi's study on a US university campus found that Muslim students had more diversity-related activities than their Jewish or Christian counterparts, but they were not more involved in religious activities than Christian students (Cole and Ahmadi 2010: 134–135). My findings were rather similar, as it seemed important to my respondents to seek friendship and company of non-Muslims, and most also appreciated the international atmosphere of Paris which brought them in contact with people from very different nationalities. Social class was a significant factor when it came to cross-ethnic relationships, however. Students belonging to higher social classes with highly educated parents already had existing networks in the host country. Students from more modest backgrounds seemed to lack these contacts, and were more likely to be lost in cultural codes, for example, when it came to socialising with the opposite sex.

Rather than suffering from direct discrimination or denigration, the students I talked to seemed to have experienced similar attitudes that Suad Nasir and Al-Amin (2006: 25) discovered among Muslim students on North American campuses: 'stereotype threat'. At the time I was collecting the data, the stereotyping as a terrorist was not mentioned very often, but stereotyping as an 'oppressed Muslim woman' had been experienced by all of the female respondents. Several male respondents also mentioned that they had been held accountable by the non-Muslim student peers for the purported 'oppression of women in Islam'.

Conclusions

In this chapter, I have reflected upon the complex ways in which religious practices are negotiated in the daily lives of Muslim foreign students in France. The fieldwork conducted among Moroccan international students revealed that there is no one, homogenous Muslim identity or way of practicing Islam. Islam can be seen as a larger cultural framework in the lives of the respondents, but they were also able and willing to negotiate some aspects such as dietary restrictions, clothing, praying and fasting and relationships with the opposite sex. Different factors determined how certain religious practices were adapted to everyday life: family background, age, political ideologies, social class, gender and age were all important.

Among the respondents were those who had left their country of origin for the search of ideological or personal freedom, as they belonged to specifically vulnerable groups such as women, ethnic or sexual minorities or disabled people (Virkama 2015b). In these cases, emigration could be a way of opting out from a value system that does not fit one's personal worldviews. The lack of particular practices could also be explained from a life-course perspective, as many people become more spiritual as they age. The students often perceived themselves to be in a liminal stage where they had not yet settled down in life, and a particular religious practice would require more stable conditions: to be married with children, have a career and possibly living back in Morocco. Being in France was also seen as a liminal, temporary stage in life, even if none of the respondents had a very set idea about when they would return to Morocco (most aspired to get some work experience in France before returning). Cultural aspects also affected the decision to not practice, for example, not to fast during Ramadan as the lack of festivities and community spirit would not make the holy month feel special. In addition, ideological reasons were important to two students, who perceived themselves as Muslims by tradition and family heritage but as socialists by ideology, and who had taken a conscious decision not to practice. Finally, there were students who had very pragmatic reasons to not take part in certain practices: health reasons, limited budget or just lack of time or enthusiasm to make special arrangements to fast, pray or buy *halal* food.

At the same time, Muslim students and university staff are also keenly observed by their non-Muslim counterparts, and at times feel that they need to answer, clarify or defend their identity, belief and practices. This is particularly true in France, where militant secularism has been on the rise, while at the same time radical Islamism has brought mainstream French society's anti-Islamic feelings to the surface. Some of my respondents felt that they were personally held accountable for each crime or injustice that took place in a Muslim country. Despite their personal relationship to faith, Muslim subjects are often first and foremost perceived as 'Muslims' by non-Muslim peers – a fact that many of the respondents found irritating, as they did not see 'Muslimness' being the most significant side of their identity. In the current atmosphere of fear and threat of radicalisation, Muslims are perhaps more than ever under scrutiny in Europe. In the United Kingdom, under the new anti-terrorism legislation, university staff are expected to report on Muslim students who may be vulnerable to radicalisation. Muslim students in Europe are, of course, aware of the Islamophobic discourses and suspicion they are facing, and many have established strategies of distancing themselves from radicalism, careful not to provoke concern by demanding special rights such as prayer rooms, the right to veil or to be provided with special meals.

The invisible Islam described in this chapter is a Muslim faith practiced in private, and which adjusts to the conditions of mainstream society. Although Muslim identity was important, the respondents showed flexibility in the way they practiced, taking into account the existing conditions. The adaptation meant that they must be willing to leave aside certain cultural practices: for example, it might be difficult to observe fasting during the Ramadan month, if the university's exam period or an important internship coincided with the dates of the holy month. Which practices are maintained and which ones are neglected is often determined by two reasons: pragmatic ones, or individual preference and taste. The respondents showed, perhaps surprisingly, little interest towards claiming more rights as Muslim subjects. For them, the choice to study in Europe had been, at least in some cases, motivated by a fascination and curiosity with the European lifestyle and the possibilities offered by Europe (studies, job opportunities or possibilities for artistic self-realization.). They perceived France and Morocco as interconnected, but separate spaces where different rules would apply. Morocco represented home, tradition, leisure and family ties, whereas France was associated with the notions of technology, modernity and professionalism (Virkama et al. 2012: 88).

To end, the main idea I wanted to promote with this chapter is that the compatibility of Muslim faith with other, seemingly opposing ideologies (such as secularism or socialism) should be discussed in light of the empirical studies. The definition of a practicing and non-practicing Muslim is also problematic, and social scientists clearly lack vocabulary that goes beyond the moderate/radical binary to describe the great variety of practices and identities that characterise different Muslim communities in today's Europe. As I have shown in this chapter, practicing or not practicing certain Islamic principles in everyday life is not necessarily about how a person feels about his or her faith.

References

Akbrazadeh, S., and Roose, J. M. (2011) Muslims, Multiculturalism and the Question of the Silent Majority. *Journal of Muslim Minority Affairs* 31 (3), 309–325.

Bartlett, J., and Miller, C. (2012) The Edge of Violence: Towards Telling the Difference between Violent and Non-Violent Radicalization. *Terrorism and Political Violence* 24 (1), 1–21.

Borgnogno, V., Streiff-Fenart, M., Ponard, L., and Wollenweider, L. (1995) *Les étudiants étrangers en France: trajectoires et devenir*. Nice: Université de Nice – Sophia Antipolis.

Briggs, R., and Birdwell, J. (2009) *Radicalization among Muslims in the UK. Microcon Policy Working Paper*. Brighton: MICROCON.

Brown, K. E., and Saeed, T. (2015) Radicalization and Counter-Radicalization at British Universities: Muslim Encounters and Alternatives. *Ethnic and Racial Studies* 38 (11), 1952–1968.

Brown, L. (2009) A Failure of Communication on the Cross-Cultural Campus. *Journal of Studies in International Education* 13 (4), 439–454.

Cesari, J. (2005) Mosques in French Cities: Towards the End of a Conflict? *Journal of Ethnic and Migration Studies* 31 (6), 1025–1043.

Cole, D., and Ahmadi, S. (2010) Reconsidering Campus Diversity: An Examination of Muslim Students' Experiences. *The Journal of Higher Education* 8 (2), 121–139.

de Gourcy, C. (2009) Partir pour revenir ou partir pour quitter? Le projet d'études d'étudiants algériens entre autonomie et attaches. In *La mondialisation étudiante. Le Maghreb entre Nord et Sud*, ed. by Mazzella, S. IRM. Paris: Kartala, pp. 97–115.

Department for Communities and Local Government (2007) *Preventing Violent Extremism – Winning Hearts and Minds*. London: HMSO.

Fetzer, J., and Soper, J. C. (2005) *Muslims and the State in Britain, France and Germany*. Cambridge: Cambridge University Press.

Geisser, V. (2000) *Diplomés maghrébins d'ici et d'ailleurs*. Paris: CNRS.

Hickman, M. J., Thomas, L., Silvestri, S., and Henri, N. (2011) *Suspect Communities? Counter-Terrorism Policy, the Press, and the Impact on Irish and Muslim Communities in Britain*. London: London Metropolitan University. Available online at: http://www.city.ac.uk/__data/assets/pdf_file/0005/96287/suspect-communities-report-july2011.pdf

Kabir, N. A. (2010) *Young British Muslims: Identity Culture Politics Media*. Edinburgh: Edinburgh University Press.

Kadri, A. (1999) *Parcours d'intellectuels maghrébins*. Paris: Kartala.

Latour, B. (2005) *Reassembling the Social: An Introduction to Actor-Network Theory*. Oxford: Oxford University Press.

Le Monde (2016) Valls rélance le débat sur le port du voile à l'université. *Le Monde*. Available online at: http://www.lemonde.fr/campus/article/2016/04/13/inter-diction-du-voile-a-l-universite-valls-relance-le-debat_4901346_4401467.html. Accessed 13 April 2016.

Marcus, G. E. (1995) Ethnography in/of the World System: The Emergence of Multi-Sited Ethnography. *Annual Review of Anthropology* 24, 95–117.

Nader, L. (1972) Up the Anthropologist – Perspectives Gained from Studying Up. In *Reinventing Anthropology*, ed. by Hymes, D. New York: Pantheon, pp. 285–311.

Nasir, N.S., and Al-Amin, J. (2006) Creating Identity-Safe Spaces on College Campuses for Muslim Students, *Change* 38 (2), 22–27.

Résistance Républicaine (2015) Ils réfusent les colis de nourriture non halal ? Qu'ils crèvent ! *Résistance républicaine*. Available online at: http://resistancerepublicaine. eu/2015/08/24/ils-refusent-les-colis-de-nourriture-non-halal-quils-crevent/. Accessed 24 August 2015.

Sayad, A. (1999) *La Double absence. Des illusions de l'émigré aux souffrances de l'immigré*. Préface de Pierre Bourdieu. Paris: Seuil.

Toguslu, E., and Leman, J. (2013) Introduction: Everyday Life Practices of Muslims in Europe. In *Everyday Life Practices of Muslims in Europe: Aesthetics and Consumption*, ed. by Toguslu, E., Leman, J., and Özdemir, S. Leuven: Leuven University Press, pp. 11–21.

Tribalat, M. (1995) *Faire France. Une grande enquête sur les immigrés et leurs enfants*. Paris: La Découverte.

Virkama, A. (2006) *Discussing Moudawana. Perspectives on Family Law Reform, Gender Equality and Social Change in Morocco*. Master's thesis. University of Joensuu. Available online at: http://epublications.uef.fi/pub/URN_NBN_fi_joy-20080053/

Virkama, A. (2015a) Maghreb, Higher Education and Academic Freedom. In the context of Post-Arab Spring Transformations. In *The Contested Role of Education in Conflict and Fragility*, ed. by Davies, L., and Gross, Z. Sense: Netherlands, pp. 137–152.

Virkama, A. (2015b) Emigration as a Political Stance? Moroccan Migrants' Narratives of Dignity, Human Rights and Minority Identities in Transnational Context. *Mathal* 4 (1), Article 5. Available online at: http://ir.uiowa.edu/mathal/vol4/iss1/5/

Virkama, A., Therrien, C., Harrami, N., and Kadri, A. (2012) Franco-Moroccan Transnational Space: Continuity and Transformation. In *Migration and Transformation. Multi-Level Analysis of Migrant Transnationalism*, ed. by Pitkänen, P., Içduygu, A., and Sert, D. Netherlands: Springer, pp. 63–101.

Wimmer, A., and Glick Schiller, N. (2003) Methodological Nationalism, the Social Sciences, and the Study of Migration: An Essay in Historical Epistemology. *International Migration* 37 (3), 576–610.

Chapter 6

'My horns come out in my attitude!'

Negotiating Jewish student identity and the politics of identification in Canada

Charlotte Shira Schallié

Introduction

This chapter analyses the findings of a focus group study with undergraduate and graduate Jewish students at a post-secondary institution in Western Canada. It will be argued that the notion of 'Jewish identity' or 'Jewishness' carries multiple overlapping – and often contradictory – meanings for Jewish students. Although our focus group participants challenged the notion of a homogenous 'group identity', their experiences with anti-Jewish attitudes and sentiments were often similar, if not identical. Jewish students who decide to publically express their identity are exposed to negative stereotyping and prejudice. Even those students who are less open about their religious and/or ethnic affiliation and self-identification are expected to act as experts on all things Jewish, especially on Israeli politics and policies. Our results also reinforce that 'Jews have often been defined . . . within the discourse of surrounding majorities' (Glenn and Sokoloff 2010: 3). It is this confrontation with the dominant culture on campus that creates the most tension and conflict for Jewish students both inside and outside the classroom.

The research findings discussed in this chapter were generated in two focus groups in 2015 with a total of fourteen Jewish students between the ages of 19 and 26, ranging from first-year undergraduate students to graduate students. The first focus group was comprised of five female student participants, one male student, plus one female Jewish community member who joined in the discussion. The second included four female students, three male students and one student who self-identified as non-binary gender. Two of the participants were students of colour. With the exception of two students – one was born and raised in an Asian country, another student immigrated to Canada from a Central American country – all participants grew up in North America. The student sample represented a remarkable diversity in their socio-cultural and religious background. Whereas some were brought up in well-established Jewish communities in metropolitan areas, others were raised in families that were the only Jews in their small town. Some of the students had a strong Jewish education – attending Jewish day school – in 'traditional' as well as 'progressive thinking' communities; others were raised in secular households. This range of experiences makes our sample size representative of Jewish student identity on a mid-sized Western Canadian university campus.[1]

The project was undertaken in partnership with my co-investigator, Moussa Magassa, who facilitated both focus group discussions, and two research assistants, Anna Jansen and Chorong Kim.[2] Our participants were recruited with the help of the Hillel director, a well-known member of the Jewish campus community. Both sessions, which lasted around 90 minutes, took place at Hillel House, which is owned and operated by the non-profit Hillel BC Society[3] and is situated adjacent to our university campus. The location was an important facilitator for our focus group session. It is not a neutral setting – if such a place ever existed – but is a popular destination for Jewish students to congregate and meet outside the classroom. Yet, the location was also chosen for symbolic reasons. Hillel House is widely known as a place where Jewish and non-Jewish students alike are welcome to attend hot lunches and Shabbat dinners. On a monthly average, 200 students (of which half are Jewish) drop by Hillel House to participate in various events, some of which are organized by the Jewish Student Association (JSA).[4] Hillel's open-house policy is not limited to shared mealtimes, but also includes a series of outreach events that foster interfaith and intercultural dialogue across campus. Thus, approaching the director of Hillel as our 'gatekeeper' in the early recruitment stage was a logical and sound choice. Hillel's endorsement was essential not only in reaching the target population, but also in gaining the trust of the community members. Another important aspect was the issue of hospitality. We were unable to provide any monetary compensation for the participants, but covered the expenses for a home-cooked dinner that was served after the focus group sessions at Hillel House. It was the sharing of food at a communal table that allowed us to personally connect and reflect on the issues raised during the two sessions.

Theory and method

Using focus groups to explore culturally and religiously sensitive topics is by no means unproblematic. One might argue that sensitive research should be conducted in one-on-one interviews or through anonymous questionnaires; yet, there are also numerous studies (Carey and Smith 1994; Kitzinger 1994; Morgan 1998) suggesting that 'people may be more, rather than less, likely to self-disclose or share personal experiences in group rather than dyadic settings' (Farquhar and Das 1999: 47). 'Safety in numbers' (Kitzinger 1994: 112) and the experience of a mutual support network within a group – especially if it is a pre-existing group – allow participants to feel more at ease when discussing difficult topics. Given the exploratory potential of focus group research, we employed 'a pragmatic version of grounded theory' (Barbour 2007: 120) incorporating 'a priori issues' (Ritchie and Spencer 1994: 180) such as those that were asked during the focus group discussion.

We designed our discussion guide with the goal of establishing broad themes that would strongly encourage group interaction but would also provide ample opportunities for personal introspection:

1   To what extent have you thought about your own identity/religion/cultural background prior to attending this focus group?
2   How do you feel about talking about these issues on an individual basis and in a group setting?
3   Have you come across any recent debates about Jewish people in Canada? If yes, did they confirm or change your views about your group in Canada? Please explain.
4   Have you experienced prejudice first-hand?

If there still was time at the end of the session, we would ask our participants if they wanted to discuss some of the questions more deeply, or bring up issues that had not been addressed. Our hypothesis, though, was that Jewish student identity in Canada would be affected by anti-Israel protests and the 'globalised new antisemitism' (Weinfeld 2004), an ideologically conflated version of modern anti-Semitic attitudes, anti-Zionism, and opposition to Israeli politics and policies.

Data analysis

In order to allow us to move beyond the descriptive stage to an analytic account, we coded the transcripts and identified patterns: themes that were repeatedly brought up, negotiated, or challenged during the discussions. Next, we produced two coding frames that allowed us to structure the patterns and establish how they might be interconnected and/or co-produced. The thematic analysis of our coding frames would provide us with a visual tool to a) explore commonalities and points of contact between patterns and b) highlight inherent contradictions (see Figures 6.1 and 6.2). The first coding frame was employed to establish the broad themes that were introduced during the first 30 minutes of the focus group discussions. The second coding frame highlights the themes that were explored in greater detail throughout the sessions. Comparing the two frames, we can see that the thematic complexity greatly increased during the remaining hour of the discussion – to the point where it became a challenge to untangle how the different themes were interrelated and affected one another.

The question of what is/what makes a Jew and what defines Jews as a group was a starting point in both sessions. As a discussion topic, it was revisited numerous times during the discussions, making it an important, complex, and confusing issue. Although all participants defined themselves as Jewish, there were considerable variances in how they defined themselves as Jewish and individually related to Judaism. Some students considered themselves to

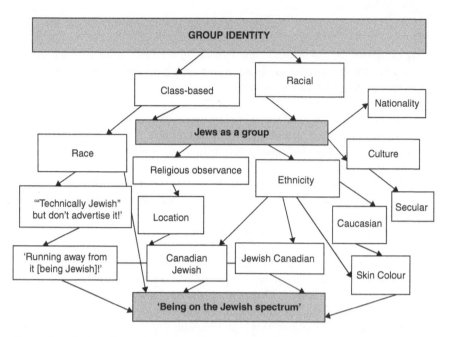

Figure 6.1 Coding Frame I: themes that were established at the beginning of the session.

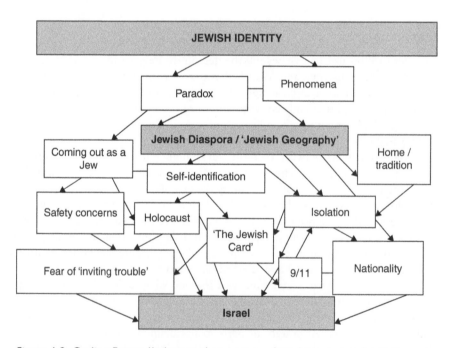

Figure 6.2 Coding Frame II: themes that were explored in greater detail throughout the session.

be a member of an ethnic or racial group, some identified themselves as culturally Jewish, and others stated that they are religious and/or observant Jews.
In most cases, participants had a difficult time situating themselves within any
one of these categories that they considered rather fluid and unstable. Yet, this
fluidity was perceived with a considerable amount of trepidation and perplex-
ity. There was consensus among the participants that these categories of self-
identification were social, cultural, and religious constructs. Nevertheless, the
students stressed that 'people' expected them to have a clearer sense of where
they positioned themselves 'on the Jewish spectrum'. Throughout the course
of the focus group conversation, it emerged that the pressure to conform to a
certain category of 'Jewishness' was not only exerted by the dominant group
but also by members of the Jewish community:

> Yeah technically I'm Jewish but I don't really practice, so I don't really know
> if I can call myself Jewish.
>   I'm like half Jewish, but I really identify as being Jewish. So does it count?
>   My Jewish identity is the strongest part of my identity.
>   I would identify as an ethnic Jewish person.
>   I am cultural Jewish but I do not believe in God . . . how can I be Jewish
> and not be religious?
>   My dad's from Israel and then I have had people who were like, oh, so
> you're not technically Jewish because your mom wasn't born Jewish. And
> then that sort of hit me.
>   I consider myself Canadian first . . . Jewish, that is my religion. But people
> see me as Jewish.

Once the students unpacked the notion of what 'Jewishness' means to them, they
moved straight into the question of how their Jewish identity co-existed with
their sense of national identity. Again, the participants stressed that it was mostly
non-Jews who prompted them to reflect on whether they would privilege their
Canadian nationality over their Jewish identity, or vice versa: were they Jewish
Canadian or Canadian Jewish (and with or without hyphen)?

The following excerpt from the transcript will illustrate how these complex
issues were co-generated and dialogically negotiated by individual focus group
participants. The narrative also highlights the degree to which seemingly separate
issues are entangled with one another and how a discussion about Jewish identity
will inevitably raise larger concerns of national belonging, religious identity, dis-
placement, and the challenges faced by Jewish diasporic communities in North
America. One focus group participant compared the question of 'what roles
Jews have to play in Canadian society' to a constant public interrogation of their
hyphenated Canadian identity, a 'pervasive questioning of Jewish loyalty'. The
brief excerpt also explicates that the issue of why 'I am a Canadian Jew, or a Jewish Canadian' matters deeply to those who are asked to subscribe to such binary

constructs. Yet, instead of internalising or rejecting these restrictive labels, our focus group participants are bending/blending opposing categories of identification. It is an act of defiance as well as resilience exemplifying the degree to which their own sense of selfhood and belonging is deeply complex and many-facetted:

MODERATOR: To what extent have you talked about your own identity or religion or cultural background prior to coming here today?

ELISHEVA: A lot.

BECKY: A lot [laughs].

EMILY: Every Jew. [Becky, Elisheva, Alejandra laugh.] I don't think it's possible to not ever think about it.

ELISHEVA: Constant discussion in my household. *Constant* discussion.

BECKY: I think it's . . . yeah, I mean, like we had said . . . lots of people are like oh yeah I'm Jewish somewhere in my family and they're just . . . they're that's . . . that's it for them and that's great and then there is people that, I mean, their entire existence is based around them being Jewish. You know what I mean, and that's. . . . . . that's literally all they do [laughs]. You know, but then I think it's such a varying . . . there's so many levels to it [Maya: yeah]. You, you aren't, some people aren't just you are or you're not.

JACKIE: You're somewhere along the spectrum.

BECKY: It's a spectrum . . . yeah.

ELISHEVA: And there is always that question which I have been asked dozens of times: are you a Canadian Jew or a Jewish Canadian? And . . . insert you know . . . American [Maya: mm-hm], British whatever. But for me . . . are you a Canadian Jew or a Jewish Canadian. And it's like many-layered.

MAYA: What's the difference?

ELISHEVA: What's the difference?

MAYA: Yeah.

ELISHEVA: Well, it's, it's like how would you . . . how would you say it yourself. I like, for me I would say I am Jewish Canadian because for me and from my point of view I am like the community I identify much more strongly with is the Jewish community. [Maya: mm-hm] You know if I go overseas and I meet other Canadians . . . that's great. I'm happy. But if I meet other people who are Jewish, it's like . . . it's a whole different experience than just meeting other Canadians.

ALEX: That's interesting.

ELISHEVA: And I, I mean it's . . .

ALEX: Mm-hm . . . that's very interesting.

ELISHEVA: Where I grew up, there is not a hu – . . . there wasn't a *huge* Jewish population, it was bigger than here in _____ [name of city], but not humongous and it was a huge part of who I was growing up. Still a huge part of who I am.

BECKY: I grew up in a town, where there was literally one other Jew.

MAYA: Wow!

ELISHEVA: I don't think that I could have done it.

BECKY: It was me and David P_____[*surname*] [everyone laughs].

ALEX: I know David P._____ [everyone laughs even more].

MAYA: Hey honesty [everyone laughs].

ELISHEVA: That is the other thing like . . .

EMILY: That's like though . . .

Everybody talks at once and is hard to understand.

JACKIE: Jewish Geography.

ELISHEVA: We get together and we play Jewish Geography, that's like you're from Calgary. Do you know so and so? It's like *yeah*, I went to pre-school with that guy.

The game of 'Jewish Geography' transcends national boundaries; it builds as well as connects diasporic communities across linguistic, ethnic, and cultural divides. 'Jewish Geography' is, as Jenna Weissman Joselit (2013) so eloquently explains, '[t]he Jewish equivalent of "six degrees of separation," the term refers to the kinship ties and social structures that bind one Jew to another. "Jewish Geography" is how we locate ourselves. It's our very own GPS'. Ultimately, it allows 'players' to grapple with estrangement and dislocation creating a pan-national sense of cultural, religious, or ethnic kinship.

It was revealing, however, that the students discussed the topic of Jewish identity and self-identification within the larger question of how they would communicate it to others. Few of our participating students had no issues or concerns bringing up their Jewish identity among non-Jews. For most participants, it was awkward or challenging to reveal that they are Jewish – regardless of how they defined their Jewishness. It was also through some of the ensuing exchanges with non-Jews that our focus group students became aware of othering processes while being confronted with racialized language and racial constructions:

My dad always told me, you know, don't be ashamed of who you are and of being Jewish.

I've sort of noticed a pattern of a lot of residence students who are Jewish [and] are sort of running away from it. They don't want to identify themselves as Jewish.

When I was growing up, I had a lot of people telling me that I didn't look Jewish . . . it was like a positive thing . . . and it took me a long time to realize that it was offensive because I have been hearing it so often.

[People would say] 'Oh I never really guessed [that you are Jewish] . . . you look normal!'

The following discussion elucidates that the assignment of favourable traits is a form of stereotyping that continues to reproduce the existing power structure delineating between insiders and outsiders. The 'Jewish girl' is provided with a set of positive signifiers that might enhance her social status but, paradoxically, will also prevent her from being accepted by members of the dominant culture as 'one of them'. Students perceive the fact that 'the Jewish girl' is singled out, 'set apart' (and thus, no longer protected by the majority culture), as a socially accepted form of segregation, a recurring theme in Jewish history, ultimately leading to the *Shoah* – the destruction of the European Jewry:

EMILY: I guess I have like pretty largely good experiences. Like I've met a lot of people . . . I've gotten acquired a bunch of friends from like pretty small rural towns and . . . I'm usually like their first Jewish friend [female students laugh] and they're like so excited.
ELISHEVA: The . . . Jewish girl.
EMILY: No, I'm serious . . . I did that once and so like usually they're pretty like, oh my God . . . like one person was like I've never met a Jew before I'm so excited and they were like really excited to meet a Jew. And they were like . . . they wanted to know stuff. People have been generally . . . they're like just kind of curious or like kind of excited which is really good, I guess. And I'm like happy to explain.
MAYA: Yeah I, I have just a question . . . and, yeah, I find it very interesting that why is it often like the Jewish kid gets identified? And, and it's sort of . . .
ELISHEVA: Easy target.
MAYA: It's just like a Holocaust in a way. It's like a Star of David, you know, like . . . and I don't know if that's because . . . like . . . I know other . . . you know if your skin color is different, or maybe you're the Chinese kid in the class. But I guess in, in like a Canadian setting, our world setting we are still . . .
JACKY: Set apart.
MAYA: Set apart. And . . .

Regardless of whether students communicated their Jewish identity verbally or symbolically (tattoos, jewelry), they were hyper-aware of safety concerns throughout the discussion. As 'Jewishness' is such a convoluted term exhibiting various signifiers, any public displays of 'Jewishness' can be interpreted in ways that are beyond anybody's control. For example, would a star of David necklace be interpreted as a sign of religious or ethnic affiliation, a cultural symbol, or an expression of solidary with the state of Israel?

> I carry the Star of David with me on my neck all the time but sometimes I do hide it depending on what the context or the situation is.
>   The director [of a Jewish sleep-away camp in the Northwest United States] always said . . . don't say [to non-Jews] that you are from a Jewish camp . . . I think he said it as a joke . . . tell them that you are from the bible camp across the lake but he did specifically make a point of being careful in public.

I don't throw 'the Jewish card' until I know the person and I feel like I can trust them.

[My parents raised] me to be stubborn and fiercely independent and proud of who I am. I won't hide and I'll never lie about who I am. That being said, there have been times when I tuck my necklace into my shirt because I don't want to invite trouble. And there are times when I'm cautious and that upsets me, it makes me really angry that I feel I have to be cautious.

The last comment, as well as the following excerpt, underscores the importance of family members and the community in fostering strong minority identities that would not be easily undermined by prejudice and bias. In many ways, the choice of wording – 'to advertise' – is telling. Not only does 'advertising' insinuate that one should make one's identity publically known, but also suggests that it might be necessary to be calling attention to it:

MAYA: [. . .] And in fact before I came [to Canada] my parents were like . . . you know don't advertise it [Jackie and Elisheva: mm-hm] . . . because it's, you know, it's not that safe.
BECKY: My dad said that to me a month ago [Jackie: really?] Yeah.
ELISHEVA: Oh my parents would never say that to me. They would encourage me to advertise it.

The importance of strengthening minority identities – such as those of Jews in Canada – becomes even more pressing when we consider the effects of ongoing exposure to bias and prejudice in a person's childhood and young adulthood. Our focus group participants displayed a considerable amount of dark humour, resilience, compassion, and a shared sense of comradery, when recollecting scenes and themes from their childhood. 'It's all in the attitude', as a student participant explained, might in fact be one of the most effective coping strategies for those who have been confronted with systemic racism. In this, the student dismantles an anti-Semitic stereotype and reclaims it on her own terms, successfully claiming ownership of it.[5]

ELISHEVA: I'll never forget my, my Rabbi growing up . . . he was American and he moved to ____ [city in Alberta] to be our Rabbi and then went on like a speaking tour with the federation of synagogues my synagogue was a part of . . . and he was down in a very rural part of ____ [name of Southern US state] speaking at a Catholic high school about diversity and how important it is to learn about other peoples' cultures and he was wearing a hat and after his talk two girls very humbly came up to him and said, you know we were just curious, we just want to know if you could take off your hat. And he said, yeah sure, why? And they said, we'd like to see your horns. [Emily laughs] And they were dead serious.
MAYA: Horns?

ELISHEVA: Horns, they were.

BECKY: You didn't know we're all born with horns [Elisheva: yeah]. And surgically removed like . . . [Jackie, Becky and Alejandra laugh].

ELISHEVA: These girls growing up in rural State in a very Christian community with no outside influences honestly thought that Jews had horns and he was *shocked*.

JACKY: Oh don't you have a pair? I have a pair [female students laugh].

ELISHEVA: It's all in the attitude.

BECKY: I don't see where the misconception is.

ELISHEVA: My horns come out in my attitude. But you know . . . It's still amazing to me that in this world this can happen.

BECKY: [. . .] It can be anything as a harmless as a joke . . . one time in high-school in grade eleven, I will never forget this. A kid that I'd known since grade three, we were talking about the Second World War and I mean you don't talk about the Holocaust until like grade twelve. Right, when you're like you should be emotionally mature enough to handle this. Grade eleven, we're talking about it and my teacher is reading a little section from the textbook. Talking about how in the ghettos in eastern Europe Jews were wearing yellow armbands, right, with the Star of David on them, and he piped up from the back of the class and said Becky where is yours? [Emily: Ohhh shit] Yeah. In front of . . .

ELISHEVA: That is very uncomfortable.

BECKY: In front of the whole class. And I just remember looking at him and looking at my teacher.

ALEJANDRA: What did your teacher do?

BECKY: Nothing.

ELISHEVA: Ohhh, that's terrible. What did you do?

ALEJANDRA: Booo [laughs].

BECKY: I left the classroom.

ELISHEVA: I don't blame you.

It does not seem accidental that our participants' first exposure to prejudice and anti-Semitism occurred in a school environment. What is revealing, however, is that educators seem often incapable of taking immediate action against overt displays of prejudice in their student population. This is not just limited to primary and secondary school levels. One student discussed a recent incident during a university business class 'when we're talking about great leaders one day and one of the students . . . said Hitler. Hitler is a great leader'. The professor failed to respond and instead proceeded to the next topic. Students commented that the same unresponsiveness, or unwillingness to respond and act – or take a strong stance against any form of prejudice and hate speech in the classroom – can be observed when the discussion turns toward the elephant in the room, Israel.

At this point, it is important to emphasise that we did not encourage students to discuss Israeli policies and politics in our focus group sessions. However, we asked them to reflect on whether and to what extent their own Jewish identity is connected to Israel as a homeland and as a modern nation-state; especially, as one participant pointed out, 'when the Jewish community in Canada is so divided' on this topic:

> The whole issue of being Jewish and . . . you know our homeland being Israel. And that just complicates things immensely in this discussion of what it means to be Jewish.
>
> I always grew up thinking that [as a Jewish person] I was directly responsible for Israel's actions.
>
> Israel as a nation-state is not my responsibility.
>
> And I think it takes someone that's quite secure in their identity and Jewish identity to say . . . and say I'm proud to be Jewish and don't think that the Israel situation really affects that and you can't criticize me for being Jewish because of the Israel situation.
>
> Even if I am not so interested in Israel's affairs as I am choosing to be an active Canadian Jew in my community, it [Israel] is being constantly fed to me by other people.
>
> You know that time at summer camp when the camp across the lake thought it would be *really* funny to deface our Israeli flag, which it wasn't funny. You know, so *everybody* has had something and that's really pathetic. You know it says something about our society.

For most Jewish students in our focus groups – regardless of whether they follow Israeli politics or show interest in current affairs in the Middle East – it is difficult, if not impossible, to separate their Jewish identity from the current situation in Israel: 'The things that Israel does affect me but that's because other people are making assumptions about me and other Jewish people'. This complicated and complex relationship with Israel becomes particularly taxing for these students when the focus turns to Israel's human rights abuses. One participant recollected that 'there was one English professor that liked to help to run Israel Apartheid week . . . I didn't take any of her classes specifically for that reason . . . what if she . . . ?' Another student commented on the fact that it was difficult for her to engage with 'more left-wing communities on campus because I am afraid that they immediately relate my Jewish identity to Israel, or they are going to trivialise my experiences as a Jew in Canada'.

At this point in the discussion, the question was raised if it was 'worth the trouble' to come out as a Jew on campus – only to be pigeonholed by the majority. Was it worth the fight to confront and contest people's assumptions of what Jewish identity entailed and meant in the current discussion on Israel? Hiding one's Jewish identity might just be easier, or at least, less complicated.

Conclusion

> My minority identity is completely invisible. I can take off my jewelry and no one will ever know.
>
> (Focus group participant)

Although there is a sizeable body of social science literature on Jewish student identity in both the United States and the United Kingdom (Goren 2014; Graham 2014; Lipstadt, Freedman, and Seidler-Feller 2005; Saxe and Sales 2006; Weinberg 2011; Yares, Elias, and Kress 2000), no comparable research project has been conducted in Canada. With this study, we hope to raise awareness of this lacuna encouraging scholars to explore this field of research from multiple interdisciplinary angles.

Our qualitative sampling, which was conducted with two pre-existing Jewish discussion groups, reflects the diversity of undergraduate and graduate students who identified as Jewish on a Western Canadian campus. The size of our two focus groups – seven and eight participants respectively – was ideal, as it allowed us to identify individual voices and seek clarification when necessary. In both discussion groups, there was a high level of participation; however, interpersonal dynamics differed greatly from one group to the other. Whereas the first session generated data mostly through group interactions, the second focus group largely consisted of one-on-one interviews in a collaborative group setting. This was, in many ways, advantageous for our research design, as it allowed us to make both inter-group and intra-group comparisons between two distinctly different focus group environments.

Our grounded theory approach was based on a participatory and dialogical research method (Freire 1970) that allowed the discussants to be in charge of their own knowledge production, selecting topics that were most salient to them. As researchers and moderators, we conducted our qualitative study both *on* and *with* our focus group members; it was therefore essential for us to provide minimal intervention, always keeping a critical distance while maintaining a self-reflective subjectivity. None of us had a previous power-over-relationship with any of our discussants.

Our findings on Jewish student identity in Canada mirror the results of previous studies on cultural-religious heterogeneity in the American Jewish population, suggesting 'that Judaism, the religion, and being Jewish in ethnic or cultural terms have been interdependent' (Klaff 2006: 416). Our study also corroborates that 'the concept of Jewish identity has been expanded to include whatever is personally meaningful to each individual' (Horowitz 2002: 24). Trying to negotiate their Jewish identity *vis-à-vis* identity constructs that students felt were imposed on them, it was the notion of 'being on the Jewish spectrum' that struck a chord with all of our focus group participants. Our results thus agree with Brink-Danan (2008: 681), who argues that 'categories of nation, practice, culture, society, class, peoplehood, language (as well as blood and soul) all emerge as meaningful ways – at times metaphorical – to understand membership'. At the same time, our study underscores that 'Jewish identity and sense of belonging depend not only on how Jews define themselves, but also, and of equal importance, on how others define Jews' (Brandes 2012: 43). The discussions also revealed that prejudice and racialized language have a significant impact on students' identity formation both on and off campus. Participants provided a variety of examples illustrating how they were affected by cultural, ethnic, and religious bias and stereotyping, some of which were alarmingly anti-Semitic in nature.

The politics of identification with Israel both as a homeland and as a nation-state proved to be the most challenging for our participants' identity formation.

Many Jewish students are perpetually and perennially – especially during Israeli Apartheid Week – reminded that their identity and sense of belonging is intricately linked to events unfolding in the Middle East. Based on their political, religious, cultural, or spiritual ties to Israel, the majority of our participants are acutely self-conscious of who they are, reluctant to discuss their Jewish identity in public. As a result, they often keep their Jewishness to themselves, or prefer to share it with others in a welcoming and community-building place such as Hillel House.

Our university's *Policy on Human Rights, Equity and Fairness* (University of Victoria 2005) reminds us that we should create 'a safe, respectful and supportive learning and working environment for all members of the university community'. Have we really come far enough to make this a reality? As educators, we have an obligation to encourage our administrators to create a campus environment that is inclusive for everybody – including those who are still in hiding because they do not feel safe to come out.

Notes

1 The University of Victoria does not keep records of students' ethnic and religious affiliations. According to the Hillel director, there are approximately 500 Jewish students on campus (which corresponds to an estimated 2.4 percent of the entire student population).
2 I would like to express my gratitude to my co-investigator and to my research assistants.
3 The first Hillel campus ministry was established in 1923 at the University of Illinois; today, there are over 250 Hillel affiliates in North America (Berenbaum and Skolnik 2007: 112).
4 The JSA is a student group at the University of Victoria.
5 The image of the horned Moses dates back to a twelfth-century mistranslation of Exod. 34: 30 ('quod cornuta esset facies sua') when the word 'beaming' or 'shining' was incorrectly translated as 'horned' (*The Oxford Dictionary of Art and Architecture* 2013).

References

Barbour, R. (2007) *Doing Focus Groups*. London: Sage Publications.

Berenbaum, M., and Skolnik, F. (2007) *Encyclopaedia Judaica* (2nd ed. Vol. 9). Detroit: Macmillan Reference.

Brandes, S. (2012) Religion, Ethnic Identity, and the Sense of Belonging. In *Dynamic Belonging. Contemporary Jewish Collective Identities*, ed. by Goldberg, H. E., Cohen, S. M., and Kopelowitz, E. New York and Oxford: Berghahn Books, pp. 31–45.

Brink-Danan, M. (2008) Anthropological Perspectives on Judaism: A Comparative Review. *Religion Compass* 2 (4), 674–688.

Carey, M.A., and Smith, M. (1994) Capturing the Group Effect in Focus Groups: A Special Concern in Analysis. *Qualitative Health Research* 4 (1), 123–127.

Farquhar, C., and Das, R. (1999) Are Focus Groups Suitable for 'Sensitive' Topics? In *Developing Focus Group Research*, ed. by Barbour, R. S., and Kitzinger, J. London: Sage Publications, pp. 47–64.

Freire, P. (1970) *Pedagogy of the Oppressed*. New York: Continuum Publishing.

Glenn, S. A., and Sokoloff, N. B. (2010) Who and What Is Jewish? Controversies and Comparative Perspectives on the Boundaries of Jewish Identity. In *Boundaries of Jewish Identity*, ed. by Glenn, S. A., and Sokoloff, N. B. Seattle: University of Washington Press, pp. 3–11.

Goren, S. (2014) Stuck in the Middle with Jews: Religious Privilege and Jewish Campus Life. *Journal of College and Character* 15 (2), 125–132.

Graham, D. (2014) *Strengthening Jewish Identity: What Works? An Analysis of Jewish Students in the UK*. Available online at: http://www.jpr.org.uk/publication?id=3642#.VyJ-0j_gKC4. Accessed 28 April 2016.

Horowitz, B. (2002) Reframing the Study of Contemporary American Jewish Identity. *Contemporary Jewry* 23 (14), 14–34.

Kitzinger, J. (1994) The Methodology of Focus Groups: The Importance of Interaction between Research Participants. *Sociology of Health & Illness* 16 (1), 103–121.

Klaff, V. (2006) Defining American Jewry from Religious and Ethnic Perspectives: The Transition to Greater Heterogeneity. *Sociology of Religion* 67 (4), 415–438.

Lipstadt, D., Freedman, S., and Seidler-Feller, C. (2005) American Jewry and the College Campus – Best of Times or Worst of Times? Available online at: http://www.bjpa.org/Publications/details.cfm?PublicationID=3150. Accessed 28 April 2016.

Morgan, D. L. (1998) *The Focus Group Guidebook. Focus Group Kit 1*. Thousand Oaks, CA: Sage Publications

The Oxford Dictionary of Art and Architecture (2013) Available online at: http://www.oxfordreference.com. Accessed 5 March 2016.

Ritchie, J., and Spencer, L. (1994) Qualitative Data Analysis for Applied Policy Research. In *Analyzing Qualitative Data*, ed. by Bryman, A., and Burgess, R. G. London: Routledge, pp. 173–194.

Saxe, L., and Sales, A. (2006) Particularism in the University: Realities and Opportunities for Jewish Life on Campus. Available online at: http://www.bjpa.org/Publications/downloadFile.cfm?FileID=3399. Accessed 28 April 2016.

University of Victoria (2005) *Policy on Human Rights, Equity and Fairness*. Available online at: http://www.uvic.ca/universitysecretary/assets/docs/policies/GV0200_1105.pdf. Accessed 29 April 2016.

Weinberg, A. (2011) *Alone on the Quad: Understanding Jewish Student Isolation on Campus*. Available online at: http://www.bjpa.org/Publications/details.cfm?PublicationID=13969. Accessed 28 April 2016.

Weinfeld, M. (2004) The Changing Dimensions of Contemporary Canadian Antisemitism. In *Contemporary Antisemitism. Canada and the World*, ed. by Penslar, D. J., Marrus, M. R., and Gross Stein, J. Toronto: University of Toronto Press, p. 43.

Weissman, J. (2013) Playing Jewish Geography from California to the New York Islands. *Forward* 10th April. Available online at: http://forward.com/culture/174188/playing-jewish-geography-from-california-to-the-ne/. Accessed 20 March 2016.

Yares, A., Elias, M., and Kress, J. (2000) Jewish Identity on Campus: Research and Recommendations for the College Years. *Journal of Jewish Education* 65 (3), 41–48.

Chapter 7

Samosas and simran
University Sikh societies in Britain

Jasjit Singh

Arriving at the Leeds University 'Faith & Culture Groups' fresher's fair in 2009, I was immediately struck by the size of the 'market' of university faith societies. At the fair, the Sikh society stall was placed opposite the Hindu society and next to the Indonesian society. The stall consisted of a table covered with a 'Khanda' insignia, a Sikh society display, a variety of leaflets produced by the British Organisation of Sikh Students (BOSS) and a box of Punjabi sweets for all who passed by. Members were charged £6 for joining the society, receiving a BOSS pack, a samosa and a membership card.

Having spent all day at the fair, the importance of the Sikh society quickly became apparent. When I arrived, I met two young Sikhs who explained that they had 'been waiting for this all week – can't wait to join Sikh society'. This feeling was echoed by two committee members who were visibly excited about being part of Sikh society. When I asked one if she felt the same way about other societies she had joined, she replied 'no, 'cos you want to do a good job for Sikh soc – Sikh soc's different isn't it? It's special 'cos it's my own people. I loved putting my Sikh soc hoodie on – loved it'. Indeed, Acland and Azmi (1998: 81) found that for minority ethnic students in particular, these societies 'helped them enormously to find friends, develop support groups and share experiences'. Furthermore, these self-support groups were 'much more successful in addressing ethnic minority needs than the formal mechanisms of support provided by the institution' (Acland and Azmi 1998: 81).

This chapter examines Sikh societies in British universities with a particular focus on the role they play in the transmission of the Sikh tradition. Beginning with an analysis of the evolution and role of South Asian faith societies in British universities, I then examine how Sikh students fit in to the world of higher education. Having understood the context which led to the evolution of Sikh societies, I examine who attends Sikh societies, what types of events take place, what makes young Sikhs want to be a part of these societies, what role Sikh societies play in religious and cultural transmission and what the interplay is between these complementary aspects of British Sikhs' lived experience. Data was gathered as part of a larger study on religious transmission among 18–30-year-old British Sikhs using a mixed-methods approach including a) semi-structured interviews with thirty 18- to 30-year-old British Sikhs who had participated in and often helped organise events for young Sikhs; b) a self-selecting online survey of young British Sikhs; c) focus groups with Sikh students across the United Kingdom; d) participant observation at events organized for young Sikhs, including Sikh camps and university Sikh society events. The chapter will include anonymised quotations from some of the interviews and survey responses.

The emergence of South Asian faith societies

As Gilliat-Ray (2000) observes, questions relating to the role of religion in higher education have been approached from the perspective of race and ethnicity, particularly focusing on rates and patterns of participation (e.g., Modood and Acland 1998). However, questions about the significance of religious identity in universities began to be raised in the late 1990s (Acland and Azmi 1998: 75), primarily as a result of the growing importance of religious identity for minority ethnic communities. Although a number of Asian Youth Movements sprang up in the late 1970s in response to the activities of the far right, as Modood and Werbner (1997: 129) observe, the 'Asian' identity was always somewhat fragile. As these movements were always having to contend with the powerful centrifugal pull of Hindu, Sikh and Muslim identities (Mehmood 1983 cited in Modood and Werbner 1997: 129), they did not survive long into the 1980s.

The first national faith-based organisation catering for members of South Asian religious traditions was the Federation of Students Islamic Societies (FOSIS), formed in 1962 to 'protect the interests of Muslim students and to enable nationwide collaboration' (Gilliat-Ray 2000: 128). Although there is little documentation regarding the activities of FOSIS during the 1960s and 1970s, Gilliat-Ray notes that 'lecture programs by eminent academics, Qur'anic study circles, and informal discussion groups reflect the scholarly bias of this now well established organization' (1997: 101). FOSIS runs an annual conference and seeks to develop new initiatives to help invigorate an organisation 'somewhat dwindling in overall popularity compared to its heyday in the 1970s' (1997: 101). In this regard, FOSIS has also linked with other Muslim youth groups, organising training camps both on its own and also with the International Islamic Federation of Student Organizations (IIFSO) in 1994.

The National Hindu Students Forum (NHSF) started in 1991 with two chapters in Sheffield and the London School of Economics (LSE) (Gilliat-Ray 2000: 128). The organisation now has local branches at over 30 higher education institutions in the United Kingdom and hosts over 4,000 active student members. A number of scholars including Brown (2006: 167), Katju (2003: 154) and Jaffrelot (2005) argue that the NHSF is affiliated to the ideology of Hindutva, being ideologically close to Hindu nationalist movements including the Vishva Hindu Parishad (VHP) and the Hindu Swayamsevak Sangh.

Between the late 1980s and early 1990s, Sikh students also begin to organise themselves into a national body. Following the formation and disbanding of the

National Union of Sikh Students (NUSS), BOSS was formed in 1992. Gilliat-Ray reported only a 'handful' of Sikh societies in 1992, 'but by 1998 this number had risen to over 50' (2000: 128). As she further observes, 'the picture that emerges from BOSS is rapid (but unsurprising) expansion over a relatively short period of time, and little documentary recording of the early history' (Gilliat-Ray 2000: 128). Although there has been some description of how and when these bodies emerged, to date there has been little examination of why both the NHSF and BOSS emerged in the early 1990s, when Asian and Indian student societies already existed to cater for the needs of minority ethnic students.

Although moves were underway in the 1970s to ensure that the specific religious needs of Hindus, Muslims and Sikhs were being met, for McLoughlin (2005: 132), it was the Rushdie affair of 1988 which gave Muslims a national and international profile, requiring Hindus and Sikhs to respond accordingly. As Jacobson (1998: 33) explains, Rushdie was significant for young South Asians as 'it was in the context of the "Rushdie Affair" that youth protests in religious terms first became noticeable', leading many Muslim youth (especially men) to be 'articulating a self-conscious identity as "Muslim" for the first time' (Jacobson 1998: 39). It was Rushdie which in turn led young Hindus and Sikhs to begin to primarily identify themselves in religious terms.

For Raj, this religious resurgence among young South Asians is also 'connected to wider processes of identity politics partially informed by the assumption of difference as the core of multiculturalism' (2000: 552). Rather than being regarded as part of an ethnic identity, the assertion of an overtly religious identity by young South Asians should be viewed as a strategy which is being used to cope with living in a pluralistic society, first because a religious identity 'includes all the positive associations of belonging to a nation-state without actually living there [which is] . . . reinforced (and assumed) by British census "ethnic" identity categories' (Raj 2000: 552), and second because the choosing of a religious identity over an ethnic identity allows young South Asians to present themselves using an 'authentic, workable, identity that is easy to comprehend' (Raj 2000: 551).

This shift from an ethnic 'Asian' identity to a more religious identity in the late 1980s/early 1990s had major consequences for the emergence of university South Asian faith societies. Arriving to study for my undergraduate degree at the University of Manchester in 1990, I remember quickly joining 'A-Soc', the 'Asian society', primarily in order to meet other South Asian students. This was a society which catered for South Asians no matter what their background, with Punjabi, Gujarati, Pakistani and Bangladeshi members. We were aware of one another's backgrounds from our names, but this was not a society for religious discussion; the emphasis was on creating shared spaces where young South Asians with similar dietary and musical tastes could socialise with one another.

At the time, there was no Sikh society or Hindu society, although an Islamic society and a Pakistani society had been formed. In 1992, I was approached by a newly arrived first-year student from Birmingham to assist in the formation of a Sikh society, as I had recently organised a trip to a local *gurdwara*.

Having completed the necessary paperwork and gathered enough signatures, the University of Manchester Sikh society was formed. Meetings consisted of discussions of passages from the Guru Granth Sahib using photocopies of English translations, along with *kirtan* and trips to the local *gurdwara*. Looking back on these events, it is clear that I was witnessing the beginnings of the establishment of Sikh societies in British universities. It must be noted that the evolution of strictly faith-based societies has not led to the total disappearance of Asian societies from university campuses. These 'Asian' societies, like the one I joined in the 1990s, still exist, offering secular spaces for young Asians to socialise with one another.

Another reason why Hindu and Sikh societies emerged at this time may be found in Knott's observation that one of the main roles of the NHSF was to 'withstand the proselytizing strategies of Muslim outreach organizations (such as Tablighi Jama'at and Hizb-ut Tahrir) and . . . [to] develop a sense of Hindu identity' (2000: 98). Having spoken to a number of those involved in establishing Sikh student groups in the 1990s, the activities of Muslim proselytising organisations on universities campuses appear to be a significant stimulus in the creation of BOSS and in the establishment of Sikh societies across the United Kingdom. Examining newspaper articles from the time, it is clear that Hizb-ut Tahrir were active in the late 1980s/early 1990s (O'Neill 1989) organising rallies at London university (Smith 1994) and Wembley in 1994 (Malik 1994). In terms of activities on university campuses, many journalists noted the presence of Hizb-ut Tahrir at the School of Oriental and African Studies (SOAS) (Gerard 1994a), Kings College London (Bright 1994), LSE (Sanders 1994), Brunel (Gerard 1994b) and Birmingham University (MacKinnon 1995). Indeed, this activity led the National Union of Students (NUS) conference of 1995 to discuss the issue of extremism and intolerance on university campuses specifically focusing on Hizb-ut Tahrir (Tyrer 2004: 35).

The British organisation of Sikh students

The exact process by which BOSS came about is somewhat lost in time, although the role of Islamist organisations on campus was certainly a major factor in the organisation's formation. What is clear from my interviews with a number of student activists who had some involvement in its inception is that BOSS was established in 1992, following the formation and disbanding of a previous attempt to form a national Sikh body, the NUSS (National Union of Sikh Students).

At this time, the establishment of Sikh societies depended very much on the efforts of individual Sikh students. As many Sikhs tended to attend their local institutions, it is not surprising that the majority of Sikh societies were initially set up in London and the Midlands, although interviewees claimed that societies were also set up in Manchester and as far north as Sunderland. As Baldeep (pseudonym), who was involved in the establishment of BOSS explained, there was a need for Sikh societies because 'all we were attached to was Bhangra societies.

Everything else but Sikhi was available and we felt something had to be done'. Much has been written about the development of the Bhangra scene on British Asian youth in the United Kingdom, with Sharma suggesting that Bhangra was 'a means for Asian youth to assert their "Asianness" and locate themselves firmly in their contemporary urban surroundings' (Sharma 1996: 35–36). In the post-Rushdie climate, the link between Bhangra and Asian-ness rather than a specific religious identity led young Sikhs to create Sikh societies, creating a distinction between what they regarded as 'religion' and 'culture'. Indeed, the relationship between the Sikh tradition and Punjabi cultural practices is constantly being negotiated by those involved in Sikh societies.

In addition, the events of 1984 when the Golden Temple was stormed by the Indian government during Operation Bluestar, and when thousands of Sikhs were killed in Delhi following the assassination of the Indian Prime Minister by her Sikh bodyguards (Nesbitt 2005: 81–83), also had an impact. As many of the young Sikhs attending university in the early 1990s watched the events of 1984 unfolding on the television screens, the formation of BOSS and of University Sikh societies allowed them the opportunity to discuss these events with their peers.

As well as assisting Sikh societies in universities all over the United Kingdom, BOSS has also organised 'Sikhi (BOSS) Camp' since 1996, an annual residential camp catering for 18–30-year-olds (Singh J 2011) and runs a store selling CDs, clothes, books and DVDs, both online and at various events around the country. Although BOSS may have originally been 'a non-political, non-profit making, independent body', it appears that the organisation has become increasingly inspired by Damdami Taksal in recent years, a group whose head, Sant Jarnail Singh Bhindranwale, was a key target of the Indian government during the events of 1984. Many of the clothes, posters and CDs on sale at Sikhi Camp and at the BOSS stall relate to the events of 1984 and to the personality of Bhindranwale.

Sikh societies today

Recent analysis of faith societies has tended to focus on the activities of Islamic societies primarily as a result of the 'preventing violent extremism' agenda, although little of this analysis has come from the academic community. Think tanks such as The Centre for Social Cohesion have observed that 'since 2006, the British government and the media have paid increasing attention to Muslim students at British universities following several high-profile cases where students or graduates took part in terrorist attacks or were convicted on terrorist- related charges' (Thorne and Stuart 2008). Despite the variety of reports arguing that young Muslims are or are not (Edmunds 2010) radicalised on university campuses, according to Abbas, 'the question as to whether the Islamic societies of universities are genuinely places where Muslims are radicalised has yet to find firm answers' (2007: 5).

In terms of the appeal of Sikh societies, Singh and Tatla note that 'Sikh students are now entering British universities in greater numbers than ever before . . . partly because of the expansion of higher education and the rise in Sikh student numbers, especially since the 1990s, coincides with their overwhelming concentration in the post-1992 "new" university sector' (2006: 159). Indeed, according to the Office for National Statistics (ONS) Census figures, 25 percent of the Sikh population in England and Wales were students in 2011 (ONS 2013). Having contacted Student Unions at a number of universities across the country in 2011, none had records available pre-2000. Consequently, any information on when various Sikh societies were established can only be based on the type of anecdotal evidence provided. As levels of activity and of membership of a particular society are directly dependent on the passion and interests of its committee, the popularity and the type of events run at various Sikh societies can vary dramatically from year to year.

Examining the types of events organised by Sikh societies and interviewing members and committee members of Sikh societies, it is clear that this is as much, if not more, a place for social interaction as for learning about the Sikh tradition. Having compared Sikh societies across the country, a reasonably standard Sikh society calendar emerges, based around term dates and key events in Sikh history; see Table 7.1:

Table 7.1 Calendar of Sikh society events

Month	Event
September	Fresher's Fair
October	Meet and Greet/Cha and Samosa
Weekly/Fortnightly	*Simran* (devotional singing) on campus – often combined with discussions or lectures
October–November	Lecture about Divali/Bandhi-Chorr – focusing on the different reasons why Sikhs and Hindus celebrate Divali
November	Sikhi Week – runs in Northern/West Midlands and London universities
November	Lecture/*Gurdwara* trip celebrating Guru Nanak's birthday
October–December	Socials at various points, usually including meals, bowling, paintballing. All take place in non-alcoholic venues
February	Continuing Simran on campus/lectures
March	Sikhi Week – runs in Northern/West Midlands and London universities
March–May	New committee chosen

As can be seen from the calendar of Sikh society events, Sikh societies only really function for around six months per year. From participant observation and examining photographs of these types of events online, it is clear that the initial meet-and-greet event is usually the most popular of the year. Following this, social events such as meals and bowling are well attended, whereas the *simran* (devotional singing) and lectures on the Sikh tradition are usually attended by smaller numbers, possibly indicating the main priorities for many members of these societies.

Increased regulation of membership of university societies, possibly due to issues with non-students attending student events, also appears to have impacted significantly on the membership of Sikh societies in 2010. An interview with Puran, the president of a Sikh society in the South of England, highlighted a number of factors leading to a decline in Sikh society attendance from the heyday of the late 1990s:

1   The role and status of South Asian University Faith Societies – As discussed, post 9/11 and 7/7, faith societies, particularly those being run for Muslim students, have been under increased scrutiny by the government and policy-makers. This increased suspicion around the role played by South Asian faith societies may have led some Sikhs to not wish to engage with faith societies at all (Grossman 2014).

2   Changes to funding of University Societies – A number of the Sikh society committee members stated that the funding they received had decreased year on year, leading to a reduction in the types and number of events organised. Changes in methods of registration: whereas previously, individuals would be recruited to join Sikh societies at fresher's fairs, where they would be able to pay the membership fee and immediately become members, members are now required by student unions to join and pay online. For Puran, the opportunity available to talk to members and to encourage them to formally join has been lost.

The interview with Puran demonstrates that both institutional changes (the requirement for online payments) and world events (9/11, 7/7) have significantly impacted on the membership of Sikh societies. In addition, the need for young Sikhs to join Sikh youth organisations such as university Sikh societies to get their questions about the Sikh tradition answered has lessened somewhat following the emergence of the internet and of the online presence of the Sikh tradition (Singh 2014).

Having been invited to lecture at Sikh societies myself, it is clear that lecturers are usually invited through personal contacts and recommendations from other committee members. As Gagan, an ex-committee member of a Sikh society in the Midlands explained, 'if you're a member of a group, it's easier to book a talk – 'cos they have networks and websites. By 'they' in this case, he was referring to Sikhs affiliated to Damdami Taksal (DDT) or the Akhand Kirtani Jatha (AKJ) (see Singh 2014), two Sikh groups to which a number of members in the Sikh

society were affiliated. Although he explained that he came from a religious background himself, Gagan inferred that people with links to the AKJ and/or DDT
could call on a wide variety of speakers, primarily because both of these groups
had access to a number of mobile, English-speaking young presenters, many of
whom had attended Sikh camps organised by these groups (Singh 2011).

Further questions regarding how speakers are booked revealed that different
kinds of Sikh society exist in different institutions. As Gilliat-Ray describes (2000:
22–46), higher education institutions have engaged with religion in different
ways depending on the history of their evolution. In addition, different types of
institutions attract different types of students. For instance, Thandi observes a
high degree of 'over-representation' among Indian students in the 'new' university sector and notes that 'there is much evidence to suggest that the entrants into
"new" universities are usually those students who have a lower "A level" score
or those who have gained admission through some other non-standard qualification' (1999: 357). The consequence of large numbers of Indian students attending local universities means that the politics of the local institution becomes more
relevant to the Sikh society.

This became clear during a focus group with members of the Sikh society
committees at two institutions in the Midlands, one at a traditional university,
and one at a post-1992 university. Many members of the Sikh society at the
post-1992 university had all attended a local *gurdwara* which had affiliated to
Damdami Taksal, meaning that talks about 1984 became popular at this particular Sikh society. Comparing the Sikh society at the post-1992 university with the
Sikh society at the traditional university in the same city, Aarti, the president at
the traditional university explained, 'Our committees are totally different – he's
got loads of Singhnia [turbaned Sikh women] on his committee. Ours is a lot
more baal [hair] cut, go out, drink – do you know what I mean? But ours isn't so
much into Sikhi, it's more about issues now like caste, homosexuality'.

Aarti, the president of the old university, noted that 'there's also the Sikh/Muslim
relationship at the new university which isn't there at ours. Muslims challenge Sikhs
more than anyone else – we don't have that at our university'. This indicates that
inter-group dynamics have as much of an impact on the types of topics discussed as
the members of the society themselves, and that the ethnic makeup of an institution
will also impact on the types of events run by the Sikh society in question.

As well as lectures, many Sikh societies organise simran on campus events.
These are usually informal events where a seminar room or lecture theatre is
'made sacred' by placing white sheets on the floor. Those students who are able
to perform *kirtan* (singing the Guru's compositions) then take it in turns to
sing compositions from the Guru Granth Sahib, usually with a projector screen
supplying translations. Many Sikh societies have simran events weekly or at least
fortnightly, as they allow for a regular event to take place without the need to
organise formal lectures on these occasions. Having attended simran events at
a number of Sikh societies around the country, again it appears that only the
very committed attend these events. These sessions play a number of functions,

allowing young Sikhs an hour a week to relax and also allowing members of the Sikh society to congregate in an informal atmosphere. It could be argued that it is these informal gatherings which are the real sites for religious transmission, as Baldeep explained:

> if there was an event and the Sikh societies were getting together, the parchaar [teaching] wasn't done at the event – it was done on route, 'cos that's when you're talking to someone face to face, or it might be a discussion.

This really brings in to question the usefulness and effectiveness of formal lectures. Although lecturers transmit facts and ideas, it appears that it is often the informal gatherings taking place around these events which are the real venues for religious and cultural transmission.

Why join a Sikh society?

Having understood what Sikh societies do, I now examine why young British Sikhs may wish to join these societies in the first place. A common response in interviews indicates a search for meaning, as one member of a Sikh society in a Northern university explained, 'I've been growing up as a Sikh, but I'm not a Sikh – I've never learnt about it, and I don't know why I call myself a Sikh'.

The most popular response provided to the question 'Why did you join a Sikh society?' in an online survey of over 600 Sikhs, was 'to meet other Sikhs'. The data gathered in the interviews and online survey highlighted this was the main reason why Sikh students join a Sikh society. As Gurpal, a member of a Sikh society committee, explained:

> me and my friend were lucky because we were living together in halls and we were the only two Singhs with Dastaars [turbans] . . . we got confidence off each another – because going to uni is a big step, because we had a partner in crime kind of thing.

Creating a sense of familiarity in a new environment was key. An 18-year-old female survey respondent explained:

> coming from Leicester where there are many Sikhs around you just want to bring that sense of familiarity back again-that's why I joined the Sikh society-to enjoy the activities they do during the year, to grasp the opportunities which help me learn more about Sikhism while at university.

It is important to also note that a number of young Sikhs chose not to join their university Sikh society for a number of reasons. Indeed, of the 567 online survey respondents who had attended university, 185 (33 percent) said that they had chosen not to join their university Sikh society because a society did not exist at their institution or because they did not feel welcome at the one that did. A 26-year-old female from London explained that she had 'joined because I was Sikh . . . by the end I didn't feel comfortable to attend all because some Sikhs were militant' whereas another 26-year-old female explained that 'the society was full of amritdhari sikhs and they were only approaching other amritdhari's to join!'. Whereas some young Sikhs did not join the Sikh society because they felt it was too 'militant', others chose not to join because they felt the Sikh society was not religious enough. A 29-year-old from Ilford thought that the Sikh society 'was not really Sikh Orientated, always running Chaa and Samosa, Nights out, paintballing etc.', whereas a 27-year-old female from Birmingham explained that 'the Sikh society at this university was contradicting, as they would discuss Sikhism and once the meeting was over head down to the student union to get drunk. I rather go to the gurdwara on my own or do part from my own house'.

Conclusion

This chapter has shown that although there are a number of similarities in the way in which university Sikh societies are organised, these societies are not homogenous, with many differences relating to locality and institutional background. Sikh societies are very fluid arenas of religious transmission, especially given that they are only active for six months a year and change committees annually. I have explained that the development of Sikh societies in British universities and of BOSS can be linked both to the emergence of a national Muslim identity following the Rushdie affair and to the activities of Muslim outreach organisations, such as Hizb-ut Tahrir.

In addition, I have highlighted the importance of the local context, especially for higher education institutions which derive many of their students from their immediate locality. If the Sikh society is comprised of a group of local attendees from a particular *gurdwara*, the societal experience will be very different to a society which comprises committee members from all over the country. In addition, institutions which offer degrees which last longer than three years are more likely to have some kind of continuity regarding participation as committee members continue to attend events.

From their heyday in the late 1990s, the popularity of Sikh societies appears to have declined somewhat as a result of events such as 9/11 and 7/7 which have led to greater scrutiny about the role and organisation of university faith societies and also because of the implementation across a number of higher education institutions of more stringent processes of membership. It also appears that the lectures organised at the Sikh societies are less important than the face-to-face interactions which young Sikhs have with one another. Ideas about tradition and authority are primarily based on the views of the committee members and are consequently derived from earlier socialisation in families, *gurdwaras* and increasingly in camps held for young British Sikhs. In terms of an arena for religious transmission, therefore, Sikh societies appear to act primarily as social arenas and secondarily as venues for religious transmission.

References

Abbas, T. (2007) *Islamic Political Radicalism: A European Perspective*. Edinburgh: Edinburgh University Press.

Acland, T., and Azmi, W. (1998) Expectation and Reality: Ethnic Minorities in Higher Education. In *Race and Higher Education: Experiences, Challenges and Policy Implications*, ed. by Modood, T., and Acland, T. London: Policy Studies Institute, pp. 74–85.

Bright, M. (1994) Police Called in as Jews Picket College Meeting of Islamic Group. *The Guardian*, 29 October.

Brown, J. (2006) *Global South Asians : Introducing the Modern Diaspora*. Cambridge: Cambridge University Press.

Edmunds, J. (2010) 'Elite' Young Muslims in Britain: From Transnational to Global Politics. *Contemporary Islam* 4 (2), 215–238.

Gerard, L. (1994a) Islamic Student Group Faces Ban After Unrest. *The Independent* (London), 29th October.

Gerard, L. (1994b) Islamic Society Barred from Campus. *The Independent*, 8th December.

Gilliat-Ray, S. (1997) Muslim Youth Organisations in Britain: A Descriptive Analysis. *The American Journal of Islamic Social Sciences* 14 (1), 99–111.

Gilliat-Ray, S. (2000) *Religion in Higher Education: The Politics of the Multi-Faith Campus*. Aldershot: Ashgate.

Grossman, C. L. (2014) Got Religion on Campus? Leave It Off Your Resume. *The Washington Post* [WWW Document], n.d. Available online at: https://www.washingtonpost.com/national/religion/got-religion-on-campus-leave-it-off-your-resume/2014/06/16/f557458e-f590–11e3–930d-ca5db8eb8323_story.html. Accessed 26 April 2016.

Jacobson, J. (1998) *Islam in Transition: Religion and Identity Among British Pakistani Youth*. London: Routledge.

Jaffrelot, C. (2005) *The Sangh Parivar*. Oxford: Oxford University Press.

Katju, M. (2003) *Vishva Hindu Parishad and Indian Politics*. Hyderabad: Sangam Books Ltd.

Knott, K. (2000) Hinduism in Britain. *In The South Asian Religious Diaspora in Britain, Canada, and the United States*, ed. by Coward, H. G., Hinnells, J. R., and Williams, R. B. Albany: SUNY Press, pp. 89–106.

Mackinnon, I. (1995) Hotline Exposes Campus Racism. *The Independent*, 31st October.

Malik, K. (1994) Muslim rally angers Jews; Islamic body accused of racism, The Independent, August 7.

McLoughlin, S. (2005) Migration, Diaspora and Transnationalism: Transformations of Religion and Culture in a Globalizing Age. In *The Routledge Companion to the Study of Religion*, ed. by Hinnells, J. R. London: Routledge, pp. 526–549.

Modood, T., and Acland, T. (1998) *Race and Higher Education: Experiences, Challenges and Policy Implications*. London: Policy Studies Institute.

Modood, T., and Werbner, P. (1997) *The Politics of Multiculturalism in the New Europe: Racism, Identity, and Community.* Basingstoke: Palgrave Macmillan.

Nesbitt, E. (2005) *Sikhism: A Very Short Introduction.* Oxford: Oxford University Press.

O'Neill, S. (1989) Young Guardian: Keeping Faith with a Circle of Awareness. *The Guardian*, 2nd August.

ONS (2013) *What Does the Census Tell Us about Religion in 2011? Articles – Office for National Statistics.* Available online at: https://www.ons.gov.uk/peoplepopulationandcommunity/culturalidentity/religion/articles/fullstorywhatdoesthecensustellusaboutreligionin2011/previousReleases. Accessed 26 April 2016.

Raj, D. S. (2000) "Who the hell do you think you are?" Promoting Religious Identity among Young Hindus in Britain. *Ethnic and Racial Studies* 23, 535–558.

Sanders, C. (1994) Terrorist Threat Denied; London School of Economics. *The Times Higher Education Supplement*, 11th November.

Sharma, S. (1996) Noisy Asians or "Asian Noise"?' In *Dis-orienting Rhythms: The Politics of the New Asian Dance Music*, ed. by Sharma, S., Hutnyk, J., and Sharma, A. London: Zed Books.

Singh, G., and Tatla, D. S. (2006) *Sikhs in Britain: The Making of a Community.* London: Zed Books.

Singh, J. (2011) Sikh-ing Beliefs: British Sikh Camps in the UK. In *Sikhs in Europe: Migration, Identities and Representations*, ed. by Myrvold, K., and Jacobsen, K. Aldershot: Ashgate, pp. 253–277.

Singh, J. (2014a) Sikh-ing Online: The Role of the Internet in the Religious Lives of Young British Sikhs. *Contemporary South Asia* 22, 82–97.

Smith, H. (1994) University Bans Moslem Militants. *London Evening Standard*, 20th January.

Thandi, S. (1999) Sikh Youth Aspirations and Identity: Some Perspectives from Britain. In *Sikh Identity: Continuity and Change*, ed. by Singh, P., and Barrier, N. G. . . New Delhi: Manohar, pp. 349–363.

Thorne, J., and Stuart, H. (2008) *Islam on Campus: A Survey of UK Student Opinions.* London: Centre for Social Cohesion.

Tyrer, D. (2004) The Others: Extremism and Intolerance on Campus and the Spectre of Islamic Fundamentalism. In *Institutional Racism in Higher Education*, ed. by Law, I., Phillips, D., and Turney, L. Stoke-on-Trent: Trentham Books, pp. 35–48.

Chapter 8

Secularism, free speech and the public university

Student engagement with Israel-Palestine in a British campus

Ruth Sheldon

In late 2010, controversy erupted at Old University[1] when the student Palestine Society organised a public talk by a Palestinian journalist that culminated in violent exchanges between participating students. The national and international media reported that the invited speaker had contravened the Students' Union's anti-Semitism policy and provoked verbal and physical aggression between members of the audience. In the immediate aftermath, the police were contacted regarding claims by Jewish students that they felt scared for their safety and the university authorities investigated these allegations. In the weeks that followed, media commentators denounced the speaker for 'glorifying' violence against the Israeli state 'in the name of Allah' and elite public figures including Members of Parliament and Jewish communal leaders accused the university authorities of allowing 'extremism' into the campus.

The following term (semester), in a context of heightened tensions between the Palestine Society and the Jewish Society, the university hosted a public debate about the academic boycott of Israel. The contrast between the reception of this debate and the prior event could not have been more marked. In the immediate aftermath of this debate, the student newspaper published an article proclaiming its success. Although the event had not 'resolved' the substantive issue, the article claimed that it had reaffirmed this institution's position as an authentically *academic* community:

> The Professor chairing the evening began with an appeal to reason from the two sides. He asked the audience to sustain a spirit of 'mutual respect, tolerance and calm' . . . 'This is an academic institution and this will be an academic debate', he [the chair] said. Afterwards, the event organisers said that they were pleased by the meeting's civil discourse.

Carefully stage managed by the institutional authorities, this debate was presented as an exemplary model of academic engagement with highly contentious questions of justice in relation to the Israel-Palestine conflict. It was also venerated in a broader sense, as a demonstration of the university instantiating Enlightenment values of free speech and civility within the public sphere.

In this chapter, I will develop the claim that this debate can helpfully be understood as a performance of secularism within the university. Of course, this may seem like a roundabout approach, as compared, for example, to studying the burgeoning activities of self-consciously 'secular' student societies. What, then, is the value of framing the terms of this academic boycott debate event in relation to secularism rather than – for example – as 'liberal', 'rationalist' or even just 'modern'? Certainly, the broader political and ethical questions raised by this activism expose the contemporary British university as a profoundly conflicted institution grappling with multiple histories and relations of power.[2] Furthermore, the raging tensions that arise in the transnational student politics of Israel-Palestine cannot be reduced to an opposition between self-identifying religious and secular groups and any attempt to explain these often visceral dynamics must attend holistically to the complex multidimensional stakes of this issue for students and institutions (Sheldon forthcoming). Yet with this caveat, the remit of this chapter is more modest: I will focus specifically on one aspect of student activism around Israel-Palestine as a locus of wider tensions between the protection of 'free speech' and prevention of 'extremism' on campus. My aims are first to connect this case with a body of scholarship that explores formations of freedom, speech, truth and subjectivity within what Talal Asad (2003) names as a dominant 'Christian secular' culture; second, to show how naming 'secularism' as one mode of power operating in relation to Israel-Palestine activism can deepen our understanding of unnamed tensions experienced by some politically active Muslim and Jewish students who may not name themselves 'religious'; and, third, to learn from the everyday practices of these students in order to think imaginatively about what constitutes 'free speech' within the contemporary university.

What is the 'secular campus'?

What do I mean when I speak of the 'secular campus' in the context of UK higher education? What is opened up by asking about the secular *campus* as opposed to secular disciplines, secular knowledge or the secular academy? The latter terms engage with the emergence of academic disciplines that explicitly oppose their truth procedures and sources of epistemic authority to those framed as 'theological'. In contrast, the notion of the secular *campus* has tended to refer to the self-proclaimed neutrality of higher education communities with regard to the religious identities of their members, so that these public institutions instantiate the doctrinal separation of church and state (Dinham and Jones 2012). In this chapter, my own use of this term is intended to connect with an emerging body of scholarship concerned with lived experiences of secularism. This work seeks to bridge the gap between more abstract genealogical analyses of secularism as an intellectual discourse and framings of secularism as affective, sensuous and relational practices, which can be studied ethnographically (Hirschkind 2011; Mahmood 2009; Motamedi-Fraser unpublished; Strhan 2012).

In one key contribution, Charles Hirschkind (2011) has asked, 'Is there a secular body?' Are there, in other words, particular non-cognitive embodied practices, sensibilities or modes of expression that we can name as 'secular'? In posing this question, Hirschkind helpfully highlights a tension, which I take up in this chapter, that the secular is somehow best approached indirectly, and yet this makes it a somehow slippery phenomenon to approach. Thus, his answer to the question challenges the reductionism of discursive approaches but notes the limitations of attempts to define secularism in terms of a determinant set of embodied dispositions. More specifically, Hirschkind emphasises that the contemporary meanings of the secular do seem to be connected with the articulation of a progressive *narrative* of the overcoming of religious error by secular reason, which differentiates the concept from the terms 'liberal', 'modern' or 'rational' (Hirschkind 2011: 641). Secularism, in other words, 'marks a relational dynamic more than an identity', it is a mode of power, a negative gesture in relation to religion (Hirschkind 2011: 644). Yet, this relation is not only discursive but also material and emotive: 'a constellation of institutions, ideas, and affective orientations that constitute an important dimension of what we call modernity and its defining forms of knowledge and practice' (Hirschkind 2011: 633). Building on this work, Anna Strhan (2012) has made a convincing case for methods that restrain from operationalising abstract definitions in order to attend to the narratives, ideas, material practices, objects and emotions, which gather into formations of secularism in specific contexts.[3]

In this chapter, I draw on these approaches as I develop a case study of secularism on campus by focusing on the dominant norms that governed an institutionally authorised public debate about the academic boycott of Israel. Learning from Saba Mahmood's (2009) discussion of free speech as a secular semiotic ideology, I explore how notions of freedom, speech and subjectivity, defined in distinction from a religious other, were realised in practice at this campus event. This means that rather than approaching the secular academy as a set of abstract disciplinary discourses, my starting point is an ethnographic study of embodied encounters relating to Israel-Palestine within university campuses.[4] By drawing on this ethnographic material, I claim that we can connect more abstract debates regarding the epistemology of academic disciplines with an analysis of secularism as a far-reaching relation of power affecting the democratic life of our institutions.

Framing rational speech against Islamic extremism

After completing the advance registration, I arrived at Old University on the evening of the public debate about the academic boycott of Israel and took a seat. The large lecture theatre quickly filled up with people wearing hijabs, keffiyehs and kippahs, sartorial signs of polarised affiliations, which contributed to a tense and expectant atmosphere. The National Union of Students (NUS) Vice President responsible for student welfare entered the room and, behind him, a middle-aged, uniformed security guard stood expressionless, hands folded, by the door. In the left-hand aisle, a student was setting up a camera in order to film the stage, supplementing the university's official audio recording of the event. The spectators hushed as the two white male academics speaking for and against the boycott (herein 'Dr Pro' and 'Professor Anti') took their seats in front of the audience. The adjudicator of the debate, 'Professor Chair', a specialist in a seemingly unrelated aspect of European politics who had been requested by the university management, was seated behind a separate table. In a plummy English accent, Professor Chair's opening remarks drew attention to the dynamic of mutual surveillance afforded by this venue, 'I'm delighted to see so many of you here. It is a deceptively large theatre and quite intimate so we can see you just as easily as you can see us'. He continued by firmly circumscribing the anticipated impulses of the speakers and audience; each speaker to be given an 'assiduously' timed fifteen minutes to make their case followed by 'a short five minute rebuttal of each other's position', at which point short audience questions and contributions would be solicited.

In stark contrast to the controversial Palestine Society meeting of the previous term, the university authorities had been actively involved in the careful staging of this debate. The stringent entry requirements, official recording, security and 'neutral' chairing of the meeting all conformed to national policy guidelines regarding the organisation of speaker events on potentially controversial subjects. A few months later, the renewed 'Preventing Violent Extremism' policy explicitly focused on the need for such procedures as part of the struggle to defend British higher education institutions (HEIs) against the perceived threat posed by 'extremist' speakers. In response, both Universities UK (2011) and NUS (2011) produced guidance on freedom of speech, the monitoring of religious societies and the introduction of checks on external speakers, which included case studies of tensions arising between Jewish societies and Palestine societies on campus.

The decision on the part of the Old University to explicitly adopt these guidelines for the boycott debate was perhaps unsurprising. In the preceding years, campus conflicts around free speech in relation to Israel-Palestine had featured in the public media, as policymakers, community leaders and interfaith organisations framed this as a key tension for university authorities (see for example, Guardian 2010). More specifically, this issue had come to be connected with discourses about religious extremism as part of a wider shift towards representing Israel-Palestine as a 'Jewish-Muslim' conflict *and* as a consequence of broader political changes to HEIs in Britain.[5] Furthermore, within Old University, the recent accusation of extremist speech at the Palestine Society meeting was just the latest controversy for an institution whose global reputation was under attack from organisations promoting this counter-extremism agenda.

A key claim of this chapter is that these political narratives constructed 'free speech' on campus in opposition to 'religious' forms of knowledge, communication and moral subjectivity. For example, the Government's 2011 *Prevent Strategy*, explicitly depicted HEIs as under threat from 'violent' and 'radical' forms of Islam. These were depicted as persuasive ideologies which influenced 'vulnerable' students through emotional processes of 'group bonding, pressure and indoctrination' to endorse violent responses to perceived injustice (Home Office 2011: 17). As such, this policy of *safeguarding* the campus posited a threat to the truthful, emotionally restrained and autonomous 'free speech' instantiated in the Western university. It demanded the exclusion of fallacious, excessively passionate and dependent/corrupted forms of speech and subjectivity associated with 'fundamentalist' religion and, specifically, Islam (Asad 2003; Asad 2009; Hirschkind 2011). And while different elite stakeholders within the higher education sector diverged over *how* to protect the values of the university, they converged in framing HEIs as the site in which secular freedom (in contrast to religious dogma) should be realised. Thus, Universities UK began its own 2011 report, *Freedom of Speech on Campus: Rights and Responsibilities* by stating:

> Universities play an important role in society as places of debate and discussion where ideas can be tested without fear of control, where students learn to challenge ideas and think for themselves, and where rationality underpins the pursuit of knowledge.
>
> (1)

In this way, as Old University instituted these guidelines at this debate, it shaped the moral campus through the exclusion of the excessive emotional, dependent forms of speech and subjectivity that it associated with theistic religion.

Regulating civil speech: Jewish identity and Zionist belief

In a paternalistic tone, Professor Chair introduced the ground rules of the meeting and of academic debate more broadly by authoritatively insisting that members of the audience display mutual respect:

> A shared will to debate rests of course on a common commitment to mutual respect as we discuss and argue . . . As chair I will rule out of order heckling or shouting. We are here in an academic institution to engage in serious debate, we will want to listen to the views being put. Otherwise there's no point in having the debate. So mutual respect means toleration, listening and I repeat no heckling or shouting . . . So if we respect each other's opinions I look forward to a very worthwhile debate.

As the debate unfolded, the protagonists dramatically evidenced their conformity to these norms with exaggerated sporting gestures, prefixing their aggressive exchanges with the civil language of 'learned friend' and 'colleague'.

In the previous section, I claimed that the discipline of dispassionate 'free speech' emerging at this debate was formed out of a negative relation to 'religious extremism'. However, there was also another narrative at stake in Professor

Chair's appeal to tolerance and respect, which contributed to the formation of secularism that emerged at this meeting. The speaker at the Palestine Society meeting of the previous term was not only accused of extremism for making claims 'in the name of Allah'. Rather, members of the Jewish society had accused him of transgressing the boundary between anti-Zionist and anti-Semitic speech. This occurred against a context of intense, high-profile disputes about the relationship between anti-Zionism and anti-Semitism in Israel-Palestine activism, which focused on claims and counter-claims regarding 'the new antisemitism'.[6] As a consequence, those hosting this debate were all too aware of the need to police the boundary between 'legitimate' and 'anti-Semitic' speech about Israel.

As Kahn-Harris and Gidley (2010) have helpfully explored, this framing of the Israel-Palestine conflict in terms of Jewish experiences of anti-Semitism forms part of a wider Anglo-Jewish discourse which highlights the insecurity of Jews as an ethnic minority in Britain. Thus, within the public spaces of the campus, Jewish students have learned to express support for Israel with reference to the threats posed to Jews as a racialised group, to affirm the distinction between 'legitimate' and 'anti-Semitic' critiques of Israel, and to avoid spiritual or theological expressions of attachments to Zionism. This has aligned Anglo-Jewish grammars for speaking about Israel with a liberal notion of balancing the right to free speech with the right to prevention from harm (Universities UK 2011: 44). According to this juridical logic, it is legitimate to critique the chosen opinions of Zionists, but this speech must be limited if it harms 'racial' subjects whose identity is not chosen.[7]

By framing free speech within the terms of respect for different *opinions*, Professor Chair contributed to a framing of Zionism – in contrast to Judaism – as propositional beliefs about the legitimacy of the Israeli state to which individuals would autonomously assent or dissent. Furthermore, his demand for tolerance drew on an opposition between free and harmful speech which took Judaism to be an unchosen ethnic identity in need of protection, and Zionism to be a set of beliefs requiring critical distance on the part of its adherents. My suggestion, following Gil Anidjar (2007), is that this is one example of a process through which Jews have been labelled according to discrete categories of 'religion', 'ethnicity' and 'race' which are the secularised products of Western Christendom. As Talal Asad (2003) and Saba Mahmood (2009) have also highlighted, this secular taxonomy assumes an implicitly Protestant understanding of the epistemic and moral subject in ways that disavow more complex, ambiguous and perhaps troubling formations of identity. In this way, as Old University sought to model a form of free speech that excluded extremism and anti-Semitism, so it implicitly constructed Islam and Judaism within its own terms.

Performing free speech

Professor Chair concluded his introductory comments on a humorous note that ironised the dramatic format of the debate, 'Surely I'm not expected to come round you like some kind of morning TV discussion programme'. Now, leaning forward, shoulders hunched, Dr Pro read out the logical steps of his carefully crafted argument, 'I'll say what the academic boycott is, why it addresses the right target, why it has a strong rationale, is efficient, high impact and potentially effective'. Anticipating his opponent's response, he raised his voice forcefully as he stated:

> The academic boycott . . . is not the preserve of anti-Semites and hypocrites, but it's timely, progressive, it's exciting, it's based on shared values, aiming at the right target with a strong rationale . . .

Then carefully prefixing his passion with a legalistic turn of phrase, he concluded:

> Indeed let me submit that where so many social movements in the contemporary world are based on religious, market, ethnic or nationalist fundamentalism of one kind of another, then a movement based on freedom and democracy speaking in the name of law and right, that opens up exciting perspectives of transnational solidarity in dark times might be one that commands our attention and even our support.

By emphatically validating universalism, scientific knowledge, academic freedom and institutional autonomy in opposition to 'fundamentalisms', Dr Pro set the stage for ensuing dynamics as each speaker struggled to embody these values and to portray their opponents in the opposite terms.

Professor Anti had been silent during this speech, looking fixedly away from his opponent, visibly containing his anger with his hand cupping his chin and covering his mouth. Now, he looked up and began to speak, loudly and clearly, categorically expressing his opposition to Dr Pro by *also* appealing to the value of scientific knowledge: 'I personally know that a cessation of links and grants with Israel would first of all have an immediate and direct effect . . . we're talking about direct disadvantage in a whole range of – not only – biomedical conditions'. Asking why Israelis institutions are 'singled out' as 'uniquely complicit' with their government, Professor Anti implicitly invoked the charge of anti-Semitism as he claimed the boycotters transgressed the logical and moral 'universality principle which is crucial to academic freedom'.

Just like the onstage protagonists, individuals in the audience now embodied abstract, predetermined political positions 'for' or 'against' the motion. Microphones picked up the sound of pages rustling as the contributors read out prepared statements. Shortly afterwards, the drama reached its apex as Professor Chair announced the final vote. Qualifying the process with 'you are not a scientific sample', he asked the audience to raise their hands either in support or opposition to the motion. I sat, fixed in my seat, struck by the rigid binary choice this presented. The 'neutral' framing of the debate had itself crystallised the polarisation of the audience; any expression of a third position, of uncertainty or ambivalence, was foreclosed by the fixed structure of format. The result was quickly announced as a victory for the opponents of boycott, an outcome which the president of the Palestine Society, Sadiq, later insisted had been apparent from the makeup of the room at the outset of the event.

From the moment that Professor Chair authoritatively expressed the contractual ground rules for the meeting, this debate circumscribed the form as well as the content of this political process. With exaggerated gestures, Dr Pro and Professor Anti engaged in a hyperbolic performance of a restrained, detached mode of speech. The main actors and audience members continued in this vein by offering statements of 'facts' about the justice of the motion, appealing to a logical grammar of consistency, universality and principled deductions while carefully avoiding any display of subjective investments or impulsive emotion. Meanwhile, Professor Chair's injection of ironic humour demanded that the audience demonstrate that they did not care *too much*, that the motion before us was not a matter of identity but rather required the adoption of critical distance.

In these ways, this debate enabled Old University to perform a juridical vision of free speech within the terms of secularist narratives. This was not only revealed in Dr Pro's explicit rejection of 'religious fundamentalisms' or in the speakers' allusions to anti-Semitism. Rather, it was indexed in Old University's dramatic conformity to a set of authorised distinctions which defined what it is to be a freely speaking subject. Shaped by an Enlightenment inheritance, this notion of freedom was predicated upon an assumed distantiation between subjects and the objects of their claims, a freedom shaped through the critical practice of objective actors, able to stand outside their emotional investments in this conflict and to autonomously *choose* whether to assent to propositions about boycotting Israel (Brown 2009; Mahmood 2009). As I will go on to discuss, set against this wider context, this vision of free speech put Muslim and Jewish students under particular pressures to conform to its terms, and it is in this sense that I claim a secular mode of power was at work.

Silencing students' voices

Writing in the student newspaper shortly after the debate, Sadiq justified the Palestine Society's decision to participate in this event, stating: 'We are willing to work with groups who we disagree with [in order]. . . to expose these disagreements and discuss them in a constructive way'. Talking with me a few weeks later, Sadiq described the internal politics of this decision in terms that resonated with the discourse of 'extremism':

> So you will get groups who are, like, not more puritanical, but in their ideological beliefs they apply that very strictly in terms of practice, so, like, we can't debate Israelis because it legitimises them . . . then you get people like me who are more pragmatic.

As another activist Yusra explained, members of the Palestine Society carefully negotiated this dominant secularist narrative, as they sought to appeal to a broader student audience within the university:

> I would say that the stereotype that Palestinian activists have is something that we're always trying to overcome. Erm so you know being leftist fanatical

or whatever, radicals, terrorists, Hamas supporting, you know we've been called a lot of things. I would say that we're trying to always come across and present ourselves in a way that is acceptable.

In this way, members of the Palestine Society at times worked *within* what they perceived to be the widely shared distinction between legitimate and extremist actors. The Palestine Society's legitimacy, their ability to 'present ourselves as acceptable' to this audience, depended on conformity to an authorised model of free speech in the university that included disciplining their emotions so as to adopt a style of restrained detachment.

Later, Sadiq explained to me that this debate had initially been intended to address internal divisions over the boycott *within* the Palestine Society and described how he personally felt conflicted about the question of academic boycott. Yet once the format was changed to an agonistic public debate with members of the Jewish Society, Sadiq raised his hand in support of the boycott, conforming to the logical 'pro-Palestinian' position demanded of him. His confession revealed how the vision of the 'free' subject, as one who makes a categorical decision about right or wrong, repressed the expression of difference, complexity and inner tensions not only amongst groups but within the self. Talking with Saniyah, a British Muslim student whose parents were Palestinian, she emphasised that her activism for Palestine was grounded not in the particularities of Islam or her family history but rather in the universal principles of human rights. She described how she had learnt over time not to get angry or over-emotional because 'that's the reaction *they* want'; instead she learned to discipline her emotions in order to speak in a logical language. Significantly, while she affirmed the rationalist practice of free speech assumed in the academic debate, an alternative model of speech – as dialogue – was too dangerous to countenance:

That's why I think dialogue is very negative in some senses because you're just gonna get angry and it's not gonna be productive and then when you get angry it becomes emotional and when it's emotional, it's not logical, so you, you need to try and maintain your thoughts and everything and not get very personal about it.

In these ways, as Muslim students negotiated the secular norms of 'free speech', so they learned to express themselves within a reductive binary grammar that silenced more complex responses to this conflict.

When I met with Justin and Ella, the Jewish Society members involved in organising the debate, they also initially represented themselves in accordance with the secular matrix of free speech. Describing the wider dynamics of this activism, Justin contrasted the 'disgusting', 'offensive' Palestine Society 'stunts' with the Jewish Society who 'do all our events to the book'. However, when in the course of our conversation I asked how Israel had come to be important to them, a different picture emerged. Justin spoke of his frustration at the demand placed on Jewish students to maintain a rigid separation between 'Jewish' and 'Zionist' activities on campus. He talked about growing up in an Orthodox community which framed a messianic relationship to Israel 'and part of me still finds that very hard to let go of'. When I clumsily asked Ella why it seemed so hard for Jewish students to articulate the role of 'religion or faith' in their activism, she responded by questioning the very framing of Zionism in terms of the religious/secular distinction:

> I think it's just really complicated. It's issues that people are uncomfortable with dealing with and feel maybe not educated enough to deal with them and people are scared . . . You know it's like 'the actions of a Zionist entity government' rather than like 'a connection of a people to a spiritual homeland for many, many years'. It's a different terminology, a different way of understanding it, which makes it easier to, to, I don't know, talk about it I suppose.

Justin added that he felt torn by his own need to participate in the secular distinction between Judaism and Zionism. For, on the one hand, he was struggling to make space for 'depoliticised' Judaism on campus, yet this was undermined by his sense that Zionism was inseparable from the 'yearning for Israel' expressed in the Torah. In this way, the very demand that Jewish students engage in detached critical judgements about the legitimacy of Israel prohibited these more complex connections from being expressed. As such, for Muslim and Jewish students alike, the model of free speech demanded at the academic boycott debate paradoxically closed down the voicing or exploration of key aspects of this conflict.

Challenging the terms of secularism on campus: what is it to speak freely?

In the course of this chapter, I have named the model of free speech upheld by one university as mediating a secular mode of power on campus. I have developed the claim that secularism can work as a hegemonic framework within our academic institutions which, as Mahmood (2009) writes, 'not only caricatures the religious Other but . . . remains blind to its own disciplines of subjectivity, affective attachments and subject-object relations' (90) To conclude, I wish to draw out two ethical implications for researchers as we contribute to specific formations of secularism within our fieldsites, disciplines and institutions (Strhan 2012). First, although it is beyond the scope of this chapter to explore this in-depth, I hope that these vignettes might open up reflexive conversations about the pressures that give rise to hegemonic secular frameworks within universities.[8] Second, I wish to frame a response to the dominant secular vision of 'free speech' within our institutions by learning from the creative practices of Muslim and Jewish students.

In 2013, I met up with Sadiq again and learned that, as he had graduated from his pressurised role with the Palestine Society, so he seemed more able to speak out of Islamic traditions with which he identified. Many months after the boycott debate, Sadiq had participated in a seminar about hate speech on campus organised by an interfaith organisation. In that context, Sadiq had sought to articulate an Islamic conception of the ethics of speech, which subtly diverged from the juridical model outlined by a representative of the student Atheist Society. He had described the ways in which Islamic traditions recognise the power of speech to unintentionally hurt and undermine people who are already situated *within* unequal social and interpersonal contexts. He talked about our responsibility to somehow recognise each other as equal participants within public life in order to enable each other to fully participate and express ourselves. In this way, Sadiq introduced an ethics of speech which challenged the assumption that speech is primarily propositional and that freedom is a property of individual agents who can be imagined in abstraction from their personal and social relationships. Rather, he gestured towards a different understanding of free speech, as somehow dependent on the quality of the relationships between those involved.

Reflecting on Sadiq's thoughtful intervention, I was struck by a resonance with the work of a student-led Israel-Palestine dialogue group based at a different institution. Here, students had also cultivated alternative ways of speaking, which contrasted with the ideal of free speech as depersonalised, dispassionate debate. There students had developed conversations over time, in which they came to reflect on their own investments in ossified narratives about Israel-Palestine. Through sharing their personal histories, and learning to trust each other as caring, rather than detached, interlocutors, it became possible to move beyond well-worn inherited scripts, to speak, as it were, in their own voices. The Jewish student who facilitated this nominally secular forum told me how his approach drew on his education within a Zionist youth movement. This helped him to shape processes of voicing, questioning and interpreting political narratives that were connected with Jewish hermeneutic, textual and ritual practices. These are traditions which challenge those analogous dualisms – including between the public and personal, the rational and emotional, and the form and content of language – which frame the secular grammar of 'free speech' on campus (Boyarin 1996; Seidler 2007).

In this chapter, I have sought to name a hegemonic model of free speech as secular in order to trace how it can silence students, and so subvert the very values it formally espouses. But I have also gestured towards a more creative role for researchers engaged with the study of religion and secularism on campus. Within a higher education landscape undergoing significant changes, the question of 'free speech' is inseparable from that of the value of the university. By attending to the ethical practices of students shaped by marginalised traditions, I suggest that an alternative vision of the university might emerge. And what might this look like? Not merely a juridical space concerned with protecting the rights of autonomous agents to demonstrate their knowledge – but rather a pedagogic community in which we come to know ourselves and speak in our own voices from within the context of ethical relationships.

Notes

1 All names of institutions, media outlets and individuals have been changed or anonymised, and media quotations relating to the events described have been altered in order to protect the identities of the students who participated in this research.

2 This includes the entanglements of contemporary universities with the violent histories of anti-Semitism; colonialism; the ongoing Orientalism, imperialism and securitisation of a post-9/11 era; and with the processes associated with twenty-first century capitalism (Dinham and Jones 2012; Philips 2012; Back 2004; Motademi-Fraser unpublished).

3 While Strhan draws on Bruno Latour's object-oriented ontology, my own approach is informed by Ludwig Wittgenstein's relational philosophical method. This helps us to question assumed dualistic oppositions (such as between discourse and reality) in our framings of religion and secularism while also attending to the formations of such bifurcations within particular socio-historical and intellectual contexts.

4 Between 2010 and 2012, I conducted participant observation at three universities, attending campus events relating to Israel-Palestine, observing online forums and conducting interviews with members of Jewish, Palestine, Islamic and Socialist Worker student societies and with a student-led Israel-Palestine forum. For further discussion of the methodological, epistemological and ethical questions raised by this research, see Sheldon (forthcoming).

5 As Kaposi (2014) observes, the rising importance of Hamas in the Middle East following their victory in the Gaza elections in 2006 contributed to shifting trans-national representations of Israel-Palestine, which has increasingly been narrated in terms of a civilizational clash between Western values and political Islam. At the same time, with growing numbers of Muslim students entering UK HEIs and participating in student politics, Palestine Societies have been subject to growing surveillance and regulation by politicians and interest groups (Sheldon forthcoming).

6 According to this theory, anti-Semitism has shifted from its traditional right-wing articulations to left-wing movements against Israel and manifests particularly in the Boycott, Divestment and Sanctions campaign (see Kahn-Harris and Gidley 2010; Kaposi 2014).

7 Following Mahmood (2009), this distinction encodes a differentiation between 'race' or 'ethnicity' as ascribed in contrast to 'religion', which is understood in Protestant terms as belief in a set of propositions and so fundamentally a matter of choice.

8 For example, we can consider how the preoccupation with excluding 'fundamentalist ideologies' entails a disavowal of the necessarily embodied sensuality of rationalist performances within the academy (Hirschkind 2011). As I argue elsewhere (Sheldon forthcoming), this should be situated in relation to the moral and epistemic anxieties experienced by universities under conditions of late capitalism and post-modernity.

References

Anidjar, G. (2007) *Semites: Race, Religion, Literature*. Stanford CA: Stanford University Press.

Asad, T. (2003) *Formations of the Secular: Christianity, Islam, Modernity*. Stanford CA: Stanford University Press.

Asad, T. (2009) Free Speech, Blasphemy, and Secular Criticism. In *Is Critique Secular? Blasphemy, Injury, and Free Speech*, ed. by Asad, T., Brown, W., Butler, J., and Mahmood, S. Berkeley: The Townsend Centre for the Humanities, pp. 20–63.

Back, L. (2004) Ivory Towers? The Academy and Racism. In *Institutional Racism in Higher Education*, ed. by I. Law, Phillips, D., and Turney, L. Stoke on Trent: Trentham, pp. 1–6.

Boyarin, J. (1996) *Thinking in Jewish*. Chicago: University of Chicago Press.

Brown, W. (2009) Introduction. In *Is Critique Secular? Blasphemy, Injury, and Free Speech*, ed. by Asad, T., Brown, W., Butler, J., and Mahmood, S. Berkeley: The Townsend Centre for the Humanities, pp. 7–19.

Dinham, A., and Jones, S. H. (2012) Religion, Public Policy, and the Academy: Brokering Public Faith in a Context of Ambivalence? *Journal of Contemporary Religion* 27 (2), 185–201.

Guardian (2010) Campus Conflict Series, Comment is Free. *The Guardian*, April-May 2010. Available online at: www.theguardian.com/commentisfree/series/campus-conflict. Accessed 27 August 2013.

Hirschkind, C. (2011) Is There a Secular Body? *Cultural Anthropology: Journal of the Society for Cultural Anthropology* 26 (4), 633–647.

Home Office (2011) *Prevent Strategy: Presented to Parliament by the Secretary of State for the Home Department by Command of Her Majesty, June 2011*. Norwich: The Stationary Office.

Kahn-Harris, K., and Gidley, B. (2010) *Turbulent Times: The British Jewish Community Today*. London: Continuum.

Kaposi, D. (2014) *Violence and Understanding in Gaza: The British Broadsheets' Coverage of the War*. London: Palgrave Macmillan.

Mahmood, S. (2009) Religious Reason and Secular Affect: An Incommensurable Divide? In *Is Critique Secular? Blasphemy, Injury, and Free Speech*, ed. by Asad, T., Brown, W., Butler, J., and Mahmood, S. Berkeley: The Townsend Centre for the Humanities, pp. 64–100.

Motamedi-Fraser, M. (unpublished) 'But God is neither like politics nor birds': Islam, Secularity and Practice in English Universities.

NUS (2011) *Managing the Risks Associated with External Speakers: Guidance for Students' Unions in England and Wales*. London: NUS.

Phillips, D. (2012) Unsettling Spaces: Higher Education Institutions in the UK. In *As the World Turns: Diversity and Global Shifts in Higher Education Theory, Research and Practice*, ed. by W.R. Allen, R.T. Teranishi, M. Bonous-Hammarth. Bingley: Emerald Group Publishing, pp. 421–432.

Seidler, V. J. (2007) *Jewish Philosophy and Western Culture: A Modern Introduction*. London: I.B. Tauris.

Sheldon, R. (2016) *Tragic Encounters and Ordinary Ethics: The Palestine-Israel Conflict in British Universities*. Manchester: Manchester University Press.

Strhan, A. (2012) Latour, Prepositions and the Instauration of Secularism. *Political Theology* 13 (2), 200–216.
Universities UK (2011) *Freedom of Speech on Campus: Rights and Responsibilities in UK Universities.* London: Universities UK.

Chapter 9

Navigating the secular

Religious students' experiences of attending a red-brick university

Lydia Reid

Introduction

'Free Speech? Not at Four in Five UK Universities' (*The Guardian*, February 2, 2015), 'Gender Segregation: The Truth about Muslim Women "Forced" to Sit away from Men' (*The Telegraph*, January 19, 2016), 'Islamic Society Students Disrupt University Lecture on Blasphemy and Make Death Threat' (*The Express*, December 4, 2015), '5 Most Controversial Things that Happened at UK Universities in 2015' (*The Huffington Post*, December 26, 2015), 'Student Israeli Society "Attacked by Protesters" at Leading London University' (*The Evening Standard*, January 20, 2016). These headlines, published in the last year (2015–16), show the extent to which universities have come under scrutiny from newspapers across the political spectrum. The media frequently depict universities as a 'battleground' by either emphasising the clashes between/within political and religious societies or the overall suppression of free speech on UK campuses. Arguably, Islamic societies have borne the brunt of this negative media attention due to issues surrounding external speakers, claims of radicalisation and gender segregation. This, alongside changes in university funding, has seen the landscape of higher education fundamentally change. The rise of the global markets has also meant that universities are increasingly in competition with one another, with students looking to league tables and student satisfaction surveys to choose where to study. Furthermore, universities have recognised the financial advantage in attracting international students (Dinham and Jones 2010: 2), whom they can charge fees of up to £16,500 per year. As a result, universities are now having to respond to an increasingly diverse student body at a time when religion (particularly Islam) is highly politicised, and where the role of universities more generally has been put into question.

Given the aforementioned changes within higher education, what is it like to be a religious student studying at a British university? The aim of this chapter, based on doctoral research carried out between 2011–13, is to shed light on how religious students from Jewish, Muslim and Christian backgrounds navigate the terrain of a red-brick university[1]. What are their experiences of studying at an ostensibly 'secular' university? What have their experiences been in joining relevant chaplaincies/religious societies? Finally, what is the nature of their interactions with religious and non-religious peers?

Research into religion and higher education

Research into higher education and religion has begun to flourish since 2010, with interest from academics, policymakers, politicians and the media. This is not just the case in the United Kingdom, and as Mayrl and Oeur (2009: 260) point out, across the academy 'religion is a hot topic' and 'historians, philosophers and educators [have] begun to question the secular ethos of many campuses'. Historically, universities have been perceived as 'secular enclaves' (Bryant 2006: 2) that have the capacity to liberalise or even eradicate personal religious beliefs; as Jonathan P. Hill notes:

> . . . sociologists of religion have primarily discussed the effects of higher education in the context of secularisation (Hammond and Hunter 1984; Hunter 1987; Roof and McKinney 1987; Wuthnow 1988). Drawing on the work of Berger, these sociological accounts contend that the encounter with alternative ideas and lifestyles on campus (i.e., pluralism) undermines the foundation of religious beliefs.
>
> (Hill 2009: 516)

This idea that religious beliefs are diminished on campus replicates the notion that as a society becomes more 'secular', its members become less religious. One of the problems with research into religious belief and higher education institutions is that there remain misconceptions about the effects of university on belief which Mayrl and Oeur point out as being overly 'normative' and 'theoretical' (Mayrl and Oeur 2009: 260). There are two key theories as to why universities are associated with loss of faith – the first concerns pluralism (as outlined in the Hill quotation) and the second pedagogy: the idea is that exposure to competing worldviews and to secular theories in the classroom is responsible for students losing their faith.

Despite this widely held assumption that the university poses a threat to religious beliefs, as posited by Caplovitz and Sherrow (1977) and Hunter (1983) (as well as by a number of my interviewees), more recent research seems to point towards a complex picture (Hill 2011: 533). For theorists such as Reimer (2010) and Sabri et al. (2008), the university is a place that 'liberalises' religious beliefs but does not necessarily eradicate them; for Hurtardo et al. (2007) and Lee (2002), the university has no or very little impact on religious beliefs, and for Hammond and Hunter (1984), the university has the capacity to make religious beliefs stronger. Of course, there are many other variables that need to be considered here, such as the range of different religious affiliations on campus, the historical context of the institution, the year of study and the measurements used for religiosity.

An important point to bear in mind, though, is that much of the research cited above has been of a quantitative nature and, while this potentially yields interesting results, there are concerns about how researchers measure religiosity and spirituality as well as the problem of generalising across institutions. Furthermore, the research cited above has been situated in a North American context, and, for that reason, comparisons with British universities have to be made with caution. Sharma and Guest (2013: 74) rightly remind us that the British context 'reflects [the] major shifts in the status of religion in wider British society. . . maintaining echoes of the historical dominance of traditional Christianity. . . a reactive secularism. . . [and] a multicultural religious pluralism'.

Guest et al.'s research 'Christianity and the University Experience in Contemporary England' is a much welcome addition to this growing area of literature. Guest et al. (2013) highlight the nuanced complexities of being a religious believer navigating the university in acknowledging that religious beliefs 'cannot be simply reduced to a matter of propositional belief'; instead, beliefs are 'more conflicted, more open-ended than our theoretical tools might lead us to understand' (24). Therefore, rather than serving to diminish religious belief, phenomena such as religious pluralism may in fact provide 'a source of inspiration to evolving, self-directed identities rather than a threat to established plausibility structures' and 'we might also expect such identities to be less vulnerable to the secularising power of higher education' than was originally thought (Guest et al. 2013: 24). Guest et al. also emphasise that the experience of university cannot be confined simply to what happens in the classroom and that there is a danger of 'decontextualisation' in research which fails to take into account institutional differences (even among universities which have a similar ethos) (Guest et al. 2013: 25). Discussing whether or not the university is a force for secularisation, Guest et al. conclude that for the most part, this is not the case, but that the peculiarity of university (in removing some students from their homes to campus accommodation and the increased level of personal autonomy) may serve to *alter* religious patterns while not necessarily eradicating them (Guest et al. 2013: 108). In addition, elite and/or traditional universities such as Oxford, Cambridge and Durham still possess a historical residue of Christianity which makes all three institutions more hospitable to Christians on campus – although, as Guest et al. remind us, it is evangelical Christianity which thrives in these universities and this does not always resonate well with *all* Christians on campus.

The existing literature in religion and higher education challenges the misconception that the university has a secularising effect on religious students. Instead, the literature points to several possible outcomes: a liberalisation of beliefs, an intensification of beliefs, an alteration to religious patterns and no effect at all.

Methodology

In order to explore religious students' experiences of navigating the terrain of the university, I utilised qualitative research methods in the form of semi-structured interviews. Particularly relevant here is Warren's statement that through interviewing we can 'understand the meaning of respondents' experiences and life worlds' (Warren 2002: 83). It is useful to view interviews as not simply a 'research procedure' but as 'part and parcel of our society and culture' (Gubrium and Holstein 2002: 4) and as capable of uncovering complex descriptions of the social world.

Since a key aspect of my research included exploring the dynamics of religious societies, I opted to do most of my recruitment directly through these, as well as the relevant chaplaincies. It is important to point out here, however, that not all religious students are members of relevant societies and/or chaplaincies; therefore, my sample is biased towards those that *are* society members (with the exception of two students). Thirty students in total were interviewed, with ten from each faith group (Jewish, Muslim and Christian). The interviewees were members of the following societies/chaplaincies: Ahlulbayt society (Absoc), Islamic society (I-soc), Jewish society (J-soc), Student Christian Movement (SCM), Christian Union (CU), Catholic chaplaincy (CC) and the university's chaplaincy. There was an equal split of genders in each faith group and I incorporated a range of intrafaith perspectives: Islam (five Shia and five Sunni Muslims), Judaism (eight Modern Orthodox and three Reform Jews) and Christianity (three Catholics, three 'liberals'[2], five evangelical Christians).

One of the challenges in taking a multi-faith approach is that the researcher must limit the number of participants in each faith group. At this stage, it is important to remember that qualitative research is not representative but it can help in providing a 'snapshot' (Guest et al. 2013: 4) of what is going on at a particular time, at a particular institution. Moreover, I would argue that the need to include a multi-faith angle is timely since many of the issues I raised at the beginning of this chapter affect *all* faith groups and sometimes occur *within* and *between* these groups.

Interviews ranged in length from half an hour to two hours, and BSA ethical guidelines were strictly followed to ensure the safety and anonymity of participants. The interviews were recorded on a dictaphone and transcribed. I used thematic analysis as a way of rationalising the data and the subsequent themes were organised under three key areas: studying at a secular university, religious and non-religious interactions with peers and experiences of chaplaincies and societies.

Studying at a secular university

> When older people from my Church heard that I was going to study Theology in a secular university rather than in a Christian Bible college, a lot of people were like: 'No, no. You can't do that. They'll make you into a liberal and you'll believe all these ridiculous things'. . . Turns out all the ridiculous things are the academic consensus for, you know, centuries on these topics.
>
> (Participant 26, Christian/CU)

The comment above provides a good starting point for linking some of the ideas referenced earlier in the chapter (such as viewing the university as a place that diminishes belief) with the views of my interviewees. The first notable point was the different ways in which the university was perceived – both in terms of the respondents' point of view, but also the views of their friends, family and local religious communities. Participant 26 (Christian/CU) talked at length about how he sought to do his Theology degree at a secular university. He used the word 'objectivity' several times to make the point that he wanted to learn about religion in an environment which he felt would be 'unbiased'. He discussed how he had been warned off studying at a secular institution precisely because of the misconceptions that I mentioned earlier. A further two students recalled similar encounters with family members or members of their local religious community who were worried that the university would diminish religious beliefs. This was particularly pertinent for those studying Religious Studies or Theology. For example, a female Jewish student (participant 30) revealed that her father had previously discouraged her from studying Theology because he knew of Jews in his community who had 'become atheist' as a result. However, despite this concern, he was entirely supportive of her studying Law at the same institution. This is significant, as it implies that the secular university is only viewed as a threat in the context of studying Theology.

Interestingly, participant 30 (Jew/non-member) also stood out as viewing the university in a purely 'instrumental' way, to borrow Bartram's (2009) terminology. This is when the university is seen primarily as a place where one obtains a degree and then enters the workforce (Bartram 2009 cited in Dinham and Jones 2010: 12). Evidence of this can be found when participant 30 states, 'the university is just a place where I go and get my degree. . . I sit in my lectures. . . I have a group of friends but that's about it really. Religion barely comes into it. I have a community at home for that'. For the most part, the religious students I interviewed tended to view the university in more 'humanistic' terms with much greater emphasis placed on personal growth and development (op. cit.). The latter finding is not too surprising since you might expect those students who belong to religious societies and/or chaplaincies to take a more humanistic approach as they are already engaging in events at university that lie outside the classroom or lecture theatre. However, it is interesting to contrast participant 30 (Jew/non-member) with participant 13 (Muslim/I-soc/Absoc), who, similarly, lived at home with his parents and commuted locally to the university. While participant 30 had little desire to socialise in the J-soc (as she perceived that it was for "out of towners"), participant 13 was much more active in his involvement in relevant societies. Participant 13, a male Shia Muslim, viewed the university in a much more humanistic way. For him, there was a conscious effort made in integrating his faith with all aspects of university life. He was an active member in both the I-soc and Ahlulbayt Society, and played football for his course and the university.

Most striking about participant 13's account of being at university was the extent to which he complemented his faith with his studies. He added:

> The title of my last essay was 'what, if anything, can we know?' so before I do all my own research (which everyone else is doing) I've first got to find out what the Islamic perspective is on this particular issue. Do I agree with it? Is it right? Why is it right? Can it be logically explained in this essay? So it's really hard in my course because I've got to put twice as much effort in when doing my research. It's not just a case of blagging it. It can't be blagged because this is about the world – do you know what I mean? Especially in Philosophy.
> (Participant 13, Muslim/I-soc/Absoc)

Whereas participant 30 (Jew/non-member) spoke about keeping her faith separate from her activities at university, participant 13 (Muslim/I-soc/Absoc) differs significantly. Participant 13 creates double the amount of work for himself in his modules by first studying the Islamic response to whichever issue he is looking at and then following it up with the reading expected in the module guidelines. Later in the interview, he elaborated on the procedure he follows and what happens if he comes across an issue where there is no Islamic consensus. His approach was unique and may only have been made possible because he was studying Philosophy, Politics and Economics, which provides scope for potentially incorporating one's own religious beliefs. Thus, an important factor here is that there will be some degree courses, such as Philosophy and Religious Studies, which will make more overt references to religion than other subjects, providing students with more of an opportunity to incorporate their own religious beliefs if they wish to.

The interaction between religious faith and degree course took a variety of forms. For some students, this interaction was positive and, for others, more challenging. Participant 27 (Muslim/I-soc) spoke about how her faith had been both challenged and enhanced by her studies in Psychology. She told me about having been challenged by evolutionary theory; she found the module particularly frustrating but she also recognised this was the dominant view in her discipline. Participant 27 also recalled an instance where her degree course and religious faith resonated well, when she learnt about a study in which people were found to be more truthful when talking in front of a mirror; she then compared this to wearing the hijab and representing Islam. Moreover, she added that

> there are a lot of things [in my degree course] that I do agree with and there's always two theories that oppose each other and Islam has given me the perfect middle ground . . . I enjoy it because it does reconcile my faith a lot . . . and a lot of the historical psychology came from the Islamic faith anyway.

Participant 27's comments go some way towards challenging the notion that the social sciences are incompatible with religious beliefs and, in this case, compatibility is achieved by attributing the origins of Psychology to the interviewee's own Islamic faith.

Among my interviewees, most of the challenges to faith were experienced by those doing Medicine and/or Pharmacy and Theology and/or Religious Studies. On a practical level for students studying Medicine and/or Pharmacy, there were issues surrounding dissections, abortions and the prescribing of contraceptives. These challenges were negotiated by drawing boundaries in conjunction with their faith. For example, participant 15 (Muslim/I-soc) talked about how, despite the fact that he was unable to dissect a dead body according to the rules of Islam, he could stand back and watch while also helping other students in his group. On the one hand, he makes the concession to be in the room and witness the dissection but, on the other hand, he himself would not make any incisions in the body. Similarly, participant 10 (Christian, CC) discussed how she was unable to prescribe contraceptives owing to her Christian beliefs; she notes:

> You're trained to help people, but at the end of the day being religious, God comes first . . . I'd do anything in my profession to help you, but some things are against my moral conscience to do certain activities.

In contrast, the challenges facing Theology and/or Religious Studies students inevitably took a more abstract form. Research carried out by Sabri et al. provides an illuminating account of the interplay between religious faith and studying for a Theology and/or Religious Studies degree. They identified a number of different interactions between the two: a 'strict division' is enforced between faith and studies, movement 'away' from a previous faith position (which, in turn, can sometimes lead to students finding a 'new' position that is different from the one they had when they first came to university) and, finally, faith stances remain 'the same' though informed by a new 'critical awareness' (Sabri et al. 2008: 44). All three outcomes emerged in the accounts of my interviewees, but interestingly they also applied to those studying subjects outside of Theology/Religious Studies.

Chaplaincies and societies

The previous section illustrates the different ways that the university was viewed by students. One of the observations I made was that students tended to make their own personal distinction as to whether or not the university was either instrumental or humanistic in its role. Most of the students believed that the university possessed humanistic qualities, and one such reason may be due to my sample being skewed towards members of religious societies and chaplaincies. Therefore, if a student has gone to the effort of joining a relevant society and/or chaplaincy, they may be more likely to view the university as having humanistic qualities. However, as pointed out earlier, membership of a society is not uniform in nature; some students attend all events, others, hardly any. The experience of committee members will be different from that of rank-and-file members, and it is important to be aware of this.

One should also be mindful of the differences between the chaplaincies and the student societies. Chaplaincies are typically run by university-affiliated religious figures and, at the time of my research, the Catholic chaplaincy operated externally to the institution. Moreover, the university's chaplaincy is meant to provide spiritual guidance to those of *all* faiths and is usually the first reference point for religious students on campus. Societies differ from chaplaincies in that they are affiliated to the Student Union and are student-led through committee members and society presidents. Religious societies tend to have two functions: socialising and education. In the case of the J-soc, its primary function is a social one since it is not a religious society and its membership includes non-religious, modern orthodox and reform Jews. Moreover, the religious makeup of the J-soc's committee members has also varied year to year, sometimes having a non-religious majority and at other times a religious majority. In the other societies included in this project (Ahlulbayt Society, Islamic Society, Christian Union and Student Christian Movement), the ratio between social and educational events varied year to year depending on the priorities of the committee members.

One of the newspaper headlines presented at the beginning of this chapter referred to tensions between a university's Israeli society and pro-Palestinian supporters; thus, one has to consider the broader political and religious landscape. Several of my Jewish interviewees raised their concerns that the National Union of Students (NUS) was being influenced by Palestinian activists in their boycotting of two Israeli companies. The NUS website makes reference to wanting to 'foster a peaceful settlement between Israel and Palestine', and, as such, they cannot support companies which may 'impact negatively' on these attempts at peace (NUS website). The NUS is committed to fostering peaceful relations between all religious faiths on campus; however, *The Jewish Chronicle* reported the NUS's decision as being 'anti-Israel' (Dysch 2012), a feeling that was echoed by most of my Jewish interviewees. There were some reports amongst my Jewish and Muslim interviewees of occasional clashes between Pro-Israel and Action Palestine groups, but these were relatively few.

Society politics had also come into play with clashes between the Lesbian, Gay, Bisexual and Transgender (LGBT) society and both the I-soc and CU. These appeared to occur when a speaker or religious society was seen as being Discriminatory:

> We [the I-soc] were attacked about our speaker and we were seen as essentially supporting homophobia and discrimination. I had to just lay the facts on the table; we weren't discriminating.
>
> (Participant 14, Muslim/I-soc)

A lot of the LGBT members often have massive issues with us, despite not being in dialogue with us; the CU's views on homosexuality is an obvious point of contention for us.

(Participant 18, Christian/CU)

The issue of homosexuality remains a contentious issue for some religious figures, and, as Dutton (2006: 470) rightly points out, this can often be at odds with the 'political correctness' agenda of the Student Union, which is 'committed to opposing discrimination on any grounds'. It is precisely these sorts of issues which the media have picked up on and universities are increasingly being seen as places that suppress free speech. However, despite the perception of there being tension between LGBT groups and religious groups, generally such instances as those described above were rare and were usually resolved without issue.

While societies have the capacity to empower students, they can marginalise them too (Sharma and Guest 2013: 60). A number of interviewees across all faith groups reported feeling 'judged' as well as highlighting that societies can be overly 'cliquey' and 'dominated' by specific denominations. Participant 15 (Muslim/non-member) recalled an incident where he and a female friend had been to visit the I-soc stall during Freshers' Week. During his encounter, one of the members challenged participant 15's friend on why she was not wearing a hijab (an occurrence also noted in Ahmad's research [2007]). This incident was significant enough for participant 15 and his friend to not sign up to the I-soc at all. Moreover, across faith groups, there was a sense that certain religious denominations 'dominated' the societies and, unsurprisingly, this tended to happen in groups that were meant to cater across religious denominations/sects (such as the I-soc and J-soc). For example, Reform Jews mentioned their unease at there being a Modern Orthodox majority that typically steered the J-soc from year to year. Participant 31 (Jewish/J-soc) felt particularly strongly about this, adding:

Most of the people who go to the religious events are orthodox and that's inevitable because they're held in an orthodox shul which makes a lot of people uncomfortable anyway, especially the services, which are segregated by gender [Reform services do not have gender segregation]. Also, they have a lot of orthodox rabbis walking around which is very off-putting.

(Participant 31, Jewish/J-soc)

Similarly, a number of the Shia Muslims I spoke to felt that the committees in the I-soc were typically made up of Sunni Muslims, and this was often used as a way to justify having their own society (the Absoc). Those religious groups that did have their own societies/chaplaincies (such as the SCM, CU, Catholic Chaplaincy) seemed to report less of a problem from 'within'.

Religious and non-religious interactions with peers

When students talked about their social relationships on campus, there appeared to be three areas where friendships emerged: on degree courses, in religious societies/activities on campus and in accommodation. This echoes existing literature on Christian students by Sharma and Guest, who point out that students experience their faith in a range of contexts: 'their lectures, halls of residence and social lives' (2013: 74). In terms of integrating with students of no religion, it was generally Christians who reported higher numbers of friends with no religion, and this was often due to their living in accommodation with non-religious students. Also, it is arguable that the demands on Christian students in terms of religious practice are such that it does not alter their relationships with non-religious students as it might with religious Jews or Muslims. The ways in which religious students managed their friendship groups was also interesting. For example, participant 17 (Muslim/I-soc/Absoc) talks about 'hanging out' with her non-religious course friends on days when she has lectures and then spending the rest of her time with her Muslim friends. She adds:

> A lot of the time who I hang around with, depends on what I'm doing. So if I want to go shopping I will just go with whoever's free. But when it comes to clubbing my non-Muslim university friends know I don't go out on nights out. So I think it's just kind of like daytime is the non-Muslim friends and night time will be with Muslim friends.
>
> (Participant 17, Muslim/I-soc and Absoc)

Participant 17 makes it known to her non-Muslim friends that there are certain activities that she cannot participate in (such as clubbing), so instead she organises different activities that they can take part in together. It is interesting that she implies that her non-Muslim friends and Muslim friends are kept separate since this reiterates a point highlighted in research with secular and religious Jews that 'when friendships [between the two] do occur they seem to be segmented' and they tend to 'entertain them one at a time' (Tabory 1992: 149). Participant 17's use of language is also significant here, as she does not use the term 'non-religious' (which is the term I used in my interview questions) but instead 'non-Muslim'. The term 'non-Muslim', while possibly denoting someone non-religious, could alternatively denote someone religious but of a different faith.

Non-religious students were often viewed in a variety of ways, but rarely were they described as being hostile to or intolerant of faith. In both Timmons and Narayanasamy's research with Christian student nurses and Guest et al.'s research with evangelical Christian students, the university was described as a place where students were respectful and tolerant of religious faith, and where students felt relaxed in their Christian identities (Timmons and Narayanasamy 2011: 461; Guest et al. 2013: 134). Furthermore, research with young British atheists showed that hostility towards *religious believers* was relatively low and that criticisms were primarily directed towards religion as an institution and religious coercion (Catto and Eccles 2013: 45). However, despite Catto and Eccles' participants appreciating religion 'as an anthropological phenomenon', the researchers also noted that 'stereotypical views persist, for example, the assumption that a Christian will be homophobic' and that religion is synonymous with conservatism (Catto and Eccles 2013: 45).

When it came to interviewees mentioning friendships with students of different faith, I was surprised that few participants spoke in detail about the nature of these friendships. Perhaps one can infer that such relationships lean more towards acquaintanceships rather than close friendships. That said, those interviewees who did mention friendships with students of different faiths tended to emphasise a common interest in religion (despite differences in affiliation). As one participant points out:

> Islam and Judaism have a lot in common in terms of religious jurisprudence, ways of thinking and also the spectrum of religious beliefs that exist within both traditions. I was speaking to one of my friends in the J-soc about this, it's a shame that political issues tend to prevent or have, until recently, prevented any religious cooperation.
>
> (Participant 14, Muslim/I-soc)

On an individual level, points of contention were managed between students with an overall acceptance of difference and the utilisation of humour. Participant 8 (Jewish/J-soc) talked about being able to 'take the mick out of each other and to use religious stereotypes but in a funny way' and participant 2 (Christian/CU and SCM) noted that when she has debates with friends of different faith, 'it's all in a jokey way'. The nature of interactions between friends of different faiths involves, on some level, the acknowledgement of difference, but also the embracing of their own faith which they can then convey in a comedic way, as can the recipient. By contrast, religious students and non-religious students do not necessarily share religion as a focal point and often this is substituted with something else that they might have in common (such as their degree course, sports and/or shopping). Overall, the students represent the relationships formed on campus between those of non-religion and those of faith as a relatively positive experience; however, most interviewees still tended to cite their closest friends as being of the same faith as themselves.

Conclusion

This chapter provided an account of how a number of religious students (from Jewish, Muslim and Christian backgrounds) navigated the terrain of a red-brick university. The literature identified a tendency to assume that universities are vehicles for secularization, and this was further enhanced by interviewees revealing that they had been 'warned' by parents or members of their local religious community about going to study at university. Significantly, recent academic research has begun to refute this idea and, instead, offered more nuanced accounts which take into consideration the possibility of: a liberalisation of beliefs, an intensification of beliefs, an alteration to religious patterns and no effect at all.

Students' engagement and perception of the university also seemed to vary, with most interviewees taking the attitude that the university has humanistic qualities (in contrast to instrumentalist qualities). Interestingly, the extent to which students viewed the university as being either humanistic or instrumentalist also fed into their willingness to engage with relevant societies and/or chaplaincies on campus. The interaction between religious faith and degree course took a number of different forms, with some participants emphasising the two as complementary and others as challenging. In the case of the latter, the nature of these challenges varied depending on whether they were practical or abstract in nature. In both cases, no students reported such challenges as undermining their faith.

Another important point to emerge from the research was the role that religious societies and chaplaincies played in shaping religious students' experiences of university (although membership of a given society and/or chaplaincy does not indicate that members' experiences are by any means identical). While chaplaincies and societies can serve to create cohesion and community, they can also be responsible for making students feel alienated and isolated. Social relationships clearly played a crucial part in students' experiences of university and it was surprising to discover that, despite the overall tendency for religious students to 'stick to their own' in terms of friendships on campus, it was 'their own' that often presented them with the biggest challenges.

Notes

1 ' Red brick' is a British term used to describe six civic universities situated in industrial cities and founded prior to World War One. The term is more broadly used to refer to institutions founded in the late nineteenth and early twentieth century.
2 Here 'liberal' denotes Christians who do not affiliate themselves to a specific denomination or movement. There were no Catholics or Evangelicals in this category.

References

Bartram, B. (2009) Student support in higher education: Understandings, implications and challenges. *Higher Education Quarterly* 66 (3), 308–314.

Bryant, A. (2006) Exploring Religious Pluralism in Higher Education: Non-majority Religious Perspectives among Entering First-Year College Students. *Religion and Education* 33 (1), 1–25.

Caplovitz, D., and Sherrow, F. (1977) *The Religious Drop-Outs: Apostasy among College Graduates.* London: Sage.

Catto, R., and Eccles, J. (2013) (Dis)believing and Belonging: Investigating the Narratives of Young British Atheists. *Temenos* 49 (1), 38–63.

Dinham, A., and Jones, S. (2010) *Religious Literacy Leadership in Higher Education: An Analysis of Challenges of Religious Faith, and Resources for Meeting Them, for University Leaders*. Religious Literacy Leadership in Higher Education Programme, York: York St John University.

Dutton, E. (2006) Political Correctness, Evangelicalism and Student Rebellion at British Universities. *Journal of Social, Political, and Economic Studies* 31 (4), 459–488.

Dysch, M. (2012) NUS Criticised for Building Boycotts Not Bridges. *The Jewish Chronicle*, 10th January.

Gubrium, J., and Holstein, J. (2002) *Handbook of Interview Research: Context and Method*. Thousand Oaks: Sage.

Guest, M., Aune, K., Sharma, S., and Warner, R. (2013) *Christianity and the University Experience: Understanding Student Faith*. London: Bloomsbury.

Hammond, E., and Hunter, J. (1984) On Maintaining Plausibility: The Worldview of Evangelical College Students. *Journal for the Scientific Study of Religion* 23 (3), 221–238.

Hill, J. (2009) Higher Education as Moral Community: Institutional Influences on Religious Participation During College. *Journal for the Scientific Study of Religion* 48 (3), 515–534.

Hill, J. (2011) Faith and Understanding: Specifying the Impact of Higher Education on Religious Belief. *Journal for the Scientific Study of Religion* 50 (3), 533–551.

Hunter, J. D. (1983) *American Evangelicalism: Conservative Religion and the Quandary of Modernity*. New Brunswick, NJ: Rutgers University Press.

Hunter, J. D. (1987) *Evangelicalism: The Coming Generation*. Chicago, IL: University of Chicago Press.

Hurtardo, S., Sax, L., Saenz, V., Harper, C., Oseguera, L., Curley, J., Lopez, L., Wolf, D., and Arellano, L. (2007) *Findings from the 2005 Administration of Your First College Year (YFCY): National Aggregates*. Los Angeles, CA: Higher Education Research Institute.

Lee, J. (2002) Changing Worlds, Changing Selves: The Experience of the Religious Self among Catholic Collegians. *Journal of College Student Development* 43 (3), 341–156.

Mayrl, D., and Oeur, F. (2009) Religion and Higher Education: Current Knowledge and Future Directions for Future Research. *Journal for the Scientific Study of Religion* 48 (2), 260–275.

Reimer, S. (2010) Higher Education and Theological Liberalism: Revisiting the Old Issue. *Sociology of Religion* 71 (4), 393–408.

Roof, W.C., and McKinney, W. (1987) *American Mainline Religion*. Rutgers, NJ: Rutgers University Press.

Sabri, D., Rowland, C., Wyatt, J., Stavrakopoulou, F., Cargas, S., and Hartley, H. (2008) Faith in Academia: Integrating Students' Faith Stance into Conceptions of their Intellectual Development. *Teaching in Higher Education* 13 (1), 43–54.

Sharma, S., and Guest, M. (2013) Navigating Religion between University and Home: Christian Students' Experiences in English Universities. *Social and Cultural Geography* 14 (1), 59–79.

Tabory, E. (1992) Avoidance and Conflict: Perceptions Regarding Contact Between Religious and Nonreligious Jewish Youth in Israel. *Journal for the Scientific Study of Religion* 32 (2), 148–162.

Timmons, S., and Narayanasamy, A. (2011) How Do Religious People Navigate a Secular Organisation? Religious Nursing Students in the British National Health Service. *Journal of Contemporary Religion* 26 (3), 451–465.

Warren, C. (2002) Qualitative Interviewing. In *Handbook of Interview Research: Context and Method*, ed. by Gubrium, J., and Holstein, J. Thousand Oaks, CA: Sage, pp. 83–103.

Wuthnow, R. (1988) *The Restructuring of American Religion*. Princeton, NJ: Princeton University Press.

The place of policies, structures and curricula

Chapter 10

Islamic Studies in UK universities

Challenging curricula

Sariya Cheruvallil-Contractor and
Alison Scott-Baumann

In 2007, the Siddiqui Report (Siddiqui 2007) recommended reform and innovation in the teaching of Islamic Studies at UK universities. Siddiqui proposed
a curriculum that reflects the living reality for young Muslims in Britain: nego-
tiating hybrid identities, facing the challenges of faith in a secular world and the
demands of academic disciplines such as sociology that often question religious
belief. Through a suite of strong research projects, we report on developments
since the Siddiqui Report and consider the current paucity of activity in this area,
with a few notable exceptions. We discuss the difficulties and the exciting possibilities of developing really new approaches to Islam in the face of neo-liberal
pressures on the one hand, conservative social groupings on the other and persistent confusion on all fronts about the role of women in faith and society.

Our curriculum analysis and proposals will be framed within an articulation of
the socio-political dimensions of the university's own identity crisis: we argue from
a strong evidence base that Islam is being politicised and even pathologised within
a troubled higher education sector. Islamic Studies can be seen as a symptomatic
case study of the difficulties within the university sector as well as a curriculum
area that urgently requires attention in its own right. Innovation and collaboration will enrich the higher education sector both within and beyond Islamic
Studies.

Islamic Studies after the Siddiqui Report

Islamic Studies is defined by the disciplinary contexts and purposes in which
it is undertaken. This includes the textual study of classical religio-intellectual
discipline and tradition, humanities and social sciences approaches that seek to
understand what the texts mean to people and communities (Izzi Dien 2007),
believers' study of divinely revealed scripture and orientalists' studies of exotic
cultures. The Siddiqui Report recommended reform and innovation in the teaching of Islamic Studies at UK universities. Siddiqui proposed a curriculum that
reflects the living reality for young Muslims in Britain. We endorse his vision by
specifying the following components: andragogy that helps to negotiate hybrid
identities and guidance in facing the challenges of faith in a secular world. This

will involve providing access to academic disciplines such as sociology that often question the relevance of religious belief in contemporary social contexts. In Britain, these different approaches or 'strands' of Islamic Studies rarely come together, which we postulate lends it an inability to respond to the contemporary challenges and needs of Islam in the West:

- a need expressed by young second and third generation Muslims to explore the 'Britishness' of *their* Islam
- a need to clarify intersectionality in British Muslim experiences that are shaped not just by their faith, but by their gender, race, social class and other social indicators
- a need, within Muslim communities and British society as a whole, to recognise the contribution of women
- and in the wake of terrorism, Islamophobia and increasing public and academic rhetoric about 'political Islam', a need to challenge the study of Muslims in contexts that view them as 'suspect' communities.

As British Islamic Studies grapples with its identity, the British university sector within which it is situated is also facing the most dangerous threats to its identity, core educational purpose and position within society that it has ever experienced. Complex issues regarding financing and the possibilities of privatisation all collided during twenty-one days in November 2015: the Department for Business, Innovation and Skills (BIS) Higher Education (HE) Green Paper about teaching excellence, the Nurse Review of research councils and proposal for a new overarching research funding body, the Spending Review and Autumn Statement 2015 with its reduction in teaching funds and many unknowns such as how much science will be favoured in funding allocations. Wrong-footed also by the government and the media, certain universities stand accused of harbouring extremists and their student societies are expressing vocal disgust both about too much and too little free speech on a wide range of contentious issues. No one has easy answers to any of these issues, so it becomes convenient to blame Islam on campus as one putative source of chaos.

The diversity of the student population and the daily worldwide political and humanitarian disasters necessitate a serious and challenging approach to Islamic Studies. As Sheikh points out, the way we teach one particular aspect of this – Islamic politics – 'goes to the root of Western civilisation's engagement with other civilisations' (Sheikh 2012: 3). By mostly excluding the peaceful everyday realities of the majority of Muslims and by emphasising radical Islam and terrorism, Sheikh finds that university curricula tend to do 'violence to balance' (Sheikh 2012: 18). Such othering of Islam may be explained as the enduring influence of orientalist approaches in Islamic Studies and also of how policymakers and politicians perceive and discuss Islam. It may also be understood as a symptom of contemporary suspicions of faith in general and Islam in particular, while noting also that today's geopolitical understandings of Islam are determined by history seen from different viewpoints (Salama 2011). However we choose to explain them, such approaches have an impact on policy, societal cohesion and, indeed, on our shared lives as Muslims and non-Muslims, and need to be challenged by educators and students. Without such challenge, the British university sector is at risk of underachieving in this area, as in others. We will investigate the current state of play regarding Islamic Studies with the aim of bearing witness to good practice and recommending future developments in curriculum, language teaching and peaceful andragogy.

Through a suite of four research projects, we recently reported on developments since the Siddiqui Report and considered the current paucity of activity in this area, with a few notable exceptions (Scott-Baumann and Cheruvallil-Contractor 2015). In this chapter, we also discuss the difficulties and the exciting possibilities of developing new approaches to Islam in the face of neo-liberal pressures on the one hand, conservative social groupings on the other and persistent confusion on all fronts about the role of women in faith and society.

Building on this previous work, our curriculum analyses and proposals are framed within an articulation of the socio-political dimensions of the university's own identity crisis: we argue from a strong evidence base that Islam is being politicised and even pathologised within a troubled higher education sector that is seen variously as an arena for developing exciting ideas (Collini 2012), a place for vocational training (Browne 2010), a compromised space that requires policing because of Islamic elements (Quilliam Foundation 2010) and a business that must pay its own way (HMSO 2015 Paper on *Fulfilling Our Potential*).

The state of British Islamic Studies

Islam, fear and academic freedoms

What do young non-Muslim adults know about Islam? Many simply want to get on with their lives, like most of us. Whereas this approach may free them to inhabit a secular world, they may also be caught off guard by the preaching, online and in their communities, of a range of approaches to Islam that can confuse. Moreover, they are surrounded by the casual prejudice and sometimes overt hostility that often demonises Islam in the media and press. According to a poll undertaken in 2013, more than a quarter of young British (18–24-year-olds) said they do not trust Muslims (BBC 2014). Within Muslim communities, there may often be distortions of faithful understanding, which is of course also true of most world religions, but here we are focussing upon Islam. Kundnani (2014: 285) argues that often:

> there is no knowledge or interest in the content of Islamic ideology, only a pulp millenarianism and what one youth worker refers to as a 'pseudo-Islam' that reduces Islam to 'a set of clichés'. . . apolitical, conspiratorial and narrowly identitarian.

The university campus can contribute to increasing clarity because universities have a centuries-old tradition of providing a safe place in which complex ideas about anything – and in this context, Islam particularly – can be discussed safely and compared with other ideas and belief systems. However, at the time of writing, the HE sector appears to be in the grip of one of its most serious challenges, a strange choking hold created by both students and university managers. Students are reacting strongly to diversities of opinion about faith and other issues by 'no-platforming' certain speakers, in other words, banning them from speaking because of views that cause offence to some. By these actions, it can be argued that democratically formulated law is being transgressed (Ali and Merrill 2016). Such refusal to allow speakers a platform, a decision implemented by university managers as well as Students' Unions, may go against the 'duty to ensure freedom of speech' that is found in section 43(1) of the Education (No.2) Act 1986. This is not a duty to 'have regard' to freedom of speech, but a much stronger duty. It is to 'take such steps as are reasonably practicable to ensure that freedom of speech within the law is secured for members, students and employees . . . and visiting speakers' (Education (No. 2) Act 1986, Part IV: 46). There should therefore be a strong defence of freedom of speech, and this situation shows how banning Muslim speakers from speaking on campus is part of a much wider pattern.

The other hand of this choking hold is epitomised by the government Prevent counter-terrorism strategy that appears to instruct university staff and students to monitor each other for signs of radicalization, although there is actually no legal basis for this, as shown in the Counter-Terrorism and Security Act 2015 (CTSA). The CTSA 2015 bases its recommendations upon the paramount importance to preserve freedom of speech in higher education to be found in the 1986 Act, as already discussed. In the light of these struggles in which Islam is often targeted, we contend that it is vitally important to support and, if necessary, re-vitalise Islamic Studies. Yet the supposedly secular nature of the modern university means that staff and students find themselves confused about how to deal with manifestations of the sacred.

Islam, Muslims and Islamic Studies: between the secular and the sacred

In current Islamic Studies provision, there is a pronounced structural divide between the secular and the sacred, in how Islamic Studies is taught and learnt, in how it is lived and in how it is perceived and discussed in contexts outside of academia. With reference to the secular and the sacred in Britain, our recent research indicates that Britain is less Christian, more secular and more religiously plural than it was a decade ago (Weller et al. 2013). According to the 2011 census, Islam is the second-largest religious group after Christianity, and British Muslims are young (according to the Census 2011, 68.75 percent of Muslims are under the age of 35).[1] These young British Muslims are seeking to critically engage with their faith and are increasingly seeking to study Islamic Studies. This is partly in order to better understand their identities as British Muslims and their roles in modern Britain (Scott-Baumann 2007, 2011a). The secular and the sacred represent a popular binary polarisation chosen by two self-identifying 'opposites'. Yet in our research, it is evident that young Muslims lead lives which have within them both secular and religious aspects, which are in constant negotiation with each other – for example, many young Muslims go to 'secular' universities and, while on university campuses, they may join religious Islamic societies and pray on campus. Similarly, as discussed by Reina Lewis, the *hijab* or headscarf that many Muslim women wear for religious reasons has also become a fashion statement (2015) that often conforms to Western norms of style, which we would argue are liberal and secular. In her work on Muslim women, Cheruvallil-Contractor (2012) postulates that Muslim women and, indeed, young British Muslims live at a 'tangential cusp' between their personal secularity and their personal faith.

The secularity and faithfulness of young Muslims has implications for how *they* want to study Islamic Studies. Some approach Islamic Studies in traditional seminaries with a desire to train in the spiritual sciences, and possibly become faith leaders. However, in our research, many young people reported that they studied classical Islamic sciences not because they wanted to become faith leaders, but simply because they wanted to become better people – British citizens who are religious but who also live and work in social environments that are secular and plural. According to Izzi Dien, the study and 'the definition of a faith as a social phenomenon needs to deal substantially with how the faith sees itself' (2007: 246). In the case of young Muslims and their aspirations of and for Islamic Studies, our research demonstrates that the popular binary between the sacred and the secular is understood by young British Muslims as artificial, and time and again in their lives they demonstrate how it can be challenged and bridged (Scott-Baumann and Cheruvallil-Contractor 2015). Indeed, Appleton shows how young adult British Muslim students are actively involved in reconciling their faith with their secularism and that they appreciate the value of university for facilitating that (Appleton 2005: 180). We suggest that it is important for young Muslims and for British society as a whole to develop curricula and pedagogies for Islamic Studies that, in responding to everyday lived realities, can similarly bridge the secular and the sacred.

There is another aspect to the secular–sacred dichotomy that is related to curricula and pedagogies used in Islamic Studies. Whereas Islamic Studies provision as taught at universities is perceived to be secular, critical and modern, Islamic Studies as taught at Muslim institutions is perceived to be confessional, non-critical and outdated. These two monoliths rarely come together, yet our research indicates that the boundaries between these two approaches are much less rigid and much more permeable (Scott-Baumann and Cheruvallil-Contractor 2015). We assert that it is imperative that opportunities for 'cross-fertilisation' are developed, which can lead to models of Islamic Studies that can enhance student employability, lead to interfaith and inter-cultural dialogue, and enable society to be more cohesive and understanding of diversity (Scott-Baumann and Cheruvallil-Contractor 2015).

Furthermore, when discussing religious matters in Britain, many people use the secular–sacred divide as shorthand for debating Islam as a contrast to the secular majority. For some key players, there seems to be a necessity to maintain this polarity by insisting upon public manifestations of those features that seem to endorse it, and this is often played out at universities, for reasons we will explore. A recent example is the furore caused in 2015 by requests for gender segregation at university student meetings: on each 'side', protagonists took up ferociously defended positions, arguing either that student groups should have choice in their social customs or that gender segregation goes against democratic ideals (The Telegraph 2016).

Yet, of course, the reality is never so dichotomous and simple; there are moral ambivalences and paradoxes at the heart of any model of religion, or secularism (and integration and assimilation). Moreover, the sacred takes many different forms, of which some are seen as mutually exclusive even by those of the same faith. Spirituality is a phenomenon that also requires consideration, whether as a sort of postmodern and secular alternative to religion, as a vital aspect of the confessional life or as a fuzzy hinterland that occupies the space beyond or outside both religion and non-religion (Cheruvallil-Contractor et al. 2013). We will therefore consider Talal Asad's (2003) assertions in his book *Formations of the secular* that the secular is not necessarily either rational or a successor to religion. We will interrogate what can be done to dismantle this binary often asserted to exist between the secular and the sacred, as well as build a broader, deeper picture to the benefit of the British university sector. Our work is predicated upon the necessity of critiquing this binary, while at the same time accepting its enduring potency and influence.

Islamic Studies in British higher education

The increasing diversity and visible religiosity of the student intake at many British universities would seem to support Asad's contention that the secular is not necessarily either rational or a successor to religion. Many faiths are represented on campus and yet they are not well reflected in the curriculum, and even Islam, the fastest growing minority faith in Britain, is poorly represented in courses. Sheikh (2012) recommends that more Muslim scholars become involved and hopes that the national and international situation will be better covered in Islamic Studies courses in the future.

About twenty-four British universities teach Islamic Studies, often within a wide range of humanities or social sciences curricula (mainly the School of Oriental and African Studies [SOAS], Oxbridge and some pre-1992 universities). Arabic may form part of Islamic Studies and is vitally important. A range of approaches may be adopted, such as area studies or anthropological or historical approaches, as identified by Bernasek and Bunt (2010). Very seldom, as at SOAS, a theological approach is followed (MA in Islamic Studies). Mainly, however, these are courses based implicitly or even explicitly upon the importance of differences between Muslim and Western cultures. The secular nature of the British campus is often held up as the triumph of the Enlightenment and the victory of reason over superstition. Western intellectual traditions are accorded privileged status and Muslim philosophies and contributions to Western thought are suppressed. Ibn Sina and Ibn Rushd were medieval Muslim thinkers whose works heavily influenced European philosophical development. Their contributions *as Muslims* are forgotten and they are often known only by their anglicised names. So Ibn Sina is known only as Avicenna and Ibn Rushd only as Averroes: 'When habitus relies too heavily upon defining as evil the less privileged one of a pair, we are faced with societal self-deception' (Scott-Baumann 2009: 158).

The enduring influence of Orientalism

The study of Islam and indeed 'Eastern' cultures in British universities has long been characterised by Orientalism, which may be understood as the study of the 'East' undertaken almost exclusively by Western scholars and researchers. While orientalists would argue that their study was sincere and was often undertaken as an 'act of prayer' (Irwin 2007), many readers of this chapter will be familiar with Said's scathing critique of orientalist approaches (1978). According to Said, the orientalists *othered* the Orient as exotic, irrational and 'manifestly different' from the occident. In emphasising the *different-ness* of these cultures, and 'in having to take up a position of irreducible opposition to a region of the world it considered alien to its own, Orientalism failed to identify with human experience and also failed to see it as human experience' (Said 1978: 328). In his book, Salama (2011) interrogates orientalism and the 'politics of exclusion', which in 'today's global politics' continue to maintain 'such a palpable polarization between Muslims and the rest of the world' (39). Achcar recommends caution as he sees a reverse form of Orientalism, one that is used by some Muslims to argue that Islamic solutions are the only ones that will modernise Islam (Achcar 2008; Scott-Baumann 2011a, 2011b).

While Said himself has now been critiqued by orientalists and others who claim that his criticism of Orientalism was too generalised and that it undermined an entire discipline of study, there is merit in the idea that in an interconnected and globalised world it is imperative that we enable students to critically interrogate the sources and methods that allow us to arrive at the knowledge that we have. In doing so, we will uncover the hierarchies in systems of knowledge that privilege the powerful few, assigning them authority and authenticity: male or female? Secular or religious? West or East? North or South? Non-Muslim or Muslim? We also need to reflect on our own positionalities as researchers, teachers and students of Islamic Studies. A recent article by an academic collective at University College London (UCL) argues that much of our intellectual thinking is underpinned by an ideology that is white and by a positioning of 'Europe (and its settler colonies) as the moral and intellectual leaders of the world'. [2] This links back to Said's bone of contention with Orientalism. And while both Said and the UCL collective may be critiqued for failing to acknowledge that they themselves may have biases, they nevertheless make a valuable and important point about the inherent biases in all so-called neutral intellectual thinking.

It is important to be aware of different hierarchies, but in the contemporary world it is no longer sufficient to do this only to reject or only challenge them. Rather, with challenge must also come symbiosis and a bridging of different intellectual traditions – where, for example, it may be possible to think both as a secular feminist and as a religious believer or to *be* both religious and secular, as for example in the life-experiences of young Muslims (Cheruvallil-Contractor 2012). In the case of Islamic Studies, it must be structured and positioned so as to appeal to and appease the intellectual demands of students and societies that are both simultaneously secular and religious at the same time. According to Siddiqui, what we need are inclusive approaches to Islamic Studies that incorporate the opinions of the different other.

We discuss such ontological stances in our book *Islamic Education in Britain: New Pluralist Paradigms* (Scott-Baumann and Cheruvallil-Contractor 2015) and methods and approaches to the design of such courses in our research report from our Higher Education Academy (HEA)-funded work on Muslim women in HE (Cheruvallil-Contractor and Scott-Baumann 2011).

Political Islam and Islamic politics

In 2012, Sheikh surveyed the higher education sector and established that in the twenty-four universities that offer coverage of Islam and politics, there is a range of subject-based approaches: theology, political theory, history, sociology and political science. Sheikh found that 'democracy', 'contemporary militancy and terrorism' and 'Islamic political ideology' appeared frequently and that, while the coverage is reasonably accurate, there is bias in topics chosen (Sheikh 2012: 4). This bias may be due partly at least to the so-called war on terror and incessant media coverage of related phenomena. In his study of British Muslims on campus, Appleton believes that insufficient account is taken of the fact that 'in terms of world affairs, Muslims are marginalised by the overwhelming preponderance of American military, cultural, political and economic power' (Appleton 2005: 173). This results in what Sheikh calls 'Doing violence to balance: excluding pacific forms' (Sheikh 2012: 18). Sheikh's analysis shows that while Sufism is a major force in Islam, it is taught much less than militant Islam. Terrorism constitutes an infinitesimal proportion of the entire Muslim population, yet the everyday peaceful realities, including peaceful politics, of the majority of Muslims receive much less attention. The language we use in such discussions has become heavily freighted: the very term 'political Islam' can be seen as synonymous with militant Islam and violent terrorist acts.

To counter this bias, Sheikh finds that Orientalism and Said's anti-orientalist stance are sometimes still taught for alerting students to the dangers of cultural stereotyping, sweeping generalisations and the imperative to understand other people (Sheikh 2012: 16–17). The use of the term 'Islamic politics' is useful, if it proves acceptable to believe that Muslims are entitled to have political views. Yet the identifiable bias towards violent acts can result in the muting of a Muslim voice of balanced criticality. By this, he means that the Muslim voice becomes disenfranchised. By extension, this process can disempower and villainize any critical voice that departs from current hegemonic narratives about Iran, Israel, Palestine, Saudi Arabia and so on, or indeed about anything at all. We see this in the current 'no-platform' approach towards speakers such as Germaine Greer with her challenging views on gender.

Sheikh also draws our attention to the absence of clear connections between Islamic politics and religious ideas, mainly because of subject boundaries and also because of an implicit orientalist bias. These artificial boundaries tend to keep Islam separate as if its identity, strengths and problems are unique. Yet Islamic Studies curricula can be enhanced to the benefit of the wider university curriculum with judicious choice of texts. In his book *The Impossible State*, Wael Hallaq (2014) provides a form of response to Achcar's identification of Orientalism in reverse: Hallaq analyses the ways in which the new worldview precludes the foundation and proper functioning of a true Islamic state. He critiques the dominant neoliberal models and contrasts them with the possibilities of Shari'a and other Islamic moral codes. By this means, Hallaq also shows what a problem many modern phenomena are for those of other faiths and of none as well as for Muslims, and his arguments therefore reach well beyond Islam.

There are also many pressing issues that spill out beyond Islam to affect the rest of the world, such as the situation in the Middle East. Judith Butler is a Jewish feminist philosopher. In her 2004 book *Precarious Life*, she demands the right for herself and for others to witness, understand and deplore the suffering of Palestinians in the occupied territories without being accused of anti-Semitism. Butler (2004) sees the universality of this crisis and looks to universities to make discussion of it possible: 'What is needed is a public space in which such issues might be thoughtfully debated, and for academics to support the commitment to academic freedom and intellectual inquiry that would support a careful consideration of these issues' (126).

British Islamic seminaries: how is Islamic Studies taught?

In Britain, as well as universities, there are Muslim *dar ul ulooms* (seminaries) that are confessional in approach and teach up to university equivalent level. They also teach a wide range of General Certificate of Secondary Education (GCSE) and advanced-level subjects to examination and are inspected by The Office for Standards in Education, Children's Services and Skills (OFSTED). There are also Muslim colleges for university-level ages that combine confessional approaches with more secular subject matters to the equivalent of a degree level. Markfield College of Higher Education (MIHE) works in collaborative partnership with Newman University and provides a range of different courses that offer a juridical, theological or secular approach.

The curriculum at MIHE offers a representative range of topics and students must study across the theological, legal and sociological themes offered. There are, for example, essay questions in Islamic law about the need to reform historical Shari'a and also about the illegality of forced marriages. There are essay questions from the 'Muslims in Britain' course that demand a critical evaluation of all the factors around Islamophobia. These examples of assignments provide a sense of the balance that is provided in these small Muslim colleges. The interdisciplinary nature of Islamic Studies could be better presented in the university sector, and skills of those in each sector can be valuable to the other. The university and the Muslim college can each also benefit from critical self-analysis. We propose that the university can and should provide more courses that would attract observant Muslims, and we will make several recommendations based on existing good practice.

New approaches to Islamic Studies

For many Muslims it is, not surprisingly, unacceptable to be persistently defined by negative phenomena such as terrorism, just as European education may contain elements of study about, say, Nazism or totalitarianism, but is neither defined nor dominated by such negative models. The everyday peaceful realities of the majority of Muslims need to be included within academic discourses about diverse Muslim communities, including those that live in Western social contexts.

Peaceful, critical andragogy

Such approaches begin with Siddiqui's assertion of the need, in British higher education, to study Islam and Muslims as an integral aspect of British society. Histories of Islamic intellectual contributions to Europe and European thought are uncovered, demonstrating that these two ends of a supposedly historical dichotomy also have deep interconnections. The inherent heterogeneity within Muslim communities is a central aspect of such approaches – it is insufficient to only acknowledge heterogeneity, it must be understood together with its influence on everyday life. Muslim experience is shaped in part by faith, but it cannot be studied in a silo, devoid of the other social characteristics – race, ethnicity, socio-economic status, gender, national identity, etc. Such an approach forms the basis of Cheruvallil-Contractor and Shannahan's MA module 'Religion, Peace and Conflict' at Coventry University. Students are given access to diverse academic and practitioner voices from the Muslim community. Discussions on art and, in particular, music from within Muslim communities give students an open and non-judgemental space where they can reflect on their own preconceived understandings of Islam. In questioning and unpicking stereotypes and hegemonic narratives for themselves, students move away from essential discourses of terrorism and towards understandings that foreground everyday peace.

Community of inquiry

Andragogy techniques have existed since language was developed for reasoned debate about complex issues. The American philosopher CS Peirce developed a 'community of enquiry' for setting ground rules in groups of adult learners that facilitate strong, honest and patient discussion. In various settings over the last twenty years, Scott-Baumann has used this approach for bringing out the preconceptions and prejudices that groups of individuals have about each other, and using that heuristic process to help them to communicate better about themselves with each other (Scott-Baumann 2010).

The faithful on campus

There is a need to acknowledge the believer's point of view (Bullock 2003) within Islamic Studies. For Muslims on campus and indeed for all faith groups, religious belief is part of their social reality (Izzi Dien 2007). These belief systems are indispensable in the choices and decisions individuals make about their lives (Jackson et al. 2007) and influence individuals' and groups' interactions with each other.

Spirituality, ethics and charity: a case study[3]

Teaching the spirituality, ethics and charity of Islam is appropriate and productive:

In 2015, Ziad Amin was a postgraduate, and, of his own volition, he designed, developed and wrote his own course for fellow students at SOAS. He advertised it in the Junior Common Room, and the course was very popular, attracting students of many and no faiths. The topic was *The Spirit of Islamic Ethics* and Ziad combined traditional texts of Imam Al-Ghazali and Abdul Qadir al-Jilani with ancient and modern Western philosophy. This combination allowed him to make connections across cultures and time, as well as to provide material that many students desire about how to live a good moral life. Ziad's ability and willingness to combine, compare and contrast the thought of both 'East' and 'West' also helped him to show how different cultural expectations can be understood in order to resolve spiritual issues and ethical dilemmas. Similarities could also be explored. Ziad saw how his course provided spiritual and intellectual nourishment that reached within and beyond Islam, and also how his teaching was able to provide a strong positive framework within which to understand Islam, oneself and oneself in relation to others. Looking back at his teaching, Ziad explained in email correspondence why it was effective:

> It's important to speak to people in a language that is relevant to their lives, and there's nothing quite more immediate than how to deal with the dynamics of yourself and of other people . . . I made a conscious decision not

to address misconceptions of Islam because I wanted to get away from the dominant defensive narrative, although I did address them if they came up. What I found, however, is that when the spiritual and moral message of Islam is the focus, the misconceptions naturally melt away.

Women in Islamic Studies

The need for all of the above – peaceful andragogy, community of enquiry, the faithful on campus – is exemplified in the case of Muslim women on campus, both in the context of their lives on campus and how they are studied. As described by Phipps and Young (2012), all women, not just Muslim women, are concerned and disturbed by the excessive sexualisation of women that occurs on campus and also by a devaluing of women' studies, feminism or gender studies. We discuss this in detail elsewhere (Scott-Baumann 2016; Scott-Baumann and Cheruvallil-Contractor 2016).

Religious and non-religious women believe in different ways and their beliefs have shaped entire belief systems. Yet women's contributions are consistently absent or less represented in academic discourses. The French feminist philosopher Michèle Le Dœuff describes this as the marginalisation of women from the processes and systems of knowledge, which in the everyday leads to a gradual erosion of their social authority and roles (Le Doeuff 1998). Muslim women and indeed all religious women's struggles are further compounded by their visibility as religious women in increasingly secular society that sometimes views religion as irrational, outdated or disconnected from contemporary contexts. Muslim women must also deal with intense media and political scrutiny. In the case of academic discourses around women's gender roles, top-down orientalist approaches that seek to replace a set of values which are perceived as inferior and oppressive often result in these being replaced with another set of values that can be similarly oppressive in their irrelevance to the everyday lived realities of the people who must live with them. By uncovering, recording and sharing women's voices, stories and beliefs, gaps in history, knowledge and understandings of faith can be filled.

Conclusions and recommendations

A greater diversity of voices must be brought to the table, allowed to speak and be seriously listened to, before any progress can be made to unpick stereotypes and allow Muslims as they are to walk out of the frame and into the political life of the twenty-first century.

(Morey and Yaqin 2011: 216)

We live in a globalised and interconnected world, which means that previous monochromatic constructions of community, identity and nationhood are no longer sufficient or fit-for-purpose. For Muslims, these discussions take place in the full glare of media and political attention. Many discussions that are taking place in communities and amongst intellectuals address difficult questions around gender roles, lost histories or histories that privilege specific voices; the threat of violent terrorism; and the conflation of this sometimes with political Islam. Muslims are also involved in a cultural recovery of their histories, art forms, music and culture. Islamic Studies needs to respond to such discussions and to the lived experiences of Muslims who are diverse themselves and who live in diverse social and political environments – from nominal/secular Muslims living in religious orthodox Saudi Arabia to deeply traditional Sufi Muslims living in super-diverse London and a range of other positionalities in between. In examining the diversity and complexity of Muslim life, it is necessary for Islamic Studies to incorporate a variety of disciplinary perspectives. New voices that have been hitherto marginalised (the faithful, women, minority, young, etc.) need to be included within Islamic Studies.

Women's contributions in particular need to be remembered and recovered. It is imperative that women – both students and academic staff – are given the opportunity to shape what is taught about women. Commonality in women's experiences can be used both to foster cross-cultural dialogue and as a platform for shared activism.

It is vital to move away from a model of andragogy that emphasises differences, as Orientalism often does, and attempt to find similarities that characterise the human condition. This can be done by challenging binaries such as secular:religious and by exploring the positive similarities shared by many students, such as the search for spiritual meaning and for the good life. Islamic Studies teachers may need training to develop andragogy that facilitates deep debate through Socratic questioning and other techniques through 'community of inquiry'.

Islamic Studies tutors need to rethink the word 'political' and use it more as George Orwell did: 'Political purposes – using the word political in the widest possible sense. Desire to push the world in a certain direction, to alter people's idea of the kind of society that they should strive after' (Orwell 2004: 5) – and also discuss other approaches, such as the secular woman's voice in Deborah Levy's (2014) feminist response to Orwell: *Things I don't want to know*. This changed emphasis would allow enhancement of the different angles from which Islam can be studied in curriculum areas; for example, sociology and religion should come together and consider their differences and similarities. Politics should not be seen as related only to militant action.

British higher education will be enriched by development of interaction and collaboration between Islamic scholars and those who teach Islamic Studies at universities in Britain. This can be done through developing collaborative partnerships between universities and Muslim colleges, and by increasing the number of practicing Muslims who teach in universities. Such interaction will improve possibilities for collaborative partnerships, such as those that exist between

Markfield College of Higher Education and Newman University, and between Islamic College of Advanced Studies and Middlesex University.

At a wider level, the higher education management and the students' union groups must urgently tackle 'no-platform' and 'safe space' policies, which are currently often used to choke freedom of speech and academic freedom. This is happening at a time when the university must reclaim its capacity to offer opportunities to discuss difficult, often irresolvable issues reasonably and not drive them underground. The scapegoating of Islam should not conceal the creeping restrictions upon the work of the university, which is to help young adults to become the citizens of tomorrow with sophistication, humility and understanding.

Notes

1 For full figures, please see http://www.nomisweb.co.uk/census/2011/lc2107ew.
2 The full piece is available at http://wire.novaramedia.com/2015/03/8-reasons-the-curriculum-is-white/.
3 We thank Ziad Amin for his case study.

References

Achcar, G. (2008) Orientalism in Reverse. *Radical Philosophy* 152, 20–30.
Ali, A., and Merrill, J. (2016), HOPE not hate chief executive, Nick Lowles, 'no-platformed' by NUS for being 'Islamophobic'. *The Independent*, 18th February 2016. Available online at: http://www.independent.co.uk/student/news/hope-not-hate-chief-executive-nick-lowles-no-platformed-by-nus-for-being-islamophobic-a6881831.html.
Appleton, M. (2005) The Political Attitudes of Muslims Studying at British Universities in the Post – 9/11 World (Part 1). *Journal of Muslim Minority Affairs* 25 (2), 171–191.
Asad, T. (2003) *Formations of the Secular: Christianity, Islam, Modernity.* Stanford, CA: Stanford University Press.
BBC (2014) Quarter of Young British People 'do not trust Muslims'. Available online at: http://www.bbc.co.uk/newsbeat/24204742. Accessed 29 February 2016.
Bernasek, L., and Bunt, G. (2010) *Islamic Studies Provision in the UK.* Report to HEFCE by the Higher Education Academy.
Browne, J. (2010) *Securing a Sustainable Future for Higher Education. An Independent Review of Higher Education Funding and Student Finances.* Available online at: www.independent.gov.uk.browne-report. Accessed 1st February 2016.
Bullock, K. (2003) *Rethinking Muslim Women and the Veil: Challenging Historical and Modern Stereotypes.* London: International Institute of Islamic Thought.
Butler, J. (2004) *Precarious Life. The Powers of Mourning and Violence.* London and New York: Verso.
Cheruvallil-Contractor, S. (2012) *Muslim Women in Britain: Demystifying the Muslimah.* London and New York: Routledge.
Cheruvallil-Contractor, S., Hooley, T., Moore, N., Purdam, K., and Weller, P. (2013) Researching the Non-Religious: Methods and Methodological Issues, Challenges

and Controversies. In *Social Identities between the Sacred and the Secular*, ed. by Day, A., and Cotter, C. Aldershot: Ashgate, pp. 173–190.

Collini, S. (2012) *What are Universities For?* London: Penguin.

Education (No. 2) Act 1986, Part IV (43), p. 46.

Hallaq, W. (2014) *The Impossible State: Islam, Politics and Modernity's Modern Predicament*. New York: Columbia University Press.

Her Majesty's Stationery Office (2015) *Fulfilling Our Potential: Teaching Excellence, Social Mobility and Student Choice*. London: HMSO.

Irwin, R. (2007) *For Lust of Knowing: The Orientalists and Their Enemies*. London: Penguin.

Izzi Dien, M. (2007) Islamic Studies or the Study of Islam? From Parker to Rammell. *Journal of Beliefs and Values* 28 (3), 243–255.

Jackson, R., and O'Grady, K. (2007) Religions and Education in England: Social Plurality, Civil Religion and Religious Education Pedagogy. In *Religion and Education in Europe: Developments, Contexts, Debates*, ed. by Jackson, R., Miedema, S., Weisse, W., Willaime, J-P. Münster: Waxmann, pp. 181–202.

Kundnani, A. (2014) *The Muslims are Coming. Islamophobia, Extremism and the Domestic War on Terror*. London and New York: Verso.

Le Doeuff, M. (1998) *The Sex of Knowing*. Translated by Kathryn Hammer and Lorraine Code (2003). London: Routledge

Levy, D. (2014) *Things I Don't Want to Know*. London: Penguin.

Lewis, R. (2015) *Muslim Fashion: Contemporary Style Cultures*. Durham NC: Duke University Press.

Morey, P., and Yaqin, A. (2011) *Framing Muslims: Stereotyping and Representation After 9/11*. Harvard: Harvard University Press.

Orwell, G. (2004) *Why I Write*. London: Penguin.

Phipps, A., and Young, I. (2012) *That's What She Said: Women Students' Experiences of 'lad culture' in Higher Education*. London: National Union of Students. Available online at: http://www.nus.org.uk/

Quilliam Foundation (2010) *Radicalisation on British University Campuses: A Case Study*. London: Quilliam.

Said, E. (1978) *Orientalism – Western Conceptions of the Orient*. New York: Pantheon.

Salama, M. (2011) *Islam, Orientalism and Intellectual History: Modernity and the Politics of Exclusion Since Ibn Khaldun*. London: I B Tauris.

Scott-Baumann, A. (2007) Collaborative Partnerships as Sustainable Pedagogy: Working with British Muslims. In *Greener by Degrees: Exploring Sustainability Through Higher Education Curricula. Section C4*, ed. by Roberts, C., and Roberts, J. Available online at: http://resources.glos.ac.uk/ceal/resources/greenerbydegrees/index.cfm

Scott-Baumann, A. (2009) *Ricoeur and the hermeneutics of suspicion*. New York, London: Continuum.

Scott-Baumann, A. (2010) Community of Inquiry. *The Study of Islam within Social Science Curricula in UK Universities: Case Studies* 1, 81–87. Available online at: Max_Farrar_Case_Studies.pdf

Scott-Baumann, A. (2011a) Developing Islamic Higher Education for a Secular University Sector: Orientalism in Reverse? In *Muslim Schools and Education in Europe and South Africa*, ed. by Niehaus, I., Tayob, A., and Weisse, W. Munster, New York: Waxmann, pp. 173–193.

Scott-Baumann, A. (2011b) Unveiling Orientalism in Reverse. In *Islam and the Veil*, ed. by Gabriel, T., and Hannan, R. New York and London: Continuum, pp. 20–36.

Scott-Baumann, A. (2016) Speak to Silence and Identify Absence on Campus: Sister Prudence and Paul Ricoeur on the Negated Woman Question. In *Feminist Explorations of Paul Ricoeur's Philosophy*, ed. by Henriques, F., and Halsema, A. Lexington: Rowman & Littlefield, pp. 37–61.

Scott-Baumann, A., and Cheruvallil-Contractor, S. (2011) Enhancing the visibility of Muslim women in Islamic Studies. In *Perspectives 2: Teaching Islamic Studies in higher education*. York: Higher Education Academy, pp. 8–13.

Scott-Baumann, A., and Cheruvallil-Contractor, S. (2015) *Islamic Education in Britain: Pluralist Paradigms*. London and New York: Bloomsbury.

Scott-Baumann, A., and Cheruvallil-Contractor, S. (2016) An Islamic Perspective: What Does Islam Offer to the Contemporary Debate? In *The Universities We Need. Theological Perspectives*, ed. by Heap, Stephen. Farnham and New York: Ashgate, pp. 118–137.

Sheikh, N. (2012) *The Teaching of Political Islam in UK Higher Education Institutions; Upping the Ante*. HEA ISN Referenced 14 December 2015.

Siddiqui, A. (2007) *Islam at Universities in England: Meeting the Needs and Investing in the Future*. Report submitted to Bill Rammell MP, Minister of State for Lifelong Learning, Further and Higher Education. Available online at: http://dera. ioe.ac.uk/6500/1/Updated%20Dr%20Siddiqui%20Report.pdf

The Telegraph (2016) 19.01/2016 Headline: Gender Segregation: The Truth about Muslim Women 'forced' to Sit away from Men. Available online at: http://www.telegraph.co.uk/women/life/gender-segregation-the-truth-about-muslim-women-forced-to-sit-aw/

Weller, P., Purdam, K., Ghanea, N., and Cheruvallil-Contractor, S. (2013) *Religion or Belief, Discrimination and Equality: Britain in Global Contexts*. London and New York: Continuum.

Chapter 11

From cognitive science to personal leadership

The role of religion and personal life orientation in curriculum development processes within the domain of religious studies

Joke van Saane

The department of Theology at Vrije Universiteit Amsterdam offers a quite unique education in the disciplines of Theology and Religious Studies. Both in bachelor and master programmes, the faculty cooperates with specific religious groups in the education of future leaders and ministers. Within the study of Theology, four different Christian denominations participate. These denominations are located at different wings in the Protestant churches, including a very traditional and theologically spoken conservative group as the Restored Reformed Church as well as the most liberal variant in The Netherlands, the Arminian Church. Within Religious Studies, students can choose different trajects (routes) as well: Islam, Buddhism and Hinduism. Half of the specialization trajects, both in Theology and Religious Studies, are taught by teachers coming from these particular religious groups. For example, a student in the Restored Reformed Church traject gets a secular course on Psychology of Religion taught by a Vrije Universiteit professor. In the same period, this student enrolls in a course on Biblical Theology, taught by a Restored Reformed professor, sharing his time between university and presbytery. The same for the Islam traject, which is partly taught by regular academic social scientists on religion, and partly by imams and Islamic spiritual care givers. As a result, the Department of Theology and Religious Studies of Vrije Universiteit Amsterdam forms a religious hub, a platform for students and teaching staff members from all different backgrounds. This construction, however successful, has implications for educational strategy.

Scientific education in the field of Theology and Religious Studies is characterized by a tense relationship between scientific detachment on the one hand and personal ideological commitment on the other. The academy has a duty to deliver students to society who are thoroughly trained and academically ready for an international academic career. These same students are also expected to be involved in their own religious tradition, being able to function as faithful and believing pastors. To be adequate in this role, they need to be equipped with all the knowledge and skills necessary in this particular religious group. It is not always easy to reach that goal within an academic context. Normative beliefs and academic descriptions, involvement and distance continuously run into one another. Moreover, personal involvement can come under pressure as a result of scientific detachment. This is, for example, the case if students from an orthodox or conservative background participate in a research course about text critics and, as a result, come to doubt their own scriptures. At the same time, a personal commitment to a religious or spiritual tradition can get in the way of a scientific analysis and a scientific attitude towards that tradition. This happens if students refuse to examine, for example, evolutionary approaches to religion, arguing that evolution theory cannot be combined with their religious beliefs. Education in Theology and Religious Studies should ensure both scientific detachment and the personal attachment to one's own tradition.

How can learning outcomes be defined within this context? It is important to distinguish between learning outcomes and faith development. A development, for example, towards an areligious or even antireligious attitude is not the preferred outcome. Nor does the faculty push the students or teachers into a liberal, tolerant, modern variant of religion; the structure and content of beliefs and traditions are left to the student or teacher. The academy in a modern secularized society, based upon the principle of separation of church and state, cannot afford any content judgments about religion, unless religious beliefs are contrary to basic human rights. The learning outcome that positively can be defined includes a form of education that combines transferring knowledge, exercising academic skills and academic distance on the one hand with a process of philosophical identity construction on the other.

The combination of these different educational elements demands different learning styles. Ball (2012) comes to the same conclusion in his project on changing theological education in Australia, based upon a switch to transformational learning. According to Mezirow (2006: 25), parallel to the distinction Habermas (1984) made between instrumental and communicative action, a distinction can be made between instrumental learning and communicative learning. Instrumental learning is aimed at controlling and even manipulating the environment or others; communicative learning includes feelings, values and intentions in its focus on others interacting with you (Mezirow 2012: 103). To validate understanding, one must assess not only the accuracy of what is communicated, but also the intention, qualifications and authenticity of the one who is communicating (Mezirow 2006: 25). Both forms of learning are essential for education in Theology and Religious Studies. Instrumental and problem-solving learning is tested via hypotheses. Measurement results are decisive in this type of learning. Communicative learning requires something different, namely a reflective discourse. A reflective discourse means above all inclusive language, so that a common understanding may arise in dialogue. In this discourse, one's own assumptions are questioned and coupled to the assumptions of the other, leading to a common understanding of differences and agreements. Communicative learning gives insight into the other, as well as insight into oneself. This type of learning cannot be tested by measurement results, but it widens the learning environment as a whole.

According to Mezirow (2012), effective participation in a reflective discourse requires not only access to accurate and complete information and the capacity of clear thinking, it also requires a form of emotional maturity (79). To participate in a constructive reflective discourse, one has to reflect upon one's own emotions and motivations. Without a certain degree of emotional maturity, this reflection will remain superficial, or even childish. Moreover, emotional maturity demands self-control in order to be able to recognize emotions in others and to deal with relationships. In other words, emotional stability covers skills such as empathy, self-control and self-confidence. These are precisely the skills that are defined in all kinds of research on leadership (see for example Van Velsor, McCauley, and Ruderman 2010; Yukl 2010) as good predictors of effective leadership. Constructive participation in a reflective discourse comes with a certain degree of personal leadership. Within the academic domain of Theology and Religious Studies, personal leadership of both students and teachers forms a fundamental condition for balancing between personal commitment and academic distance.

At Vrije Universiteit Amsterdam, education in Theology and Religious Studies is not an isolated subdiscipline. This form of education is complicated by the connections between university and all kinds of religious and societal groups. Even within the educational programmes themselves, different religious groups actively participate. This connection with society and religious groups ensures that the faculty inevitably has to deal with the facts of pluralization and secularization. To be clear, these processes of pluralization and secularization do not imply a marginalization of religion. On the contrary, the world news underlines the significance of religion.

The world news about religions and religious (terrorist) behaviour demonstrates that there can be no absolute internal perspective on religion against an absolute external perspective. Violent and irrational forms of religious behaviour reveal the fact that an absolute internal perspective on religion can even be dangerous. This is not only the case if a literal interpretation of their own sacred text leads to the justification of killings and rape (Hood et al. 2005), but also if traditional and conservative guidelines sabotage, for example, scientific forms of healing diseases (van Saane 2010). However, an absolute external perspective cannot serve as an alternative, while such a perspective can only describe this state of affairs, not being able to influence these practices. To be able to influence religious behaviour and cognition, one needs to understand the other, as well as one's own norms and values.

Education in Theology and Religious Studies takes place at the interface between internal and external perspectives. Science is never absolutely neutral or value-free. It is always marked by the presuppositions of its practitioners. The interfacial and discursive context of education requires reflection upon the own presuppositions, by teachers and students. This reflection is conditional for dialogue; discussions with the other imply discussions with oneself (van Eersel 2011).

The learning outcomes of the programmes at Vrije Universiteit do not include degrees of belief or disbelief. Students are equally free to embrace rather orthodox religious beliefs or to join atheist groups. However, the learning outcomes do include statements about reflection. Students reach their goals if they feature the proper cognitive science and academic skills, if they can formulate their own perspective in a dialogical manner and if they are capable of reflection upon their own process of identity development.

To achieve this combination of goals (cognitive and academic skills, dialogical skills and reflection skills) within one program several conditions must be met. First and for all, the standards for the teaching staff are rather high. Application of different teaching methods, interactive education, differentiation of assignments, organizing students' teamwork, guidance on internships and instruction based upon real problems are parts of the basic assessment of teaching staff. Especially in a multi-faith context, discussion is a way of teaching (Brookfield and Preskill 2005). This implies continuous processes of professionalisation and sufficient organizational conditions.

Beside these staff requirements, a second condition can be formulated. All programs should embody multi-faith education, education from different religious traditions instead of education from just one religious tradition (Baird 2013). Of course, the latter is the more traditional form of education in Theology and Religious Studies. But that traditional form of theological education is no longer sufficient. The modern Western secularized society requires well educated and credible religious leaders who have thorough knowledge of different religions, complementing the knowledge of their own religion.

Within religious groups, sometimes resistance to multi-faith education can be found based on the fear that students will switch to another religion. However, research by Roozen (2011) and Graham (2012) indicates a strengthening and deepening of students' commitment to their own religious tradition if education takes place in a multi-faith context.

Multi-faith education inevitably demands forms of dialogical learning. However, studies on multi-faith education show that dialogical learning does not necessarily come easily. It proves to be important for the students not only to build social relations with others, but also to spend enough time with 'equals'. The last element is easily forgotten in a context of dialogue and relations. Beside the balance between relating to others against building their own network, the attitude and passion of the teaching staff appear to be important. Students need passionate role models who can be partners in discussions about religious and spiritual reflection. These discussions increase all the time. Connected to dialogical learning and multi-faith education, inevitably a process of identity formation occurs. Both students and teachers experience the urgency to discuss this process. Faced with other religious convictions, students develop two patterns (Baird 2013). In the first pattern, initial fear and resistance is followed by confrontation and curiosity. The result is usually a reinforcement of the original personal belief. The second pattern shows a development from seeing the religious other through the eyes of their own religion to seeing the other through the eyes of his own religion.

This second pattern creates space to take over the other's perspective. Students need to learn how to enter into these debates without losing self-control.

Multi-faith education can take place in different forms. The exchange of cognitive knowledge about other religions is an often-used educational form. It is also possible to expose students to another religious experience, for example, by participating in holy services. At Vrije Universiteit Amsterdam, we experiment with Scriptural Reasoning, a practice of inter-faith reading. Small groups of students from different religious traditions (Jews, Muslims, Christians) gather to read short passages from their scriptures with the goal of deepening the understanding of scriptures. There is no need for the participants to agree or even to accept one another's texts as scripture. In other cases, debates are organized, and religious places and institutions are researched by religiously mixed groups of students.

The third condition for a successful educational program with a focus on identity construction and dialogue is focused on curriculum development. In the field of Theology and Religious Studies, curriculum development typically aims to maintain and improve the knowledge and wisdom of one's own tradition – Christian, Muslim, Buddhist. Usually, these curricula are organized around systematic contents, encyclopedically arranged (Ball 2012). However, it is very doubtful whether this corresponds to the way students learn, especially when this learning takes place in a multi-faith context. A curriculum that is more centred around the student rather than centred around the cognitive content will provide better conditions for engaged learning, leading to personal goals of development of the students. This does not necessarily mean that the content is reduced, but that the content is transferred in a more integrative manner. Integration is not so much a feature of a curriculum, but a characteristic of the individual learning process of students (Kanarek and Lehman 2013). The curriculum should encourage students to connect the knowledge learnt to their own lives and experiences. This advocates a curriculum with a clear opportunity for reflection by the students. Reflection should not take place in the form of separate reflection assignments. Research studies on reflection skills in education programs show that this will not work. In most cases, students experience separate reflection assignments as useless, finding it hard to connect these assignments with the whole of their study and lives. It seems to be more useful to construct distinct units in the curriculum which serve as a platform for reflection. These units should be part of the regular program, for the duration of the program. Constructed in this way, reflection forms part of the learning itself; students need time to understand what they are taught, and to give meaning to it (Smith 2013).

Effective learning strategies result from a process of transformation; the existing perspective is transformed into another perspective (Mezirow 2006). This process goes along with the practice of learning, especially when students bring their values, beliefs and assumptions under critical reflection and rational discussion. If they do so, long-standing meaning schedules and meaning perspectives can be transformed. Learning is a process of differentiation of meanings. In other words, learning itself is a process of change and transformation. Existing knowledge and experience should be connected to more meanings of the same phenomenon.

This can be confusing. Not only new knowledge must be recorded, also 'old' knowledge comes under discussion. Everything we learn leads to change. Learning is not just cramming information, learning is changing, learning is reflection, learning is transformation, learning is adaptation.

If providing for new visions is accompanied by a process of self-reflection and self-examination, students are capable of exploring new options, options for knowledge, behaviour and choices. The university is the place *par excellence* to carefully try out new options. What happens if I behave differently? What happens if I do something else? The university is a place of practice and imagination. Of course, this does not happen automatically, a real trial requires the opportunity in time and space to do so, experiencing a sense of security. If done fully and freely, this exploration of new options can lead to the creation of a new frame of reference (Mezirow 2012: 82). This can be in the form of a new cognitive frame, or in the form of the existing frame of reference embraced again, as a reflected and conscious choice. A frame of reference is a perspective of meaning, the structure of assumptions and expectations which filters out our impressions. A changing frame of reference leads to a different view to the world, with different expectations, judgments and explanations. That is all part of a change of reference.

This places demands on the educational program, and on the faculty and the university offering the program. This requires hospitality, an atmosphere in which one feels invited to participate (Graham 2012). If there is a reciprocal exchange of assumptions and ideas, accompanied by a willingness to question those assumptions and ideas, something new can arise. This is not an easy activity, or a reduction of academic standards. On the contrary, hospitality does not make learning easier, but hospitality ensures that the pain and tension in the learning process can be tolerated. Learning is a process of transformation, of change. Change takes effort and time; change provokes resistance. If we must learn that we do not know something or a lot of things, if we must test shaky hypotheses and assumptions, if we call into question existing knowledge and if we criticize one another, we need hospitality: a light tone and self-critical humour.

Critical reflection is facilitated by student-centred education strategies. Crucially, education has not so much to do with teaching activities, but with the student's learning process. There is no education if there is no learning. Starting with the student involves needing to know something *about* the student. That knowledge is necessary to take into account who they are, what they already know and can do and how they have structured their knowledge. In doing so, a stepping stone is provided between what they are currently learning and their previous knowledge. This integration conditions deeper forms of knowledge and skills, resulting in mature discernment and compassion as student characteristics. Ball (2012) recommends a focus on learning and assessment tasks that promote deep learning strategies (158). Students need to be invited to formulate a personal and coherent statement of theological understanding, utilising both critical academic skills and relevant vocational application.

Beside the opportunity for reflection within the curriculum and a focus on the student as an actor in the learning process, I distinguish a last condition for a constructive process of identity formation. This condition is inevitably related to the former ones, focusing on self-directed teaching and learning strategies. I argue for a teaching strategy known as 'self-directedness in learning' (Gijbels et al. 2014; Mezirow 2012). This learning strategy refers to an instruction method in which the learner takes the primary responsibility for the learning experience, both when it comes to identifying learning needs and setting goals, in order to produce appropriate forms of learning and assessment of learning outcomes. Self-regulation and self-control are central to this learning strategy. If this learning and teaching strategy is applied consistently in education, the emphasis lies on the self-management of students. As a result, students need to develop some resilience and a personal sense of responsibility for feedback and responding to feedback. Students with a self-directed learning style are proactive, they think forward and they develop adaptive capacities. This learning style does not fit with passive consuming students. After all, all components of the learning process, including targets, strategies, implementation and evaluation, are the responsibility of the student. Obviously, teachers must be professional. Of course, the organization of education must be in order. But students may also be expected to be observant and to find themselves responsible for their own learning processes. To give meaning to newly acquired perspectives can be facilitated by an education or university; however, it is ultimately a process that is in the hands of the student himself.

So, a constructive process of identity formation within the context of academic education requires a reflection part within the curriculum, a central focus on the student and a strengthening of self-directed learning and teaching strategies. Formulated in this way, reflection on identity is a form of personal leadership.

Van Saane (2012) describes the self-knowledge of the leader and thorough knowledge of followers as strong predictors for effective leadership. Self-consciousness and knowledge about the goals and dynamics of the group are helpful factors in increasing the purposiveness of leadership. This means that effective leaders are not characterized by one uniform set of personality traits and skills, to be used in every situation. It means that in different situations, different traits and skills are needed. To develop and show the right traits and skills, it is necessary to know your range of skills and traits. Credible leadership is above all professional leadership, self-conscious and appropriate in the specific situation. I assume a parallel between theories on leadership and education on the domains of Theology and Religious Studies. In these disciplines, students are educated to become professionals in religion and meaning. Education leads to professions such as ministry in very diverse religious traditions, spiritual care, policymakers, journalists, religious entrepreneurship and research. All these varieties have one requirement in common: credibility and professionalism is dependent on self-insight and on insight in the professional context.

For several reasons, the focus in education is usually on the second form of insight, insight in the professional context. This insight is developed by the transfer of cognitive knowledge and by dialogue about that context in relation to their own world perspective.

A lot of innovations have improved the transfer of cognitive knowledge in higher education in the last decade. In most cases, the knowledge is interdisciplinary and offered as complicated cases to be solved by the students in group sessions. Assessment methods have been adapted, new teaching methods were introduced and information and communication technology (ICT) has become indispensable to monitoring and conditioning the whole learning process. A continuous renewal and innovation of education is going on, accompanied by a strong focus on quality assessment in higher education. The first form of insight, self-insight, necessary to increase the professionalism of students, seems to be much harder to conduct and to control.

Education in the field of Theology and Religious Studies can only be constructive if the program balances between a strict academic outside perspective on the one hand, and a personal committed perspective on religion on the other. This requires a highly professional teaching team, able to transfer knowledge as well as to function as a role model for students. A multi-faith context is a constructive way to foster interreligious debates, for example, through the practice of Scriptural Reasoning. These forms of education are strengthened by accurate dialogical assignments, forcing students to reframe their meaning systems. These education practices flourish in an academic environment, characterized by intense forms of supervision, self-directed learning strategies and development of personal leadership.

Teachers and students need to stimulate each other to develop traits such as emotional stability, self-trust, authenticity, flexibility and empathy. Personal leadership means being in control of yourself, your study, your environment, your life as a whole. Clawson (2008) calls personal leadership the 'level three leadership', with an emphasis on feeling and thinking, rather than on behaviour. Focusing on personal leadership requires opportunities for reflection, a certain degree of freedom for students and a clear choice for self-directed teaching and learning styles. From an attitude of self-consciousness, one can take responsibility for him or herself and for the greater good. Ideally, self-knowledge goes hand in hand with awareness of the other, openness, a sense of purpose and a wide horizon. However, the world is not always an ideal one. For students, especially the younger ones, it is a very risky journey to abandon your own beliefs and presuppositions in order to reach a state of openness for the other. This can lead to confusion, or even conversion. In all curricula, we need time for reflection and interpersonal meetings.

Personal leadership within higher education means that someone not only knows his or her own personality, but that he or she is also able to use that knowledge to foster the learning process. Personal leadership goes along with an attitude of openness, attention and consciousness. Higher education in Theology and Religious Studies does not only aim to produce students with excellent professional knowledge. These students should also be willing and able to conduct the religious dialogue in society, totally aware of their own limits and capabilities, focused on growth and development, open to new insights and experiences. Education in the field of Theology and Religious Studies is education to personal leadership.

References

Baird, J. (2013) Multifaith Education in American Theological Schools: Looking back, Looking ahead. *Teaching Theology and Religion* 16 (4), 309–321.

Ball, L. (2012) *Transforming Theology. Student Experience and Transformative Learning in Undergraduate Theological Education.* Eugene, OR: Wipf and Stock.

Brookfield, S. D., and Preskill, S. (2005) *Discussion as a Way of Teaching. Tools and Techniques for Democratic Classrooms.* San Francisco: Jossey-Bass.

Clawson, J. G. (2008) *Level Three Leadership. Getting below the Surface.* London: Pearson.

Gijbels, D., Donche, V., Richardson, J. T. E., and Vermunt, J. D. (2014) *Learning Patterns in Higher Education. Dimensions and Research Perspectives.* London and New York: Routledge.

Graham, S. (2012) Christian Hospitality and Pastoral Practices in a Multifaith Society: An ATS Project, 2010–2012. *Theological Education* 47 (1), 1–10.

Habermas, J. (1984) *Reason and the Rationalization of Society. Volume 1 of the Theory of Communicative Action.* Boston: Beacon Press.

Hood, R. W. jr., Hill, Peter C., and Williamson, W. Paul (2005) *The Psychology of Religious Fundamentalism.* New York and London: The Guilford Press.

Kanarek, J., and Lehman, M. (2013) Assigning Integration: A Framework for Intellectual, Personal, and Professional Development in Seminary Courses. *Teaching Theology and Religion* 16 (1), 18–32.

Mezirow, J. (2006) An Overview of Transformative Learning. In *Lifelong Learning. Concepts and Contexts,* ed. by Sutherland, Peter, and Crowther, Jim. New York: Routledge, pp. 24–38.

Mezirow, J. (2012) Learning to Think Like an Adult: Core Concepts of Transformation Theory. In *The Handbook of Transformative Learning. Theory, Research, and Practice,* ed. by Taylor, E. W., and Cranton, P. San Francisco: Jossey-Bass, pp. 73–96.

Roozen, D. (2011) Educating Religious Leaders for a Multi-Religious World: Outcomes and Learning from the 2009 Parliament of the World's Religions. Available online at: www.parliamentofreligions.org

Saane, J. van (2010) A Cultural Psychological Approach to Evangelical Faith Healing Groups. *Mental Health, Religion & Culture* 13 (4), 411–415.

Saane, J. van (2012) *Geloofwaardig Leiderschap. (Credible Leadership)* Zoetermeer: Meinema.

Smith, B. H. (2013) Teaching the Devout Student: Faith and Scholarship in the Classroom. *Teaching Theology and Religion* 16 (2), 132–149.

van Eersel, San (2011) *Towards Dialogue. Teacher/Student Interaction in Interreligious Communication.* Münster: Waxmann.

Van Velsor, E., McCauley, C. D., and Ruderman, M. M. (eds.) (2010) *The Center for Creative Leadership Handbook of Leadership Development.* San Francisco: Jossey-Bass.

Yukl, G. (2010) *Leadership in Organizations.* Upper Saddle River, NJ: Pearson.

Chapter 12

Do religion and belief have a place in 'the student experience'?

Duna Sabri

In recent years, the concept of the 'student experience' has acquired totemic status in higher education (Sabri 2013). Shaping both national policy and higher education research, this has coincided with a burgeoning interest in many aspects of student life, including choice and access to higher education (e.g., Reay et al. 2005), experiences of learning and curriculum (e.g., Clegg 2011; Quinn 2006), mental well-being (as evidenced in the creation of the charity Student Minds), and progression and attainment (Richardson 2008). Students of different social backgrounds, ethnicities, national origins, and ages have all received considerable attention from researchers in higher education, to name but a few lines of inquiry.

Within this wide-ranging interest in students' experiences of higher education, religion and belief are relatively under-explored. In part, this may have arisen, not simply as an oversight, but as an aversion to the phenomenon of religious belief, reflecting both academic cultures and the personal life experiences of researchers. As Craig Calhoun (Modood and Calhoun 2015) has suggested, such aversion can be indicative of an underlying 'distaste (which itself is not just a reflection of disinterest or different beliefs but also of personal trajectories moving away from parental or community religious beliefs, and sometimes of a class-tinged understanding of what respectable people talk and even think about)' (22).

Where religion is considered in relation to student life, it is often framed in the context of equalities legislation in which religion is understood as a social practice that is to be accommodated and respected. This is exemplified by Weller et al.'s (2011) report for the Equality Change Unit on the experiences of staff and students in relation to religion and belief, which seeks to provide guidance to higher education institutions that would enable them to meet their obligations under equality legislation, including the Religious and Racial Hatred Act 2006 and the Equality Act 2010. The themes pursued in this report include participation and access, accommodating religious observance, discrimination and harassment, and good relations. The concern with how the social practice of religion should be accommodated within different elements of the higher education system is particularly informed by the public sector equality duty which the 2010 Equality Act introduced. This implies a vision of equality that is more focused on social relations than on the rights of individuals. In particular, the duty 'to foster good relations between people who share a relevant protected characteristic and people who do not share it' situates religious commitment as of equal status to an absence of commitment. The effect of this is to flatten out significant differences that may be implied in various religious and non-religious ways of engaging with the educational process, constructing these differences as equivalents in terms of equality responsibilities towards students. Religion is also, in this context, constructed in static terms – as identities, beliefs, and practices that are fixed and unaffected by the process of learning.

What is largely absent, then, is a more forensic questioning of what difference religion might make to the nature of students' engagement with higher education, particularly in relation to the practices of learning and teaching. The aim of this chapter is to contribute to this neglected issue by exploring briefly the ways in which religion has been, or could be, conceived of across three domains relevant to learning and teaching in higher education – educational research on learning, national policy on religion in relation to learning environments, and institutional policy and practices relating to religion in learning and teaching. In undertaking this analysis, it will seek to demonstrate both some limitations in the ways in which religion has been thought about in these contexts, and some potentially fruitful alternative ways of thinking about the relationship between religion and the student experience of learning. Drawing on a range of writing from specialists in educational studies and religious studies, the chapter seeks a more dynamic and complex picture of that relationship than has thus far emerged.

Educational research

Students' university experience, and in particular the educative aspects of it, have been theorised in several ways. Among the most dominant seams of literature is that of Approaches to Learning (AL), based initially on a study of students' reading (Marton and Säljö 1976). This research tradition came to dominate the higher education landscape through its inclusion in programmes for the professional training of university teachers and as a basis for their evaluation in the design of the National Student Survey (NSS). The AL literature has been widely critiqued (Haggis 2009; Sabri 2011) as not taking account of students' characteristics or social contexts, but neither the original AL literature nor these critiques touch on the possible significance of students' religious beliefs. This omission remains consistent in the subsequent use of the AL literature for higher education policy interventions. For example, the Higher Education Funding Council for England (HEFCE) website that offers access to NSS data for research purposes allows for the results to be viewed by gender, age, ethnicity, socio-economic class, and school type, among other characteristics. Data on religious affiliation are absent, however, possibly, but perhaps only partly, because the data were not widely collected by institutions before the 2010 Equality Act came into force in April 2011.

The concept of student engagement which has underpinned the US-based National Survey of Student Engagement does not directly address students' religion either, but it does contain two relevant items: the first on spiritual practices, 'In your experience at this institution, how often have you participated in activities to enhance your spirituality (worship, meditation, prayer, etc.)?'; and the other on interactions with diverse peers, 'In your experience at this institution, how often have you had serious conversations with students who are very different from you in terms of their religious beliefs, political opinions, or personal values?' (Kuh and Gonyea 2006: 43). Kuh's study explores correlations between these two items and students' learning. Essentially, the question posed is whether religiosity appears to impede or sustain learning. Kuh's conclusion is that there are small positive associations between religious participation and interaction with students from very different religious and political beliefs and personal values, and that religious observance does not seem to hinder engagement in higher education. Kuh's concern is to reassure those who are worried that a resurgence in religious observance may hinder liberal learning and his answer is 'not to worry' (Kuh and Gonyea 2006: 46). While Kuh's study is enlightening within the parameters of survey research, it gives us no insight into the causal mechanisms that might lie behind his correlations. Furthermore, it treats religious observance as a static student characteristic rather than as a social practice which may grow, recede, or fluctuate over time.

We have to look to past and, to some extent, forgotten conceptualisations of students' learning for an understanding of learning that accommodates religion and belief not simply as an attribute, but as a developing and possibly transforming aspect of students' experience. This is the work of William Perry (1999), whose longitudinal study of college students in the 1950s and early 1960s provided a foundation for several studies of students' epistemological development. Perry delineated nine positions in a scheme of 'ethical and intellectual development' distinguished by changing conceptions of 'Authority', a term which changes its meaning in accordance with the students' position. In the earlier positions, the term denotes those who possess the 'right answers' or who 'falsely pretend' that they do, usually a university lecturer. In the later positions, students understand 'authority' (the use of lowercase is deliberate) as a differentiated concept that is constructed by power, expertise, and culture. The second crucial aspect of Perry's scheme is the curriculum that the students encounter. In Perry's scheme, students' beliefs about what knowledge is, how it is acquired, and what makes it valid or 'true' are central to the different positions. To begin with, students believe they can accrue the right knowledge through obedient hard work; as a diversity of opinion becomes discernible, they begin to doubt the expertise of the tutor/Authority or rationalise the situation by assuming that the curriculum is designed to get students to find the 'right answer' for themselves. Uncertainty is gradually accepted as legitimate as students move away from a dualistic position toward a relativistic one. At position 5, the students 'may subordinate dualistic right-wrong functions to the status of a special case, in context'. In the subsequent positions, students form a personal view in a relativistic world, making an initial commitment, and come to experience a process of ongoing reflection on their identity and selfhood.

Perry believed that students moved through these positions in a cyclical fashion, in relation to each new intellectual domain as they encountered it. Religious commitments did not feature strongly in his scheme: his interest was more generally in how students implicitly or explicitly imputed structures to the world 'in which they construe the nature of knowledge, of values, and of responsibility' (1999: 1). He is exceptional among educational theorists to have integrated religiosity and belief at all in his scheme: he suggests that 'Position 5 [Relativism] represents the point of critical division between "belief" and the possibility of faith . . . To become faith it must first be doubted' (146). Perry distinguishes between 'belief' and 'faith', explaining:

> If one later commits oneself to faith in an Absolute, *there is a criterion which reveals that this Commitment has been made in the context of a relativistic world.* This criterion is one's attitude toward other people with a belief or a faith in a different Absolute. They cannot appear as alien, as other than human; one must, however paradoxically, respect them. In one sense they 'must' be wrong, but in another sense, no more so than oneself. The moral obligation to convert them or annihilate them has vanished.
>
> (146, emphasis in original)

It is worth noting that Perry situated his scheme in the social context of 1950s and 1960s America and took care not to generalise his work to other generations or beyond the particular elite social context within which his research was conducted. We might also contextualise Perry and his work as taking place in 'a secular age' (Taylor 2007) when religious belief is 'no longer axiomatic' and, for many, 'faith never even seems an eligible possibility' (Taylor 2007: 3).

Nevertheless, Perry not only sees religious belief as a dynamic part of students' educative experience, but also elaborates its relevance to students' social interaction with peers, lecturers, and others in their environment. Certainty is his crucial criterion: it implies a rejection of the legitimacy of others' beliefs, whereas doubt opens up the possibilities for exchange that leads to growth. It is interesting to note that we have to go backwards in the history of educational theory (Perry's work was first published in 1968) to find a well-elaborated conception of religion and belief in higher education. There have since been several US studies that have replicated Perry' work and developed it, and, within the United Kingdom, there is at least one small-scale study that has analysed the relationship of students' faith stance to their conceptions of intellectual development (Sabri et al. 2008). In addition, there have been some in-depth considerations of the interplay between particular pedagogic approaches and students' faith (see Fairweather 2012). It is important to note that the interplay between religious faith and academic practice is not always seen in productive terms: in an exploration of the place of religion in contemporary art, Elkins (2004) explores five ways in which students' art practices position religion and spirituality, but he concludes that 'modern spirituality and contemporary art are rum companions: either the art is loose and unambitious or the religion is one-dimensional and unpersuasive' (Elkins 2004: 116). Elkins, however, also argues that the talk about the relationship between the two should continue and that it should be 'slow and careful' (116). Perry's work, while not without its critics, does offer a way of conceptualising religion and belief as problematic to learning and therefore as central to what is arguably the most fundamental part of 'the student experience'.[1]

National policy

Perry's understanding of the dynamic ways in which religious belief could change in the wider context of a student's epistemological development offers a positive account of the ways in which religion can be shaped dynamically through the learning process. By contrast, as Mathew Guest (2016) puts it, at a national policy level in Britain, 'radical transformation through learning is only raised when considered as a threat'. The most recent UK government guidance to higher education institutions in England and Wales does recognise that students' religious and political commitments are dynamic and capable of transformation while at university, but in terms that illustrate Guest's point:

> Some students may arrive at RHEBs [relevant higher education bodies] already committed to terrorism; others may become radicalised whilst attending a RHEB due to activity on campus; others may be radicalised whilst they are at a RHEB but because of activities which mainly take place off campus.
>
> (HM Gov 2015)

Stevenson (2013) has argued that it is only in relation to points of conflict and especially instances of (Muslim) religious extremism that policy discourse at a national level engages with religion and belief. The role that religion plays in equalities policy for higher education should also be noted, such as the Office of Fair Access's advice to universities which includes religion as a protected characteristic under the terms of the 2010 Equality Act. But national equalities policy relating to religion and higher education remains largely abstract and vague, with detailed implementation left to the discretion of individual institutions. By contrast, Stevenson is right to note that it is only in the context of anxieties about extremism that national policy on religion in higher education becomes more detailed and actively engaged. It seems that over the past decade or so, since the 7/7 bombing in London, government guidance and rhetoric has progressively become less nuanced and less trusting of the professional knowledge of those who work in higher education. The 2008 'Promoting Good Campus Relations, Fostering Shared Values and Preventing Violent Extremism in Universities and Higher Education Colleges'

(DIUS 2008) has morphed into the most recently issued 'Prevent Duty Guidance: for higher education institutions in England and Wales' (2015) which supplements the Counter-Terrorism and Security Act 2015. This most recent document has elicited considerable critique from academics in particular. For example, a group of eminent academics and students writing in *The Independent* newspaper (Lister et al. 2015) argued that Prevent was based on the misapprehension that extremism, radicalisation and terrorism were driven primarily by ideological beliefs. They also felt that the presentation of the requirement to report students suspected of being 'radicalised' as 'safeguarding' acted to depoliticise what is actually a very political subject that needed to be the focus of open debate. There continues to be robust opposition to the latest Prevent requirements, with delegates at the conference of the Association of University Administrators voting two to one in favour of a motion that Prevent duties 'endanger freedom of expression and contribute to a long-term decline in academic liberty' (Grove 2016).

Prevent guidance seems to conceive of 'the religious student' as a particularly vulnerable individual who must be protected from radicalisation and a descent into terrorist intent. Guest speakers seem to be perceived as an enduring means of influencing students, who are conceived as empty receptacles. What is abundantly clear is that government policy has lost faith that academia can challenge and transform students' thinking and requires staff to report suspects. The academics who wrote in *The Independent* newspaper (among whom are several specialists in the field of the sociology of religion and Islamic studies) assume that higher education is experienced as a place of intellectual exchange and freedom of expression, and conceptualise the student as both willing and capable of making use of this environment. Such a view has, so far, had little influence on national policy.

Institutional policy and practices

Recent policy relating to religion and belief, at the level of individual universities, has so far been focused on issues of internationalisation and equality and diversity. Internationalisation, as Stevenson (2014) has observed, has been driven in Western universities first by a commercial imperative and more recently by a focus on employability, where students develop a sense of global citizenship through intercultural exchange. Stevenson notes that culture is often poorly defined in this context, with the consequence that religious elements of international cultural exchange are generally ignored. However, the integration of religion and belief within internationalisation has potentially far-reaching implications because it is perceived to hold benefits for both home and international students, local and international staff. There is also a wide reach in terms of the aspects of student and staff experience to which it is deemed to be relevant: from application to graduation, employability, and alumnus status for students; and from recruitment to retirement for staff. As yet, these possibilities remain largely unexplored.

Institutional policy on religion and equality has been primarily concerned with accommodating and, to some extent, celebrating diverse religious beliefs. While these aims are reasonable, even laudable, they do not engage with religion and belief critically. The stance of accommodation is particularly supported by the construction of students as consumers whose expectations must be satisfied and by the limited construction of religion as a protected characteristic. If religious beliefs are taken to be more than attributes but a matter of agency, then students need to be able to engage in negotiation about their needs and the capacity of their institution to accommodate them. This is paramount not just in relation to the distribution of resources, but also in instances when there are serious clashes of values, for instance between religious beliefs and gender equality. In 2013, Universities UK (the body composed of higher education vice chancellors and principals) was embroiled in controversy surrounding its guidance on gender segregation when the issue became a focus for both students' protests and comment from (former) Prime Minister David Cameron, who saw the body as elevating religious accommodation above gender equality (Syal and Weaver 2013). The Universities UK advice was primarily informed by interpretations of universities' legal obligations, but it is arguable that the law represents a minimum requirement rather than a limitation to the issues to be considered at an institutional level. Otherwise, there is a tendency to treat students as passive recipients of university provision which might in turn lead to rigid understandings of 'needs' and exclude the possibilities for social learning and professional development (for both staff and students).

The Equality Act of 2010 that has brought religion into line with other protected characteristics has underpinned a view of religious commitment as a fixed attribute and as an aspect of students' needs which must be accommodated. For example, among the initiatives that are typically underway are the production of new monitoring data on religious affiliation, the provision of prayer or contemplation spaces, and extra-curricular celebratory events that promote inter-faith dialogue. The variation among institutions in taking forward such initiatives can be fruitfully analysed through the framework of religious literacy (see Dinham, this volume) which assists universities in understanding their own positions. In its focus on the role of leadership in religious literacy, this approach very significantly points to an interplay between the worldview with which students come to university and what the university offers in response. This moves us away from treating religion and belief as internal to the student and towards a critical analysis that problematizes that response.

The failure to think, at the level of institutional policy, about the significance of religion in relation to student learning in particular is a crucial omission. It is in this domain that assumptions potentially can be questioned and intellectual and moral development is most sustained. While higher education cannot be reduced to curriculum, its relevance seems currently underplayed. In this context, it is important that universities become more confident and proactive in thinking about the nature of their educational mission in relation to religion. As Modood and Calhoun (2015) argue in a stimulus paper prepared for the Leadership Foundation for Higher Education, universities should rethink their outlook as purely secular institutions to one in which they understand themselves as having a responsibility to lead debate about the role of religion in society. Rather than being excluded or avoided, religion might then be allowed a place across a wide range of intellectual inquiry. As they put it:

> The challenge . . . is not just for religion to be the main focus of discussion on some occasions and to handle those occasions without exacerbating conflict. It is for religion to be part of discussions of many topics on other occasions without dominating or derailing the discussion
>
> (Modood and Calhoun 2015: 22)

What is envisioned here is an environment in which religion and belief can be included in discussions with students in a way that is proportionate to the topic in hand and legitimate in the university space. Perhaps through inclusion of religion and belief, there is more potential to avoid an emotionally charged approach (from both those who hold and those who do not hold religious beliefs) that results in the derailment of critical debate.

Conclusion

This brief review suggests how far there is to go before attention to religion and students' experiences of learning are more fully integrated into educational research, as well as relevant national and institutional policies. In the absence of such work, religion can be both silenced and a focus of conflict within the classroom. In one published account of the latter, a lecturer described how:

> Buying into the current claim that Christians suffer persecution in the UK, many appear compelled to resist the academic critique of the traditions and texts they hold dear. Recently, a group of students in a lecture refused to undertake the work set because they didn't want to apply postmodern perspectives to what for them was a sacred text.
>
> (The Guardian, February 2014)

The sense of powerlessness in this lecturer's account chimes with a colleague's recent comment to me about the feeling that a students' religious commitment is something that is off bounds in the course of critical debate and 'cannot be challenged . . . because the message itself is off limits'. His experience was also that students quite often hold back from exposing their religious beliefs in the knowledge that what they really think is too controversial in the academic environment in which they are operating. This view was certainly evident in a study of students in the disciplines of theology and philosophy which demonstrated that some students with strong religious convictions would find ways of masking these in classroom interactions and their assessed work, for fear that disclosure of their beliefs would have adverse effects for them (Sabri et al. 2008). Paradoxically, then, the lack of a professional language for thinking about how religious convictions could constructively be talked about, and critically thought about, in the classroom creates conditions in which both bold religious claims by students are hard to challenge and students can also feel uncomfortable exploring intellectually their religious beliefs and experiences. A default position for academics can therefore be that religious views are fixed, resistant to change, and have to be circumvented in some way for 'real' intellectual work to take place. Interestingly, similar points of view do not necessarily pertain in relation to students' political commitments. So in a pedagogic context, the religious student can be conceived of as an exceptional and particularly 'difficult' case.

To move beyond this current impasse, academics will benefit from educational research that adopts a constructive and dynamic view of the interaction between religious belief and learning (such as offered by Perry's understanding of students' epistemological development), national level policy which moves beyond constructing religious belief in the learning environment primarily in terms of social risks, and institutional policies in which universities think more creatively and confidently about their educational missions in relation to religion. It is crucial that future institutional practices embrace the possibilities for conflict and challenge in both individual students' development and in the context of their social interactions with peers and staff members. The ways in which religious belief interacts with the learning process will also require more reflection in different disciplinary learning environments, with these interactions potentially taking somewhat different forms across the arts, humanities, and social sciences, as well as the mathematical, biological, medical, and physical sciences. The relevance of religion and belief should be explored across these various learning contexts because it makes pedagogic sense to engage with the prior conceptions that students bring with them and the implications these might have for learning in those particular disciplines.

This will not be a one-off or easy process. As historians, sociologists, and anthropologists of religion are well aware, religious beliefs even within a single tradition can be fluid and diverse, as well as occupy a complex relationship to religious identity and practice (e.g., Orsi 2006). The phenomenon of students' 'lived religion' (McGuire 2008) is likely to be far more complex than textbook definitions of religious beliefs. A student's religious belief will also be experienced and performed in its intersections with their gender, age, sexuality, ethnicity, and class (Ahmad 2001; Wilkins 2008). The form and significance of religious belief in a student's life, and the ways this shapes their experience of the learning process, will therefore be highly diverse with implications unique to each particular student.

Yet, despite these complexities, there is also considerable potential to develop more constructive ways of thinking about the relationship between religion and students' experiences of learning simply by acknowledging that this is an issue to be addressed. By bringing our intellectual curiosity to this issue, the place of religious belief in the learning process can begin to be seen less as an implacable problem and more as an opportunity for new forms of collaborative intellectual inquiry which remind us of the very purpose of higher education.

Note

1 It is worth noting that there are some similarities between Perry's positions and Fowler's (1981) stages of faith, though the latter are conceived, following Piaget, as taking place over a life-cycle as opposed to within the higher education environment.

References

Ahmad, F. (2001) Modern Traditions? British Muslim Women and Academic Achievement. *Gender and Education* 13 (2), 137–152.

Anonymous (2014) Teaching Religion: My Students Are Trying to Run My Course. *The Guardian*, 8th February 2014.

Clegg, S. (2011) Cultural Capital and Agency: Connecting Critique and Curriculum in Higher Education. *British Journal of Sociology of Education* 32 (1), 93–108.

Department for Innovation, Universities and Skills (DIUS) (2008), *Promoting Good Campus Relations, Fostering Shared Values and Preventing Violent Extremism in Universities and Higher Education Colleges.* Available online at: http://webarchive. nationalarchives.gov.uk/20100222165247/http:/www.dius.gov.uk/publications/extremismhe.pdf. Accessed 15 March 2016.

Elkins, J. (2004) *On the Strange Place of Religion in Contemporary Art.* New York and London: Routledge.

Fairweather, I. (2012) Faith and the Student Experience. In *Religion and Knowledge: Sociological Perspectives*, ed. by Guest, M., and Arweck, E. Aldershot: Ashgate, pp. 39–55.

Fowler, J. W. (1981) *Stages of Faith.* San Francisco: Harper Collins.

Grove, J. (2016) Prevent 'stopping students speaking out in class'. *The Times Higher Education*, 31st March 2016.

Guest, M. (2016) Can Universities Still Provide a Transformative Experience? *Open Democracy*, March 2016. Available online at: https://www.opendemocracy.net/ transformation/mathew-guest/can-universities-still-provide-transformative-experience. Accessed 20 March 2016.

Haggis, T. (2009) Student Learning Research: A Broader View. In *The Routledge International Handbook of Higher Education*, ed. by Tight, M., Mok, K. H., and Morphew, C. C. New York and London: Routledge, pp. 23–35.

HM Government (2015) *Prevent Duty Guidance: For Higher Education Institutions in England and Wales.* London: Home Office. Available online at https://www.gov.uk/ government/uploads/system/uploads/attachment_data/file/445916/Prevent_Duty_ Guidance_For_Higher_Education__England__Wales_.pdf. Accessed 20 March 2016.

Kuh, G.D., and Gonyea, R.M. (2006) Spirituality, liberal learning, and college student engagement. *Liberal Education* (Winter), 40–47.

Lister, R., Armstrong, K. et al. (2015) Prevent Will Have a Chilling Effect on Open Debate, Free Speech and Political Dissent. *The Independent*, 10th July 2015. Available online at: http://www.independent.co.uk/voices/letters/prevent-will-have-a-chilling-effect-on-open-debate-free-speech-and-political-dissent-10381491.html

Marton, F., and Säljö, R. (1976) On Qualitative Differences in Learning: I-Outcome and Process. *British Journal of Educational Psychology* 46, 4–11.

McGuire, M. (2008) *Lived Religion: Faith and Practice in Everyday Life*. New York: Oxford University Press.

Modood, T. and Calhoun, C. (2015) *Religion in Britain: Challenges for Higher Education: A Stimulus Paper*. London: The Leadership Foundation for Higher Education.

Orsi, R. (2006) *Between Heaven and Earth: The Religious Worlds People Make and the Scholars Who Study Them*. Princeton, NJ: Princeton University Press.

Perry, W. G. (1999) *Forms of Intellectual and Ethical Development in the College Years – A Scheme*. New York: Holt, Rinehart and Winston 1968, 1970 and San Francisco, CA: Jossey-Bass. 1999.

Quinn, J. (2006) Mass Participation But No Curriculum Transformation: The Hidden Issue in the Access to Higher Education Debate. In *Perspectives and Practice in Widening Participation in the Social Sciences*, ed. by Jary, D., and Jones, R. Birmingham: C-SAP, University of Birmingham.

Reay, D., David, M. E., and Ball, S. J. (2005) *Degrees of Choice: Class, Race, Gender and Higher Education*. Stoke-on-Trent: Trentham Books.

Richardson, J. T. E. (2008) *Degree Attainment, Ethnicity and Gender: A Literature Review*. York: Equality Challenge Unit/Higher Education Academy.

Sabri, D. (2011) What's Wrong with 'the student experience'? *Discourse: Studies in the Cultural Politics of Education* 32 (5), 657–667.

Sabri, D. (2013) Student Evaluations of Teaching as 'fact-totems': The Case of the UK National Student Survey. *Sociological Research Online* 18 (4), 15.

Sabri, D., Rowland, C., Wyatt, J., Stavrakopoulou, F., Cargas, S., and Hartley, H. (2008) Faith in Academia: Integrating Students' Faith Stance into Conceptions of Their Intellectual Development. *Teaching in Higher Education* 13 (1), 43–54.

Sheridan, L. (2006) Islamophobia Pre and Post September 11th 2001. *Journal of Interpersonal Violence* 21, 317–336.

Stevenson, J. (2013) Discourses of Inclusion and Exclusion: Religious Students in UK Higher Education, Access and Widening Participation. *Journal of Widening Participation and Lifelong Learning* 14 (3), 27–43.

Stevenson, J. (2014) Internationalisation and Religious Inclusion in UK Higher Education. *Higher Education Quarterly* 68, 46–64.

Syal, R., and Weaver, M. (2013) Universities UK Withdraws Advice on Gender Segregation in Lectures. *The Guardian*, 13th December 2013.

Taylor, C. (2007) *A Secular Age*. Cambridge, MA: Belknap Press of Harvard University.

Weller, P., Hooley, T., and Moore, N. (2011) *Religion and Belief in Higher Education: The Experiences of Staff and Students*. London: Equality Challenge Unit.

Wilkins, A. (2008) *Wannabes, Goths and Christians: The Boundaries of Sex, Style and Status*. Chicago: Chicago University Press.

Chapter 13

Developing religious literacy in higher education

Adam Dinham

Higher education (HE), we are told, is increasingly for all. Governments and vice chancellors have been encouraging 'widening participation', to include more students from more backgrounds in more programmes in more institutions. At the same time, universities continue to reflect their mediaeval roots (directly, or by pastiche), hanging on to the gowns and hoods, titles and roles, of a feudal age, in which learners sit at the feet of their revered professors, advancing from Bachelor, to Master, to Professor of their subject, should they stick around long enough. The mediaeval universities were an essentially religious settlement, organised monastically, and in which the primary subjects read were Theology and Medicine. Their legacy is part of the contemporary higher education landscape.

This presents a tension because things have changed. In 1700, there were seven universities in Britain (just two in England). In 2016, there are 133 members of Universities UK, the main representative body for higher education institutions (HEIs). The relationship between British universities and religion also changed dramatically over that period. It was not until 1871 that religious tests were fully abolished at Oxford and Cambridge, and the Victorian expansion of the university sector was in part motivated by the goal of establishing countermanding secular centres of higher learning that would be open to everyone (Gilliat-Ray 2000: 22; Graham 2005: 7–9; Rüegg 2004: 61–64). Anglican chaplaincies remain a strong feature of higher education in this milieu. Up until the 1950s, there was a widespread view that the primary reason for making most chaplaincy appointments was to serve the interests of the Anglican Church (Gilliat-Ray 2000: 29). This model of chaplaincy has since given way to one in which chaplains are understood to serve the whole university and frequently define themselves as 'multi-faith'.

In teaching and learning too, there has been considerable change. In all the British Commonwealth countries, the presence of theology reduced by 60 percent between 1915 and 1995, though in some contexts underwent revival from the 1980s on, although this time in new forms focusing especially on Islam or the intersection between religion and public life (Frank and Gabler 2006: 92–116). The link has also been made between the retreat of religion in universities and the emergence of academic disciplines and their attendant communities of scholars that challenged hitherto dominant forms of thinking (Edwards 2006: 84). Each discipline, according to Edwards, has developed its own procedures and vocabularies for understanding its subject matter, and, as they have done so, alternatives to the dominant forms of theological knowledge have inadvertently emerged. The sciences, the social sciences, then the humanities in turn 'declared their independence from religion' (Edwards 2006: 84; Wittrock 1993).

Yet increasing awareness of religion – driven largely by anxieties about extremism, sex, and money – have prompted some to suggest that 'religion is back' (Micklethwait and Wooldridge 2010) for universities as for other institutions and public spaces. The rolling back of welfare states and the turn to faith groups to plug the gaps, 9/11, and the new law on equality (which includes non-religious beliefs, such as atheism and humanism, as well as traditional religion and non-religion, such as environmentalism and veganism) all draw attention back to what was always there anyway, and they press for a renewed public conversation. Yet we have largely lost our ability to talk about it. Schools are implicated because they too are in a muddle on religion and belief. Recent research on school religious education (RE) is revealing of the conundrum (see Dinham and Shaw 2015 at www.gold.ac.uk/faithsunit/reforreal). Religious education is required in schools, but not in the national curriculum. Places for RE teacher training have been reduced, yet in schools, RE is a growing subject choice. Nevertheless, it remains often questioned in terms of status and academic seriousness. The relationship between teaching and learning, formation, and a national statutory requirement for a daily Act of Collective Worship is vexed. As a recent RE Council report observes, the RE community is in crisis (RE Council 2013). A crucial challenge is how to work out a place for education – in schools and universities – which emerges out of a Christian past, and to some extent present, while at the same time taking fully and authentically on board the real religious landscape, which is Christian, secular, plural, and non-believing. The real complexity is that it is all of these things at once. Universities pick up where schools leave off, confusing students further with a sub-textual re-playing of the old science–religion arguments, built deeply in to the epistemologies of most subjects. Professional training – much of which has also now moved into the universities – consolidates the challenge, behaving as though the service-using public is largely not religious.

The higher education challenge begins in – and reflects – wider society. Public discourse – such as it is – tends to resonate with somewhat untested assumptions: that the West is largely secular; that religions tend to cause wars, oppress women and gay people; that they want to hold people in orthodoxies which constrict their freedoms and creativities. Likewise, it is generally supposed that the public sphere is a secular sphere, by which is usually meant a somehow neutral sphere when it comes to religion and belief. Thus, in their book *Religion and Change in Modern Britain*, Linda Woodhead and Rebecca Catto write about:

> a characteristic assumption of the post war period: that religion has become a purely private matter with no public or political significance. So long as this idea prevailed, both in scholarship and in society, it was possible to treat

religions as discrete entities which could be analysed solely in terms of their inner logics.

(Woodhead and Catto 2012: 2)

They challenge this, saying that religion is not an *aside* to economics, politics, media, the law, 'and other arenas' (Woodhead and Catto 2012: 2), but is indeed integral to them. 'Private religion, public sphere' is an antinomy which makes less and less sense as the religion and belief landscape becomes increasingly apparent once more. How can universities reflect this? There are nettles here which have not been grasped because of the even bigger questions which they raise – what can be meant by national values and identity, and what is the proper role of Christianity in the apparatus of state under circumstances which have changed so dramatically and which are now so highly plural?

Universities

Restoring order in how we think about religion and belief is a pressing task for education at all levels, and universities have a particular part to play. This was explicitly recognised in policy and practice, as well as in theory, when in 2009 the Higher Education Funding Council for England (HEFCE), a government body in England, began to engage in a discussion with academics about religion in the universities, which I was appointed to direct.

At first, a driving force in this conversation for many of those interested in it was anxiety about extremism on university campuses. But I wanted to argue for a different way of thinking about this. My first point was that extremism is a tiny minority problem, although it is absolutely right to take it very seriously indeed because the consequences can be catastrophic when things go wrong. I also argued that extremism on campuses is itself both rare and notoriously hard to judge (see Dinham and Jones 2012). Indeed, radicalism and contestation are what universities *should* be for, so where does one draw the line? But most importantly, I felt an approach based on anxiety about extremism casts religion and belief as a problem first and foremost, and I wanted to argue that this need not be the starting point. I thought it would be much more effective – and much more realistic – to set religion and belief in their proper context and seek engagement rather than solutions. After all, religion and belief are not 'something else', 'somewhere else'. They are highly present and pervasive, especially in the light of globalisation and migration, which put us all into daily encounter with a rich diversity of religion and belief, whatever our own religion, belief or none. In particular, if governments want faiths to fill the welfare gaps, and faiths are visible again as a result, we need to be good at talking about faiths again. We need education to equip us to do so.

The Religious Literacy Leadership in Higher Education programme has been one response, working in universities in the first instance, though subsequently broadening its reach to work with employer groups and service providers as well, and crucially also in schools. Universities are a good place to start because, first, they are places of peculiarly intense encounter, especially but not exclusively amongst young people. They are often even more plural and mixed than the rest of society around them, though sometimes the precise opposite is true – which brings with it a different set of problems. They are also precisely designed to encourage debate about interesting and difficult issues. Many Western societies have become quite good at discussing race, gender and sexual orientation, for example. But on religion and belief, they are stuck.

Second, universities embody what liberalism takes to be a range of essential freedoms – namely, freedom of speech and freedom of thought. These are the basis of academic freedom; however, religions are sometimes seen as an obstacle to such freedoms.

Third, universities reproduce and reflect a particular post-religious way of thinking, intellectually, which tends to reject religion as distracting nonsense. As these assumptions are produced and reproduced in university settings, they are part of the formation of minds which underpins the conversation in wider society. So, it turns out to matter very much what universities think about religion, even though they may have thought of themselves as secular and therefore neutral on the matter.

These may be pressing reasons for taking religion more seriously in university operations, but this still leaves the vexed question of whether and how to take religion seriously in curricula. How, if at all, should teaching and learning respond? This question goes for education all the way up and down, from primary school level to PhD and professional education and training. In some subjects, of course, religion is simply a topic of relevance, as in History and Religious Studies itself. In others, it is a cultural legacy to be decoded and understood, as revealed in the growing tendency to teach 'Introduction to the Bible' to students of English Literature so they can manage Milton or Donne. In others again, it embodies the opposite of the rational, scientific method which predominates in higher education, and in relation to which practically all other disciplines have cut their teeth. As such, it is an utter irrelevance, as in Richard Dawkins's comparison between astrology and astronomy. In some cases, this produces hostility against all religious ideas. This is likely to feel painful for students who, as some of our research shows, can feel uncomfortable to hear lecturers be quite rude or offensive about their beliefs or about belief in general. In the social sciences, unlike race, gender, or sexual orientation, religion has rarely been a variable. It simply does not often count as a topic to be counted.

So where are we now? I have observed a lamentable quality of conversation about religion: at the same time, a pressing need for a better quality of conversation in order to avoid knee-jerk reactions which focus only on 'bad' religion. Universities understand that they have got to get better at providing really excellent student experience, and what is starting to emerge alongside is a bigger debate about the role of religion in teaching and learning. This all reflects a crucial contention in the rest of society about the re-emergence of religious faith as a public category at all. How and what we teach and learn about religion and belief in this milieu will be a key part of how we handle these identities in the context of community relations, public services, trade and commerce, and foreign affairs in the decades to come.

Doing religious literacy

The Religious Literacy in Higher Education Programme has enabled an understanding and evolution of a concept and a practice of religious literacy which is intended to provide the beginnings, at least, of a discourse – a language and a grammar, as the term implies – for talking better about religion and belief. This starts with challenges to the theoretical assumptions which underpin the conversation. It goes on to a practice of religious literacy, conceived of as a journey.

As programme director, and with my board of academics and senior sector administrators, it was immediately obvious that here was an issue of enormous significance and urgency, yet with almost no language which could adequately begin to address it. I liken it to the state of public discourse on race in the 1960s and gender in the 1970s – that is to say, hugely prominent but largely unformed. Developing a discourse seemed like the pressing task, and it needed to be both thoughtful and theorised on the one hand, and publicly accessible and practical on the other. Where to start?

I began with an analysis of the religious literacy challenge in higher education contexts. This involved theoretical engagement with the relationship between religion and universities, alongside empirical research work to understand the preoccupations of university leaders, the stances this could lead to, and the practical challenges of university as big operations. In terms of theoretical engagement, a literature review quickly revealed a paucity of attention to religion in higher education at all, though there is more in the United States than in the United Kingdom and elsewhere. A body of literature has emerged that has examined the history of religion in higher education (Hart 1999; Reuben 1996; Roberts and Turner 2000), the recent 're-emergence' of religion on university campuses (Edwards 2008; Wuthnow 2008), and the implications of increasing religious diversity for teaching and research (Edwards 2006; Tisdell 2008). Partly inspired by the widely discussed 'deprivatisation' of religious traditions and communities of faith since the end of the Cold War (Berger 1999; Casanova 1994; Habermas 2007), this literature has renewed an old debate about the responsibilities of universities in a world marked by the 'complex co-presence' (Ford 2004: 24) of a variety of often competing religious and secular philosophical traditions. As with the US literature, what UK literature there was focused on religion and belief as a surprise and as a risk to be managed.

A number of scholars based in the United Kingdom (Ford 2004; Gilliat-Ray 2000; Woodhead 2012: 28) and the United States (Prothero 2007) have argued that the education system, and particularly universities, could play a vital role in improving the quality of these vexed conversations. For example, Ford has contended, as part of a comprehensive rationale for the public role of universities in relation to religious faith, that HEIs 'ought to be taking far more seriously than they do their responsibility to contribute to the coming century by engaging with the issues arising from the simultaneously religious and secular character of our world' (Ford 2004: 25). Similarly, Graham (2005: 243–261) has argued that universities have a vital role to play as part of a society's cultural infrastructure, and that one part of this role is consideration of both religious and secular spiritual values. A different take on the same issue is provided by Gilliat-Ray (2000: 59), who chooses to stress not the role that universities can have in educating about religion, but bringing young people from diverse backgrounds into contact. 'Universities', she observes, 'are sites of cultural engagement and exploration, and if issues of religious diversity, rights and representation cannot be debated and explored in this context, then where else?'

Another rich theoretical seam focuses on the post-religious mindedness of the HE sector, steeped as it is in the principles and practices of scientific method and Enlightenment philosophy. Thus, it is possible to describe the changes to UK HE in terms of a decline in dominant traditional forms of religion followed by burgeoning religious diversity: HE in the United Kingdom has undergone a process of secularisation, rapidly followed by an increase in diversity that heralds what has been called a 'post-secular' phase. This can be illustrated by looking at university chaplaincy, for example. Up until the 1950s, there was a widespread view that the primary reason for making most chaplaincy appointments was to serve the interests of the Anglican Church (Gilliat-Ray 2000: 29). However, this model of chaplaincy began to give way in the 1960s and 1970s, with chaplains starting to serve the whole university.

This analysis in turn gave way to an engagement with more recent literature, especially in the sociology of religion, drawing attention not so much to the post-religious as the post-secular, and to dramatic changes in the real religious landscape, and how to think about it. Thus, the UK 2011 Census tells us that Christianity remains the largest religion in England and Wales, but is down from 71 percent to 59 percent. We know that Muslims are the next biggest religious group, with 4.8 percent, and is the most increasing group, up from 3.0 percent. Meanwhile, the proportion of the population who reported they have no religion has now reached a quarter in the United Kingdom, and this is an increase from 14.8 percent to 25.1 percent. According to other sources and other questions, *what* we believe has changed too. Belief in 'a personal God' roughly halved between 1961 and 2000 – from 57 percent of the population to 26 percent. But over exactly the same period, belief in a 'spirit or life force' doubled – from 22 percent in 1961 to 44 percent in 2000 (see Woodhead 2012).

Of course, the data are hugely debatable and other sources say different things, but the trends are clear enough. They point to how religious forms have been changing in this period, as well as the religious mix and the mix of religion and non-religion. Society continues to be secular, but also Christian and plural, and its religion is more informal. All of these things are happening together. It is important to grasp this through learning because there appears to be a *real* religious landscape and one imagined by policymakers, professions, and publics, and there is a growing gap between them (see Dinham 2012).

At the root of, and consolidating the muddle, the conversation is usually couched in terms of society as somehow secular – and this is usually equated with neutrality. The conversation about religion is impeded by the paucity of the conversation about the secular too. Yet the secular frequently appears in the debate in just as fuzzy a form as much that is said about religion. These complications leave a lot to be desired, drawing as they often do on old tropes and stereotypes about religion causing wars and fuelling the oppression of minorities. Hence, we hear primarily about sex, money, and violence, and the dominant discourse has split into three areas of anxiety, each of which plays out in higher education:

1   How do we prevent atrocities in religion's name? This finds expression in the security agenda, reflected in the UK government's Prevent policies (see Dinham 2012), to which many students' unions have especially objected
2   How do we respond when atrocities happen? This is expressed in the cohesion agenda, reflected in universities in the language of 'widening participation', but also raising questions about how to learn well about religion and belief diversity in disciplinary contexts which have largely bracketed it out; and
3   How do we engage with the religion and belief which is there in ordinary everyday life, regardless of its role in cohesion and security, and their opposites? The dilemmas here have given rise to many university controversies about public speakers, accommodating Ramadan during exam periods, the replacement of Christmas services with 'winter celebrations', and the provision of *halal* and *kosher* food in canteens (amongst many more).

Following this analysis phase, the programme then turned to empirical research to flesh out what these analyses mean and how they play out in practice. The focus was two-tiered. There was one focus on university leaderships to find out what preoccupies them, and where this sits in the overall analyses; and another with operational staff in practical settings such as admissions, accommodations, timetabling, and catering (amongst others) to find out what sorts of issues were being encountered.

Religious literacy leadership

In research undertaken with vice chancellors and other staff in 2009–10, we found two helpful considerations (see Dinham and Jones 2012). The first was about the sort of stances universities think they take in relation to religion and belief. The second was what motivates practical action in relation to religion and belief. In relation to the first, we identified four university stances, or 'types', which appear to be easily translatable into a range of other sectors and settings across wider society (Dinham and Jones 2012). In the first type, society is conceived of as a secular space where public institutions remain as far as possible neutral and education avoids mentioning religions or belief. We called this group 'soft neutral'. A similar but firmer line actively seeks the protection of public space from religious faith, asserting a duty to preserve public bodies, such as universities, as secular. We called this group 'hard neutral'. Others saw religious faith as a potential learning and formation resource upon which to draw. A larger number of the vice chancellors we spoke to took this view, with many stressing that their campus is friendly to religions and religious people, and comfortable with religious diversity. We called this group 'Repositories and Resources'. The fourth approach we identified aims to offer education 'for the whole person', incorporating a specifically religious or belief dimension. This perspective was more common in universities which were founded as religious institutions. We called this group 'Formative-Collegial'.

The second issue we asked about was what sorts of matters about religion preoccupy vice chancellors and other university leaders. Here we found that practical and policy concerns inflected the debate. Vice chancellors were concerned about issues in four key areas. First, they were focused on legal action arising out of possible discrimination on the grounds of religion and belief; second, about campus extremism and violence; third, about being able to market their universities to students of all religion and belief backgrounds and none; and fourth, especially about appealing to international students, including those from all parts of the world, and from all religion and belief traditions, identities, and backgrounds. These were very concrete and practical concerns, and could be primarily characterised in terms of anxieties detectable in wider society, about being sued and being bombed. On the other hand, they were interested in the potential opportunities, as well as the risks (in terms of 'widening participation' and attracting international students). This too reflects an interest in faith groups in wider society for what they can bring to the table, in welfare, and in the provision of schools particularly.

We also looked at who attended religious literacy programme training events (in 2010–11) and found that the majority were from chaplaincies and equalities teams in universities. This reflects a widespread assumption amongst our sample that 'religion' is something that is done in the chaplaincy primarily, with little resonance or relevance in the wider life of the institution. The risk is that religion is 'bracketed off' in this way, rather than understood as something which pervades universities and wider societies.

Religious literacy practices

We finally conducted case study research in three universities to understand the narratives of religious faith as they are experienced by students and staff. This enabled us to dig down in to the many practical ways in which faith plays out in universities much more widely. We found students who had not felt able to attend for interviews, exams, or Saturday lectures because of clashes with religious events. There were anxieties about public speakers and what to 'allow' them to say on topics like Israel and Zionism. Timetabling staff were worried about how to handle the exam periods for the years after 2014 when Ramadan coincides with it. Canteens and bars were taking all sorts of stands for or against halal food, alcohol-free events, and single-sex socials, and there were bitter rumours in one institution that the Muslims were receiving subsidised lunches. There were sports societies whose members were ribbing a Sikh for wearing the 5 Ks (worn by orthodox Sikhs: *kesh* – uncut hair; *kara* – armband; *kangha* – comb; *kacchera* – knee length shorts; and *kirpan* – sword). Residences were struggling with kosher kitchens and women-only halls. Campus banks either could or could not handle the requests of Muslim students for halal borrowing for student fees, while counselling services felt they could not discuss religion with religious students.

The theoretical and empirical work would never be useful if it was not also linked to action, and the programme had an action orientation built in from the outset. The intention was to translate what we found theoretically and empirically into training, and this was developed in a wide range of areas. We devised training workshops for vice chancellors and their senior delegates, designed to draw their attention to the critique and analysis we have undertaken and to stimulate university leaderships to consider their own stances and how these affected the tone and practice of their institutions. We also delivered training workshops to upwards of 600 HE staff – academic and administrative – from more than 100 Universities, exploring the analyses and stances evolved from the leadership work, but also working to induce bottom-up solutions to concrete dilemmas in student services, timetabling, accommodation, food and alcohol, dress and etiquette, and a whole range of practical issues and settings. This included our devising specialist workshops on religion and belief law, and in conflict resolution, in partnership with expert bodies in these areas. All of this was reflected upon and fed back in to the process over a number of years (see Dinham and Jones 2012).

A religious literacy framework

The experience of this process of thinking, researching, training, and reflecting has reified a religious literacy framework which is intended as a way of thinking about religion and belief, not only in university spaces, but across wider society. Underpinning it are a number of key observations which make it much more than a simple acquisition of knowledge. First, religious literacy is a problem of the developed West (including New Zealand and Australia), in that it is ill-conceived secular-mindedness – what I have sometimes called subconscious secularity – that assumes a post-religious world, and seeks to act as though it is one. The secular paradigm, in all its varying and contested forms, is itself a product of Western intellectual life and tradition, rooted in Enlightenment philosophy, scientific method, and the discipline of sociology, representing a shift from explanations of the world based in God – 'theo-logy' – to explanations rooted in the immanent – 'socio-logy'. Second, religious literacy is a liberal endeavour. It stands in the liberal values of human rights, social justice, and freedoms of speech and thought, and invites people of all religions, beliefs, and none to engage with religion and belief diversity in this spirit. It does not extend as far as respecting and tolerating any and all expressions of religion or belief, where those expressions cut across liberal ones. It is thereby normative, in that it has purposes and goals: peaceful encounter across religion and belief differences. Third, religious literacy is context-specific. One size does not fit all. Understanding and responding to the religion and belief landscape of any particular sector or setting is the key task of religious literacy, and within the overall critiques and values set out, it must be approached anew each time. Thus, religious literacy requires a journey which, in my conception of it, takes place in four parts.

First, we have to understand religion as a category, drawing especially on sociology of religion to understand the real religious landscape, and how to think about it critically – including how to think well about the secular. In our HE work, we have repeatedly observed a tension between readiness to use the terms 'religion' and 'secular' on the one hand, and a lack of definition of those terms on the other. There, as in wider society, there is limited understanding of how much religion and belief have changed in the twentieth century, and the dominance of the idea of secularity in sociology as the primary lens through which to understand religion has translated into its dominance more broadly. Yet the notion of secularity is both widely misunderstood and highly nuanced. In HE, we found that it is often used to mean 'neutrality'. There is no shortage of resources for thinking more carefully about these terms and simple vague reference to 'secular universities' will not suffice. Thus, Wilson's classic proposal that religion is losing its social significance (1966) is taken on by Berger's suggestion that religion will disappear to a vanishing point (1967). Davie counters with the observation that people are believing without belonging (1994), and Hervieu-Leger inverts this to add that people are also belonging without believing (2006). Woodhead concludes that while traditional religion may be in decline, new spiritual and informal forms are thriving (2012), which Bruce dismisses, saying that all this religion talk is nothing but a last gasp before it finally disappears, as originally predicted (2011). Clarity about what is meant by religion is key. Does it refer to the traditional religions – the world religions – and if so how many of them count? Or does it encompass non-traditional, revival, and informal modes too, such as Druidism, Paganism, and Spiritualism? Might it extend to 'beliefs', such as atheism and agnosticism? Or to non-religious beliefs, such as secularism and humanism? Clarity about the secular is crucial too, since it is so often the context in which the conversation is assumed to take place. Being clear about these categorical issues is the first stage in moving towards religious literacy.

Second, we have to understand dispositions – what emotional and atavistic assumptions are brought to the conversation and what are the effects of people's own positions in relation to religion or belief? We know that higher education is steeped in both the religious-mediaeval and the post-religious Enlightenment, and carries forward aspects of each at the same time, though often in sub-textual ways. In operations and practice, HEIs still tend towards the mediaeval (using ancient titles, dress, and ceremonies), and being arranged residentially, such as the old monastic colleges, even when those inheritances are pastiche, rather than continuations. Yet in teaching and learning, they largely eschew religion from curricula, having organised around disciplinary communities formed at least in part against the old epistemologies which they were developed to replace. This is a significant issue in general, in that students have come almost entirely to lack a framework for thinking or engaging well with religion and belief, just at the point at which globalisation, migration, equality, and human rights discourses put them into daily encounter with the greatest religion and belief diversity in history. It is also a significant issue specifically for students of the professions since professional training has come so markedly into the universities, where students need to be prepared for practice with publics who will be just as diverse. Moving from the sub-textual and atavistic – the largely untested assumptions and emotions which underpin so much learning – to the expressly understood will be crucial if students are to engage thoughtfully with the religion and belief they encounter. One example of the challenge is the common use of the acceptable notion of spirituality in social work as a proxy for the unacceptable term, religion.

Only once these issues have been addressed can one pass on in to knowledge, based on identifying what we need to know, in each specific setting, and having the confidence and wherewithal to know who and what to ask. In the professions, a social worker practicing in Solihull will need different religious literacy knowledge than a medic in Manchester or a lawyer in Leeds. Inside the universities, the demographic of each will also vary significantly and there is both an immediate task – of being ready to engage with the religion and belief encounter at hand – and a formational one – of being able to translate that into any contingent space in the future. It is obvious that nobody can know everything. An engagement with religion and belief as identity, rather than tradition, is required as a release from the notion that we can and ought to learn the A-Z of a *tradition* in order to have religious literacy. Rather, it is about recognising that the same religions and beliefs are different in different people and places. Sometimes they differ within the same person, from one day to the next.

Finally, there are skills – how does what I know translate into skilful encounter, and am I clear what the encounter is for? If it is to improve interfaith relations, I need different skills than if it is to appoint a person to a job, marry someone I love from another faith, or resolve a conflict from a desk in the Foreign Office. Identifying what these skills are is a task for research in to the challenges and obstacles of religion and belief in specific sectors and settings. For example, in social work and nursing, there is a rhetoric in curricula about spirituality, but this appears to translate into very little engagement with religion or belief in classrooms and practice settings. Knowing more about why not will facilitate and support revisions to curricula which prepare social workers and nurses for the encounter.

It has been suggested that religious literacy can go one step further to enable a renewed encounter with the wisdoms which reside in religions and beliefs. For David Ford and Mike Higton, this is reached through the study of theology and its application to everyday life (see Ford and Higton 2015). These are, after all, 'wisdom traditions'. This draws attention to how strange it seems that millennia of insight, experience, drama, and poetry should be set aside exclusively in favour of the natural scientific paradigm of modernity and its social scientific followers. That in turn draws our attention to the serious reform that would be needed to universities' current ideas of what counts as knowledge if we are to engage with such 'wisdoms'. These are fundamental epistemological issues which need to be addressed.

The future

On religion and belief, religious literacy is at the root of a good future. It may only be needed – or the categorical and dispositional parts anyway – in the first half of this century, as we regain the conversation through education in school and universities, and as a generation is equipped for the task. In the meantime, equipping the public sphere *now* with the ability to have the conversation will be the urgent task of professional training and continuing professional development in every sector and setting. Theology and Religious Studies programmes across British HE are recognising this, and courses in 'Religion and. . . ' are beginning to emerge. How the other disciplines engage is crucial, and new work is beginning to analyse this already (see Baker and Dinham 2015 at www.gold.ac.uk/faithsunit/reimaginingreligion).

More generally, religious literacy challenges rather than reproduces the oversimplifications of declining religion and a secular trajectory. Across the West, these have come to be expressed in terms of the catastrophic polarisation of an enlightened Europe and a perennially backward Islam, and this plays out in anxieties about 'good campus relations' and Prevent in university campuses. Charlie Hebdo encapsulates what goes wrong with the conversation and how pressing is the religious literacy need. Islam is, after all, a civilised and civilising force, at the forefront of architectural, artistic, social, scientific, and political innovation for centuries. It does not need to look more like Europe, as Europe and Islam infuse each other, as well as diverge. Religious literacy means recognising this. It also means pulling perspective on the real religious landscape, which is neither post-Christian not post-religious, nor dominated by Islam.

Arendt writes, 'for the first time in history, all peoples on earth have a common present. . . every country has become the almost immediate neighbour of every other country, and every man feels the shock of events which take place at the other end of the globe' (Arendt 1955: 83). This 'unity of the world' could result in 'a tremendous increase in mutual hatred and a somewhat mutual irritability of everybody against everybody else'. Or it could simply demand a growing up to the realisation that the West's story of religion is not the only one and it will not survive such globalisation if it chooses intransigence. This both applies to and is informed by the West's universities. Some talk of the post-secular future. But we are all of this at once – secular and post-secular; religious and post-religious. These ideas are sedimented, not relegated. Some envisage a frightening and sinister future. But one of the Enlightenment's successes, as discovered by and within the universities – the detachment of the spheres of theos from politics – will be best sustained by a public sphere which can retain the distinction but welcome both. As holders of the Enlightenment as well as inheritors of the religious, universities are challenged to rethink their practices, but also their assumptions and epistemologies about religion and belief, and how they are learnt.

References

Arendt, H. (1955) *Men in Dark Times*. San Diego, New York and London: Harcourt, Brace and Company.

Baker, C., and Dinham, A. (2015) *Reimagining Religion and Belief for Policy and Practice*. Available online at: www.gold.ac.uk/faithsunit/reimaginingreligion

Berger, P. (1967) *The Sacred Canopy: Elements of a Sociological Theory of Religion*. Garden City: Doubleday.

Berger, P. (1999) The Desecularisation of the World: A Global Overview. In *The Desecularization of the World: Resurgent Religion and World Politics*, ed. by Berger, P. Grand Rapids, MI: William B. Eerdmans, pp. 1–18.

Bruce, S. (2011) *Secularization: In Defence of an Unfashionable Theory*. Oxford: Oxford University Press.

Casanova, J. (1994) *Public Religions in the Modern World*. Chicago: Chicago University Press.

Davie, Grace (1994) *Religion in Britain since 1945: Believing without Belonging*. Oxford: Wiley-Blackwell.

Dinham, A. (2012) *Faith and Social Capital after the Debt Crisis*. Basingstoke: Palgrave Macmillan.

Dinham, A., with Jones, S. (2012) Religion, Public Policy & the Academy: Brokering Public Faith in a Context of Ambivalence? *Journal of Contemporary Religion* 27 (2), 185–201.

Dinham, A., and Shaw, M. (2015) *REforREal: The Future of Teaching and Learning about Religion and Belief* at www.gold.ac.uk/faithsunit/reforreal

Edwards, M. (2006) *Religion on Our Campuses: A Professor's Guide to Communities, Conflicts and Promising Conversations*. New York: Palgrave Macmillan.

Edwards, M. (2008) Why Faculty Find It Difficult to Talk about Religion. In *The American University in a Postsecular Age*, ed. by Jacobsen, D., and Jacobsen, R H. Oxford: Oxford University Press, pp. 81–98.

Ford, D. F. (2004) The Responsibilities of Universities in a Religious and Secular World. *Studies in Christian Ethics* 17 (1), 22–37.

Frank, D. J., and Gabler, J. (2006) *Reconstructing the University: Worldwide Shifts in Academia in the 20th Century*. Stanford, CA: Stanford University Press.

Gilliat-Ray, S. (2000) *Religion in Higher Education: The Politics of the MultiFaith Campus*. Aldershot: Ashgate.

Graham, G. (2005) *The Institution of Intellectual Values: Realism and Idealism in Higher Education*. Exeter: Imprint Academic.

Habermas, J. (2007) *Religion in the Public Sphere*. Unpublished Lecture. Available online at: http://www.sandiego.edu/pdf/pdf_library/habermaslecture031105_c939cceb2ab087bdfc6df291ec0fc3fa.pdf

Hart, D. G. (1999) *The University Gets Religion*. Baltimore: Johns Hopkins University Press.

Hervieu-Léger, D. (2006) The Role of Religion in Establishing Social Cohesion. In *Religion in the New Europe*, ed. by Michalski, Krzysztof. Budapest: Central European University Press, pp. 45–63.

Higton, M. and Ford, D. F., (2015) Religious Literacy in the Context of Theology and Religious Studies. In *Religious Literacy in Policy and Practice*, ed. by Dinham, A., and Francis, M. Bristol: Policy Press. pp. 39–54.

Micklethwait, J., and Wooldridge, A. (2010) *God Is Back: How the Global Rise of Faith Is Changing the World*. London: Penguin.

Prothero, S. (2007) *Religious Literacy: What Every American Needs to Know – And Doesn't*. Boston: Barnes & Noble.

Religious Education Council of England and Wales (2013) *A Review of Religious Education in England*. London: Religious Education Council of England and Wales. Available online at: http://resubjectreview.recouncil.org.uk/media/file/RE_Review.pdf

Reuben, J. A. (1996) *The Making of the Modern University: Intellectual Transformation and the Marginalization of Morality*. Chicago: University of Chicago Press.

Roberts, J. H., and Turner, J. (2000) *The Sacred and the Secular University*. Princeton, NJ: Princeton University Press.

Rüegg, W. (2004) *A History of the University in Europe: Volume 3, Universities in the Nineteenth and Early Twentieth Centuries (1800–1945)*. Cambridge: Cambridge University Press.

Tisdell, E. J. (2008) Spirituality, Diversity and Learner-Centred Teaching: A Generative Paradox. In *The American University in a Postsecular Age*, ed. by Jacobsen, D., and Jacobsen, R. H. Oxford: Oxford University Press, pp. 151–165.

Wilson, B. R. (1966) *Religion in Secular Society: A Sociological Comment*. London: Pelican.

Wittrock, B. (1993) The Modern University: Three Transformations. In *The European and American University since 1800*, ed. by Rothblatt, S., and Wittrock, B. Cambridge: Cambridge University Press, pp. 303–362.

Woodhead, L. (2012) *Religion in Britain Has Changed, Our Categories Haven't*. Available online at: http://faithdebates.org.uk/wp-content/uploads/2013/09/1335118113_Woodhead-FINAL-copy.pdf. Accessed 1 October 2015.

Woodhead, L., and Catto, R. (eds.) (2012) *Religion and Change in Modern Britain*. London: Routledge.

Wuthnow, R. (2008) Can Faith Be More than a Sideshow in the Contemporary Academy? In *The American University in a Postsecular Age*, ed. by Jacobsen, D., and Jacobsen, R.H. Oxford: Oxford University Press, pp. 31–44.

List of contributors

Kristin Aune is Senior Research Fellow at the Centre for Trust, Peace and Social Relations, Coventry University. She has published widely on sociology of religion, gender, feminism and higher education. Her books include *Women and Religion in the West* (co-edited, Ashgate 2008), *Reclaiming the F Word: Feminism Today* (co-authored, Zed 2013) and *Christianity and the University Experience* (co-authored, Bloomsbury 2013), and she has published in journals including *Gender & Society, European Journal of Women's Studies* and *Journal of Contemporary Religion.* She is a founder board member of the International Association for the Study of Religion and Gender. She is currently co-directing the research project 'Chaplains on Campus: Understanding Chaplaincy in UK Universities'.

Nicholas A. Bowman is an Associate Professor in the Department of Educational Policy and Leadership Studies as well as the director of the Center for Research on Undergraduate Education at the University of Iowa. His research interests cover several topics in postsecondary education, including diversity experiences, student retention and graduation, university admissions and prestige and methodological issues in studying the impact of colleges and universities. He is a co-author of the third volume of *How College Affects Students,* which synthesised thousands of studies from the United States, United Kingdom, Canada, Australia and New Zealand. His work has also appeared in top journals, including Review of Educational Research, Educational Researcher, American Educational Research Journal, Sociology of Education, Personality and Social Psychology Bulletin and Social Psychological and Personality Science.

Sariya Cheruvallil-Contractor is Research Fellow in Faith and Peaceful Relations at the Centre for Trust, Peace and Social Relations, Coventry University, the United Kingdom. She specialises in the Sociology of Religion with particular emphasis on democratic research methodologies that work with and for research participants to capture the nuance and complexity of societal diversity, pluralism and everyday lived experiences of religion or belief. She is the author of *Muslim Women in Britain: Demystifying the Muslimah* (Routledge 2012), co-author of *Religion or Belief, Discrimination and Equality: Britain in Global Contexts* (Bloomsbury 2013) and *Islamic Education in Britain: New Pluralist Paradigms* (Bloomsbury 2015) and co-editor of *Digital Methodologies in the Sociology of Religion* (Bloomsbury 2015).

Adam Dinham is Professor of Faith and Public Policy and Director of the Faiths and Civil Society Unit, Goldsmiths, University of London. With degrees in Theology and Religious Studies (BA, MA Cambridge University), Applied Social Studies and Social Work (MA Brunel University) and Politics (PhD, Goldsmiths), his work focuses on religious literacy in the public sphere, the role of faith-based organisations in the mixed economy of welfare and theories and practices of faith-based social action. He convenes an international policy-practice-research network on faith and civil society and is director of the Religious Literacy Leadership Programme; Professor of Religious Literacy at VID University, Oslo; Honorary Professor of Religion, Leadership and Society at the University of Sheffield UK; and Fellow of the Westminster Abbey Institute for Faith and Public Life.

Mathew Guest is Reader in the Sociology of Religion in the Department of Theology and Religion, Durham University. His past research has mainly focused on the sociology of contemporary Christian movements, especially as framed by the dominant institutions of western culture. Between 2009 and 2012, he was Principal Investigator of the research project 'Christianity and the University Experience in Contemporary England', and continues to publish work on the changing shape of the university as a site for the expression of religious identities. He is now researching how perceptions of Islam are forged and challenged within higher education institutions in the United Kingdom. He is the co-author (with Kristin Aune, Sonya Sharma and Rob Warner) of *Christianity and the University Experience: Understanding Student Faith* (Bloomsbury, 2013).

Jonathan P. Hill is Associate Professor of Sociology at Calvin College. He is author of *Emerging Adulthood and Faith* (Calvin College Press, 2015) and co-author of *Young Catholic America: Emerging Adults In, Out of, and Gone from the Church* (Oxford, 2014). He has published articles and book chapters on higher education and religious faith, volunteering and charitable giving. He also directs the National Study of Religion and Human Origins, a project that explores the social context of beliefs about human origins.

Tristram Hooley is Professor of Career Education at the University of Derby. His research interests include the intersection of identity and work, education policy and the role of new technologies in career, education and employment. He is a Senior Research Adviser to the Careers & Enterprise Company,

Adjunct Professor at the School of Linguistics, Adult and Specialist Education, University of Southern Queensland; a fellow of NICEC; a Winston Churchill Fellow; and a member of the Editorial Board of the British Journal of Guidance and Counselling. With Paul Weller, he has written a number of papers on religion and belief.

Lydia Reid is a Post-doctoral Researcher based at St. John's College Durham and is currently working on the project 'Equipping Christian Leadership in an Age of Science'. Part of her role on the project is to survey and interview clergy on their views towards science. Prior to this, Reid completed her PhD in Sociology at the University of Manchester (in 2014), which explored religious university students' experiences of studying at a red-brick university. Reid is due to publish a monograph (based on her doctoral research) in 2017 with Mellen Press. Her research interests lie in the areas of higher education, science, secularisation, non-religion and qualitative research methods.

Duna Sabri is a visiting Research Fellow at the Centre for Public Policy Research, Kings College London. She began her career as a Researcher on equality issues at Royal Holloway's Centre for Ethnic Minority Studies before working at the Learning Institute at the University of Oxford in educational development for nine years. Since completing her DPhil at Oxford on the assumptive worlds of policymakers and academics. Her work has involved universities with diverse missions addressing questions such as why students leave, how to understand the inequalities in outcomes among students of different ethnicities, assessment practices and the interplay between students' identities and university experiences. Her publications explore the concept of 'the student experience' and its deployment in higher education policy. She is currently working on an analysis of how students' familial contexts support their higher education experiences and an exploration of the parameters of universities' roles in determining students' employment outcomes.

Charlotte Shira Schallié is an Associate Professor of Germanic Studies at the University of Victoria, Canada. Her research interests include post-1945 German/Swiss literature and film, transcultural studies, Jewish identity in contemporary cultural and religious discourse, Holocaust education and community-engaged scholarship. Her recent publications on religious and cultural identity of university students are: 'The Dark Side of the Academy: Antisemitism in Canadian and German Students' in *The Journal for the Study of Antisemitism* (October 2013) (co-authored with Wassilis Kassis); 'Prediction of Anti-Muslim Sentiment on Campus: A Cross-Cultural Analysis of Prejudice in Two University Populations' in *HIKMA – Journal of Islamic Theology and Religious Education* 5.9 (October 2014) (co-authored with Wassilis Kassis, Sonja Strube and Judith von der Heyde); and 'Empirische Ergebnisse zum Zusammenhang von Geschlechterrollensterotypen und antimuslimischen

Vorurteilen. Ein international komparativer Blick' in *Rechtsextremismus als Herausforderung für die Theologie* ed. Sonja Angelika Strube. Freiburg i.B.: Verlag Herder, 2015 (co-authored with Wassilis Kassis and Judith von der Heyde).

Alison Scott-Baumann is Professor of Society and Belief in the Centre of Islamic Studies, Department of Near and Middle East, School of Oriental and African Studies (SOAS) at University of London. She has been working with Muslim groups in Britain, Pakistan and India for almost twenty years and uses philosophy to develop robust research ethics for working towards social justice. She established a groundbreaking Muslim teacher training programme in 2000 and supports Muslim colleges who seek partnership with British universities. She is the author of *Ricoeur and the hermeneutics of suspicion* (Continuum 2009), *Ricoeur and the negation of happiness* (Bloomsbury 2013) and co-author of *Islamic Education in Britain: New Pluralist Paradigms* (Bloomsbury 2015). She co-edited *Iris Murdoch and the moral Imagination* (McFarland 2010).

Ruth Sheldon is a Research Fellow in the Department of Psychosocial Studies at Birkbeck College, University of London. Her research focuses on the ethnographic study of ethical, theological and political encounters within public institutions and urban settings. Her book *Tragic Encounters? The Palestine-Israel Conflict in British Universities* is forthcoming with Manchester University Press. She is currently working on a research project entitled 'Psychosocial Components of Ethical Monotheism', which is exploring everyday relations between Jewish, Muslim and Christian neighbours in London.

Jasjit Singh is a Research Fellow in Religious and Cultural Transmission based at the University of Leeds and a recognised expert on Sikhs in Britain. His research examines religious identity and processes of religious and cultural transmission among British South Asians with a focus on British Sikhs. His research interests include Religion and Youth, Religion and Media, Religious Identity, Sikh Studies and Religion in Diaspora. Jasjit has an emerging track record in publications including peer-reviewed journals and edited collections. He regularly presents his work in both academic and non-academic contexts, including at national and international conferences, public lectures and on national and Sikh media. Jasjit is a visiting fellow at the Faiths & Civil Society Unit at Goldsmiths University of London and is a member of a number of academic networks including 'Sikhs in Europe', 'Religious Literacy Leadership in Higher Education' and the 'Religion and Diversity Project' in Canada.

Jacqueline Stevenson is Professor of Education Research and Head of Research in the Sheffield Institute of Education, Sheffield Hallam University. She is a sociologist of education with a particular interest in policy and practice relating to equity and diversity in higher education; widening participation, access and student success; pedagogic diversity; and the stratification and marketisation of higher education. Key areas of interest are the social and academic experiences of religious students; the access, retention and success of refugees in higher education; and Black and minority ethnic students' degree attainment and success.

Joke van Saane is Professor of Education Theology and Religious Studies and Psychology of Religion at Vrije Universiteit Amsterdam, Department of Theology. As Vice Dean of Education, she is responsible for all educational affairs of the faculty. Research themes are leadership, innovative education in theology, conversion and the relation between religion and (mental) health. Key publication: Saane, Joke van (2012) *Geloofwaardig Leiderschap. (Credible Leadership)* Zoetermeer: Meinema; Saane, Joke van (2010) A Cultural Psychological Approach to Evangelical Faith Healing Groups. *Mental Health, Religion & Culture* 13 (4), 411–415.

Anna Virkama is a sociologist and anthropologist whose research interests include everyday transnational practices and social change, international student mobility, sociology of education and qualitative methods with a special focus on ethnography. She earned her Master's Degree in Social Sciences in 2006 from the University of Joensuu in Finland, and is currently finalizing a PhD thesis on Moroccan student migration as a joint degree with University of Tampere in Finland and University of Paris VIII in France. She has conducted ethnographic research in France and Morocco, and published articles and book chapters on emigration and human rights, academic freedom in Maghreb and migrants' transnational practices.

Paul Weller is a Professor in the Centre for Trust, Peace and Social Relations at Coventry University; Non-Stipendiary Research Fellow in Religion and Society at Regent's Park College, University of Oxford; and Emeritus Professor, University of Derby. He is Director of Religion and Belief Research and Training Ltd and Trustee of the Multi-Faith Centre at the University of Derby. His research focuses on religion, state and society, and particularly matters relating to religion or belief freedom, discrimination and equality in public life. He is editor of *Religions in the UK: Directory, 2007–10* (Multi-Faith Centre at the University of Derby, 2007); author of *Time for a Change: Reconfiguring Religion, State and Society* (T & T Clark, 2005); author of *A Mirror for Our Times: 'The Rushdie Affair' and the Future of Multiculturalism* (Continuum, 2009); and co-author of *Religion and Belief, Discrimination and Equality: Britain in Global Contexts* (Bloomsbury, 2013).

Index